Slavery, Law, and Politics

SLAVERY, LAW, AND POLITICS

*The Dred Scott Case
in Historical Perspective*

DON E. FEHRENBACHER

OXFORD UNIVERSITY PRESS
Oxford   New York   Toronto   Melbourne
1981

Oxford University Press

Oxford   London   Glasgow
New York   Toronto   Melbourne   Wellington
Nairobi   Dar es Salaam   Cape Town
Kuala Lumpur   Singapore   Jakarta   Hong Kong   Tokyo
Delhi   Bombay   Calcutta   Madras   Karachi

This book is an abridged edition of
The Dred Scott Case:
Its Significance in American Law and Politics,
Copyright © 1978 by Oxford University Press, Inc.
First published by Oxford University Press, 1981
First issued as an Oxford University Press paperback, 1981

Library of Congress Cataloging in Publication Data

Fehrenbacher, Don Edward, 1920-
Slavery, law, and politics.
Abridged ed. of the author's The Dred Scott case,
its significance in American law and politics.
Bibliography: p.
Includes index.
1.   Slavery in the United States—Law and
legislation.   2.   Scott, Dred.   3.   Slavery in the
United States—Legal status of slaves in free states.
I.   Title.
KF4545.S5F432   346.7301'3   80-25574
ISBN 0-19-502882-1
ISBN 0-19-502883-X (pbk.)

Printed in the United States of America

printing, last digit: 10 9 8 7 6 5 4 3 2

For
Virginia
with love

Preface

This book is an abridged edition, with some minor revisions, of *The Dred Scott Case: Its Significance in American Law and Politics* (Oxford University Press, 1978). In order to retain as much of the original text as possible within the desired limit on total length, it has seemed advisable to dispense with documentation entirely. Anyone who wants badly to know the authority for a particular statement or the source of a particular quotation can find it, with just a little trouble, in *The Dred Scott Case*. Footnotes aside, this abridgment is approximately half the length of the original volume but incorporates all of its chapters and major themes. I have cut much illustrative and collateral material and have found it disconcertingly easy to make stylistic economies. The result is a book less rich in detail but more to the point—suitable, I hope, for academic use and for the enlightenment of the general reader.

Again I acknowledge with gratitude the help of Charles Lofgren, Carl N. Degler, Walter Ehrlich, Robert W. Johannsen, William M. Wiecek, Carol Clifford, Virginia Fehrenbacher, and Sheldon Meyer and the editorial staff of Oxford University Press. Also Green Library, the Law School Library, the Institute of American History, and the office staff of the Department of History at Stanford University; the Library of Congress, the National Archives, the Library of the United States Supreme Court, the

Missouri Historical Society, the Maryland Historical Society, the Ohio State Library, the Historical Society of Pennsylvania, the University of North Carolina Library, and the University of Virginia Library; the National Endowment for the Humanities, and the *Journal of Southern History* for permission to reprint in Chapter X some of the material that first appeared in my article, "Roger B. Taney and the Sectional Crisis," XLIII (November 1977), 555-66, copyright 1977 by the Southern Historical Association.

November 1980   D.E.F.

Contents

Introduction   3

1. Slavery and Race in the American Constitutional System   7

2. Expansion and Slavery in National Politics   41

3. Toward Judicial Resolution   72

4. The Taney Court and Judicial Power   102

5. The Dred Scott Case in Missouri   121

6. Before the Supreme Court   151

7. The Opinion of the Court   183

8. Concurrence, Dissent, and Public Reaction   214

9. The Lecompton and Freeport Connections   244

10. Not Peace but a Sword   273

11. In the Stream of History   295

Selected Books for Further Reading   309

Index   313

Slavery, Law, and Politics

Introduction

On Friday morning, March 6, 1857—a crisp, clear day for residents of Washington, D.C.—public attention centered on a dusky, ground-level courtroom deep within the Capitol. Ordinarily, the Supreme Court carried on its business before a small audience and with only perfunctory notice from the press, but today the journalists were out in force, and the room was packed with spectators. A murmur of expectancy ran through the crowd and greeted the nine black-robed jurists as they filed into view at eleven o'clock, led by the aged Chief Justice. Recent acrimonious debate in Congress had once again failed to settle the sectional conflict over slavery in the federal territories, but the Court was now ready to issue an authoritative ruling on that subject and, incidentally, to decide the fate of a man named Dred Scott.

Neither of the two litigants was present in the courtroom. Scott remained at home in St. Louis, still a hired-out slave eleven years after he had taken the first step in his long legal battle for freedom. As for his alleged owner, John F. A. Sanford languished in an insane asylum and within two months would be dead. But then, both men had been dwarfed by the implications of their case and were now mere pawns in a larger contest.

Roger B. Taney, almost eighty years old, began reading from a manuscript held in tremulous hands. For more than two hours the audience strained to hear his steadily weakening voice as he

delivered the opinion of the Court in *Dred Scott v. Sandford.**
Other opinions followed from some of the concurring justices and
from the two dissenters. When they were finished at the end of
the next day, only one thing was absolutely clear. Nine distinguished white men, by a vote of seven to two, had decided in
the court of last resort that an insignificant, elderly black man
and his family were still slaves and not free citizens, as they
claimed.

What else had been decided was fiercely debated then and
ever afterward. Critics argued that on some points Taney did not
speak for a majority of the justices. Yet none of his eight colleagues directly challenged Taney's explicit assertion that his was
the official opinion of the Court. Critics also insisted that Taney's
most important pronouncement was extrajudicial, but only the
Court itself, in later decisions, could settle such a question by accepting or rejecting the pronouncement as established precedent.
Rightly or not, permanently or not, the Supreme Court had written two new rules into the fundamental law of the nation: first,
that no Negro could be a United States citizen or even a state
citizen "within the meaning of the Constitution"; and second,
that Congress had no power to prohibit slavery in the territories,
and that accordingly all legislation embodying such prohibition,
including the Missouri Compromise, was unconstitutional.

Public reaction was prompt and often intense. There was a
roar of anger and defiance from antislavery voices throughout
the North, well illustrated in the notorious remark of the New
York *Tribune* conceding the decision "just so much moral weight
as . . . the judgment of a majority of those congregated in any
Washington bar-room." From southerners, in contrast, came expressions of satisfaction and renewed sectional confidence at this
vindication of their constitutional rights. Meanwhile, northern
Democrats and certain other conservatives were confining themselves, for the most part, to exclamations of relief at the settlement of a dangerous issue and pious lectures on the duty of every
citizen to accept the judgment of the Court.

The public response to the decision proved to be more im-

---

* The defendant's last name, Sanford, was misspelled in the official Supreme
Court report.

portant than its legal effect. As law, the decision legitimized and encouraged an expansion of slavery that never took place; it denied freedom to a slave who was then quickly manumitted. But as a public event, it aggravated an already bitter sectional conflict and in some degree determined the shape of the final crisis.

No doubt the Dred Scott decision is of historical significance primarily because of its place in the configuration of forces and events that produced the Civil War. Yet the decision also has revelatory value in the study of other forces at work and other historical problems. For instance, unlike Taney's pronouncements on slavery, which defended a minority section with partisan fervor, the racial theory underlying his opinion was majoritarian. For proof of the Negro's degraded status, he relied heavily upon examples taken from the free states. Without the northern record of increasing discrimination he would have found it much more difficult to exclude Negroes from citizenship. Although the principal conclusions of Taney's opinion were soon wiped away by the Civil War and subsequent constitutional amendments, the spirit of the opinion survived for a century in the racial sequel to emancipation.

Furthermore, although the Dred Scott decision was essentially a vain effort to turn back the clock of civilization and permanently legitimate a "relic of barbarism," in at least one respect it had a distinctly modern ring. American courts in the late twentieth century are no longer mere constitutional censors of public policies fashioned by other hands. They have also become initiators of social change. Government by judiciary is now, in a sense, democracy's non-democratic alternative to representative government when the latter bogs down in failure or inaction. The Dred Scott decision nevertheless remains the most striking instance of the Supreme Court's attempting to play the role of *deus ex machina* in a setting of national crisis. The decision, in fact, provided an early indication of the vast judicial power that could be generated if political issues were converted by definition into constitutional questions.

For most of its eleven-year history, Scott's legal struggle for freedom aroused scarcely any public interest as it proceeded by an anomalous route from a Missouri trial court to the Supreme

Court of the United States. In the beginning, it posed a fairly simple legal problem for which precedent seemed to provide a ready-made solution. At each stage of litigation, however, new and bigger issues were injected into the case. Thus it grew steadily more complex and in the end became critically important to the entire nation.

The three principal subjects with which Taney dealt at length in his opinion were: 1) the black race generally and free blacks in particular; 2) the institution of slavery; and 3) the territorial system. Of these, the first is not mentioned at all in the Constitution; the second is referred to in three separate passages, but never by name, and the third is treated in one brief and ambiguous clause. The textual basis for constitutional interpretation was therefore meager. In each instance, moreover, there was a peculiar hybridism that fostered confusion. The so-called "free" Negro, though not a slave, was excluded from many of the privileges and opportunities associated with American freedom. Slaves were in some respects persons and in other respects property. And territories were likewise something betwixt and between, being neither colonies nor self-governing states but rather a distinctive American combination of the two.

Altogether, the Dred Scott case was legally complex and invited a judicial investigation of remarkable scope into matters of perplexing ambiguity for which the constitutional guidelines were often vague and discrepant. The Court, as a consequence, had much freedom of choice and found it easy to treat broad political and historical questions as though they were legal issues susceptible of judicial settlement. In fact, citation of legal rules and precedents was only a secondary bulwark of Taney's opinion, which depended primarily upon the interpretation of American history that he proposed to write into constitutional law.

Such an event cannot be examined in any narrow context without the risk of considerable misunderstanding. For it is integrally part of a complex pattern of thoughts and actions extending far backward and well forward in time from the year 1857. Studied in breadth and depth, the Dred Scott decision becomes a point of illumination, casting light upon more than a century of American history.

❧ 1 ❦

Slavery and Race
in the
American Constitutional System

The first African Negroes in the British North American colonies were brought ashore at Jamestown in 1619. During that same year, Virginians organized the first representative assembly on the continent, and thus, in a sense, slavery and self-government arrived simultaneously. The irony seems plain enough now, but for more than a century it did not scratch the surface of colonial consciousness. By the eve of the American Revolution, slavery was not only legally established in all thirteen colonies but so firmly implanted in the southern colonies that blacks constituted about 40 per cent of the population.

The theoretical foundations and essential nature of the institution were much the same from Maine to Georgia. Yet the daily life of a New England house servant bore little resemblance to the life of a field hand on a South Carolina rice plantation. There were significant variations even in the legal structure of slavery from colony to colony, and the institution in practice took many forms, reflecting many varieties of social context and individual personality. In all the colonies, to be sure, African slavery was lifelong and hereditary. At law, a slave was reduced in considerable degree from a person to a thing, having no legitimate will of its own and belonging bodily to its owner. As property, a slave could be bought and sold. As animate property, he could be compelled to work, and his offspring belonged abso-

lutely to the master. Thus a slave was in some respects like a domestic animal, being an item of wealth, virtually a beast of
burden, and a creature requiring constant supervision and restraint. Classification of the slave as property could nevertheless
go only so far before it was overtaken by the ineluctable fact of
his humanity. Both conscience and interest dictated that in certain respects he must be treated as a person. For instance, criminal law held the slave fully responsible and punishable for his
own misdeeds, like any free man. And the principal moral justification for slavery—that it lifted savages up toward civilization
and heathen up to Christianity—certainly contemplated slaves as
men, and men, indeed, with immortal souls. Plainly, in law as
well as in life, a slave was both person and property. This dualism often proved embarrassing for slaveholders and confusing for
lawmakers, but southerners learned that it could also sometimes
be advantageous.

Introduction of the peculiar institution into the thirteen colonies had been essentially undeliberate and uncontroversial. By
the 1760s, however, new currents of liberal thought from the
European enlightenment, which contributed so much to the ideology of the American Revolution, were also encouraging uneasy
reflection on the rationale of slavery. And then the rhetoric of the
colonial struggle with England brought out in strong relief the
ugly paradox of freedom and servitude in America. If words
were read for their plainest meaning, slavery was incompatible
with the fundamental assumption of the Declaration of Independence—that all men are created equal and endowed by their cre-
ator with the inalienable rights of life, liberty, and the pursuit of
happiness.

The antislavery tendencies of the Revolutionary period were
not inconsiderable. State after state took steps to end the African
slave trade. Abolition of slavery itself was achieved in New England and Pennsylvania, and it seemed only a matter of time in
New York and New Jersey. Virginia in 1782 gave strong encour-
agement to private manumissions by removing earlier restrictions
upon them, and both Maryland and Delaware subsequently followed her example. By the 1790s, abolition societies had appeared in every state from Virginia northward, with prominent

men like Benjamin Franklin and John Jay in leading roles. And Congress in 1787 prohibited slavery in the Northwest Territory with scarcely a dissenting vote. One can see in this early movement against slavery, with its promising but limited achievements, the contours of a revolution which failed—failed, however, not because its supporters lacked *sincerity*, but rather because they lacked the *intensity* of conviction that inspires concentrated effort and carries revolutions through to success. The great men of the time gave the movement their sympathy and formal endorsement but always had other more pressing claims on their sustained attention. Also, they were inhibited by their desire for continental unity, by a tender concern for the rights of private property, and, in the South, by racial fears that made universal emancipation difficult to visualize. In the end, there was a strong disposition to settle for moral gesture and a reliance on the benevolence of history.

What this incomplete revolution did produce, of course, was a fairly clear-cut division of the new nation into slaveholding and nonslaveholding states—all at the very time when the foundations of a national government were being laid. The division proved to be a remarkably even one, both in number of states and in population. It was also ominously geographical, reinforcing old economic differences between the North and the South. The elements of sectional conflict were thus assembled, as James Madison pointed out more than once to members of the Constitutional Convention. In a context of so much change and uncertainty, the men of 1787 were not very well prepared to make indelible decisions about slavery for themselves and their posterity.

Slavery had in fact been an obstacle to American union since the beginning of independence, contributing especially to the financial weakness of the Articles of Confederation. Efforts to apportion the expenses of the Confederation among the states according to their populations had foundered on the question of whether slaves should be counted in the enumeration. Instead, the Articles as finally adopted provided for apportionment according to the value of real estate—a formula that proved unworkable.

At the Constitutional Convention, the first major struggle was between large and small states over the distribution of legislative power. But after the Great Compromise began to take shape, establishing proportional representation in one house while retaining state equality in the other, the old sectional dispute about counting slaves promptly resumed. The stakes had changed, however, and both sides more or less reversed their previous arguments. When it had been a question of apportioning governmental expenses according to population, northerners had insisted that slaves be included in the enumeration; southerners had replied that slaves were property and therefore to be excluded. But in 1787, when apportionment of seats in the House of Representatives was the issue, southerners wanted slaves to be counted equally with free men, while northerners emphatically disagreed and in some instances even asserted that slaves must be regarded as property.

Ready at hand, however, was a familiar design of compromise—the so-called federal ratio, which, although approved by Congress in 1783, had never been put to use. Now brought forward in the Convention, it won acceptance by a narrow margin. By the terms of this settlement, both representation and direct taxes would be apportioned among the states "according to their respective numbers," determined by adding to the total of free persons "three fifths of all other persons." The compromise went over rather smoothly in the Convention and in the state ratifying conventions that followed. But as the years passed, it looked more and more like a major victory for the South, especially when the link with direct taxes proved to be unimportant. The three-fifths clause augmented southern representation in the House by 30 per cent or more. Yet, in spite of growing northern resentment, the clause never became a major public issue, partly because it was too securely locked into the constitutional system.

The political effects of the three-fifths compromise were one thing, but in addition, what did the compromise say about the nature and status of slavery within the American constitutional system? Certainly, by its reference to "other persons," the clause gave formal recognition to the existence of a system of bondage in the country. But did this mean that the clause, which spoke only of *persons,* nevertheless recognized and legitimated the treatment of slaves as *property?* The affirmative answer soon adopted throughout the South was also widely accepted in the North. Yet this interpretation ignored the possibility that some of the framers (and perhaps a majority of the framers some of the time) intended to give slavery only a limited kind of national recognition in the Constitution. At one point in the Convention proceedings, for instance, James Madison, a slaveholder who had supported the three-fifths compromise and who certainly regarded slaves as property in Virginia, protested that it would be "wrong to admit in the Constitution the idea that there could be property in men."

Much confusion resulted not only from the association of *slavery* with property, but also from the association of *representation* with property in eighteenth-century thought. Among Convention delegates there was widespread acceptance of the Whig principle that political representation should to some extent reflect differences in wealth. But while the principle had been applied to individuals in the suffrage and office-holding qualifications of the various states, no one had found a practical way to compute the proportionate wealth of the states themselves. In the end, as Charles C. Pinckney of South Carolina later explained, the Convention decided that "the productive labor of the inhabitants was the best rule for ascertaining their wealth." The solution adopted, in short, was simply to count the producers of wealth—that is, to use population as an index of property values in the states. Thus, in the apportionment of direct taxes (and therefore of representation also), slaves were not treated as property any more than free persons were treated as property, but both were used as measures of wealth. The three-fifths compromise did not necessarily imply that a slave was 60 per cent human being and 40 per cent property. Instead, it incorporated a differential estimate of his wealth-producing capacity *as a person.* It reflected a widespread belief in the relative inefficiency of slave labor. Therefore, neither in its wording nor in its historical context does the clause lend significant support to the property-holding aspect of slavery. Perhaps this is why it received no mention whatever in Taney's Dred Scott opinion.

Slavery provoked only one other major disagreement in the Convention, and it was over the future of the African slave trade. Delegates from Georgia and the Carolinas insisted vehemently that their states must be free to permit the trade or prohibit it, as they chose. This would require a special restriction on the general powers of Congress to lay taxes and regulate foreign commerce. The outcome, after extensive debate, was a compromise worded as follows: "The migration or importation of such persons as any of the states now existing shall think proper to admit, shall not be prohibited by the Congress prior to the year one thousand eight hundred and eight, but a tax or duty may be imposed on such importation, not exceeding ten dollars for each person." In spite of its circumlocution, the purpose of the clause was obvious, and Congress at the first opportunity prohibited importation of slaves. But here again, as in the case of the three-fifths compromise, one must ask what the passage indicated about the status of slavery in the American constitutional system.

By the slave-trade clause, according to Taney in 1857, "the right to purchase and hold this *property* is directly sanctioned and authorized for twenty years." But the clause actually authorized nothing except a tax on the importation of persons. Otherwise, it merely stayed the hand of Congress in the exercise of a power presumably granted elsewhere in the Constitution. It would have been just as accurate to say that the clause authorized the future abolition of the slave trade and thus amounted, by Taney's own logic, to a delayed repudiation of the slave system. Some delegates did in fact regard the clause as a major step toward total abolition.

Whether intended or not, the vagueness of the clause lent variety to its interpretation. Thus the awkward euphemism for slaves could be read as including free immigrants also. At the same time, the use of the words "importation" and "duty" seemed to recognize the property-holding aspect of slavery—but then it was a recognition scheduled for cancellation in twenty years. Even the authority to impose a tax or duty was symbolically ambiguous, as Congress soon discovered. Measures unsuccessfully introduced in 1789 and again in 1804-06 were defended on the antislavery grounds that taxation would constitute a public censure of the slave trade, and they were opposed on the antislavery grounds that such taxation would degrade human beings by classifying them as merchandise.

Neither the three-fifths clause nor the slave-trade clause offered slavery any positive protection under the Constitution. The fugitive-slave clause, on the other hand, became the basis for the most notorious kind of federal intervention in behalf of the institution. Its wording too was ambiguous: "No person held to service or labour in one State, under the laws thereof, escaping into another, shall, in consequence of any law or regulation therein, be discharged from such service or labour, but shall be delivered up on claim of the party to whom such service or labour may be due." Read literally, the clause seems to include apprentices and other persons bound to service for a limited period. Thus, unlike the three-fifths clause, it drew no distinction between free and non-free persons. And its terminology, unlike that of the slave-trade clause, carried no connotation of property. Not in what it said, but only in how it was universally understood, did the so-called fugitive-slave clause acknowledge the existence of slavery in America.

The clause was not a significant issue in the Convention. Introduced late in the proceedings, it aroused little debate and received unanimous approval. There is little evidence to support the assertion frequently made in later years that without it the Constitution would have failed. Placement of the clause in Article Four, rather than in Article One, suggests that it was designed as a limitation on state authority and not as an extension of federal power and responsibility. That is, the purpose was to guard against personal-liberty laws, rather than to provide for a national fugitive-slave law. The very language of the clause seems plainly directed at the states, not at Congress. Nevertheless, both Congress and the Supreme Court eventually came to the opposite conclusion.

Of course there were other passages in the completed Constitution that would come to bear upon the institution of slavery—

including the commerce clause, the territory clause, and the provision for admission of new states. None of them reveal anything, however, about the "intent of the framers" as far as slavery was concerned. Even the three clauses that did deal with slavery were uncoordinated and ambiguous, embodying no ruling principle except compromise for the sake of union, but their want of coherence does not entirely obscure a certain elemental drift or tendency.

To begin with, the Constitution neither authorized nor forbade the abolition of slavery. It dealt only with peripheral features of the institution. All three of the slavery clauses treated slaves as "persons," and just one (the three-fifths clause) expressly differentiated between free and unfree persons. None used the word "property." One (the slave-trade clause) contained language that seemed to reflect the property-holding aspect of slavery, but another (the fugitive-slave clause) seemed almost to repudiate ownership of men by designating a slave as a "person held to service or labour," and an owner as "the party to whom such service or labour is due." The temporary nature of the slave-trade clause made it a dubious sanction for perpetual slavery. In addition, the operation of the clause was restricted to the original states, and this, together with congressional enactment of the Northwest Ordinance, indicated a disposition to make slavery the exception rather than the rule in an expanding nation.

Perhaps most revealing of all was a last-minute revision of the fugitive-slave clause. As it came from the committee of style, the clause began: "No person legally held to service or labour in one state." The revised version read: "No person held to service or labour in one state, under the laws thereof." Because of its contextual ambiguity, the word "legally" would have permitted the inference that the Constitution explicitly affirmed the legality of slavery. The framers, in shifting to the phrase "under the laws thereof," lent strong support to those antislavery spokesmen of a later day who would insist that slavery was without national existence and strictly the creature of local law.

The pattern that emerges is one of acknowledging the legitimate presence of slavery in American life while attaching a cluster of limitations to the acknowledgment. And one returns always to the striking fact that in the three clauses dealing with slavery, the word itself was deliberately avoided. This should not be dismissed as mere fastidiousness. The law inheres most essentially in the text of the document, not in the purposes of those who wrote the document, although the purposes may be consulted to illuminate obscure meaning. The sharp contrast here between text and purpose has its own significant effect. It is as though the framers were half-consciously trying to frame two constitutions, one for their own time and the other for the ages, with slavery viewed bifocally—that is, plainly visible at their feet, but disappearing when they lifted their eyes.

2

From time to time at the Constitutional Convention there had been confrontation between a slavery interest and an antislavery sentiment. The interest was concentrated, persistent, practical, and testily defensive. The sentiment tended to be diffuse, sporadic, moralistic, and tentative. This distinction between interest and sentiment remains appropriate for at least the first half-century of national history. An antislavery interest of significant proportions was especially slow to develop, even slower than a proslavery sentiment.

Antislavery sentiment received considerable lip service even from the slavery interest in the early years of the Republic, and the first American constitutions, including those of the southern states, made no direct mention of the peculiar institution. Constitution-making, after all, was a noble enterprise, infused with a good deal of moral grandeur. Overt recognition of slavery did not fit well with solemn discussion of fundamental law, the social compact, and bills of rights. In the day-to-day operations of government, however, interest would usually have the advantage over sentiment.

American Negro slavery had originated in international custom and colonial practice, reinforced by the express or implied support of the English government. Over the years, it had ac-

quired a legal structure consisting essentially of local common
and statute law in the thirteen colonies. Slavery under the new
federal Constitution of 1787 remained almost entirely the legal
creature of local (state) law. In this respect it was not unlike
marriage, property-holding, inheritance, and other basic social
institutions. Codification of slaveholding law began during the
colonial period and continued right up to the Civil War. The
slave codes varied substantially from state to state and were supplemented by a large body of local regulations. In behavioral
terms, the so-called law of slavery was the work, not only of
those persons who drafted it but also of everyone charged with
enforcing it—including sheriffs, constables, patrols, judges, jailors, masters, and overseers. But as a body of written rules, it was
primarily the work of state legislatures and state appellate courts,
with the latter standing first in the sheer bulk of their contribution. The content of this state law of slavery has been described
in detail by numerous historians. Here, it is sufficient to note certain major characteristics discernible in a cluster of fifteen systems that were similar but by no means uniform, and stable but
by no means unchanging.

In criminal law, the slave was regarded essentially as a person, responsible and punishable for his offenses. The law of private rights (civil law), on the other hand, treated slaves primarily as property. Thus, even though he was punishable as a
person for any crime he might commit, he was not suable as a
person for any injury he might do. Damages, if they were to be
collected at all, had to be collected from the slaveholder.

The criminal law of slavery as it moved westward tended to
lose some of its severity—not because westerners were more ten-
der-hearted but because the times were becoming more enlightened. The slave code of Arkansas, for example, was considerably
less severe than the codes of Virginia and South Carolina, which,
locked in the colonial tradition, remained the harshest in the
South. For slaves as well as free men, the cruel physical punishments of earlier times were eliminated or at least diminished
everywhere in the nineteenth century. The list of capital offenses
grew longer as a consequence, however, and the inappropriate-
ness of imprisonment for slaves left whipping as the standard

punishment for lesser offenses. The Georgia code of 1861 specified that jailors and constables should be paid one dollar "for
whipping a negro," but set the limit at thirty-nine lashes, not
"inhumanly" done.

Perhaps the most notable development in the slave law of
the nineteenth century was the increasing procedural protection
given slaves accused of capital offenses. In many southern states
this came to include nominal equality with white persons in respect to the rights of trial by jury and appeal, the right to counsel, and immunity from coerced self-incrimination. The changes
were wrought by legislative action and by certain enlightened
appellate judges, some of whom insisted upon bringing the slave
generally within the protection of the common law. Such amelio-
rative tendencies did not reflect any erosion of proslavery conviction in the South; for in protecting a slave's person one also
protected a master's property, while at the same time offering
refutation to the abolitionist indictment of slavery as totally unjust and inhumane.

The ultimate purpose of slave codes was to prevent insurrec-
tions and other dangerous forms of servile resistance, such as ar-
son and poisoning. Southern legislatures grappled continually
with the problem of security, becoming especially active in the
1830s after the Nat Turner rampage and the emergence of Garrisonian abolitionism. Much of the security legislation laid restrictions on white behavior considered subversive in its influence on slaves. Laws forbade teaching slaves to read and write,
trading with slaves, gambling with slaves, or supplying them with
liquor, guns, or poisonous drugs. In addition, severe penalties
were established for the utterance of abolitionist doctrines and
the circulation of abolitionist propaganda. The fear of insurrection was also manifested in laws subjecting the free black population to increased restraints and disabilities amounting virtually
to persecution.

If the state law of slavery were the whole story, then even in
all its great bulk and variety it would be a relatively simple
story of each state's enforcing its own law within its own jurisdiction. The complexity results in large part from the interplay
and conflict of overlapping jurisdictions. For one thing, there

was the remarkable extent to which slavery, though given very limited recognition in the Constitution, became a matter of concern to the federal government in the routine conduct of its business.

The influence of the slavery interest was greatly enhanced, for instance, by the location of the national capital on the north bank of the Potomac River and by the predominance of southern leadership in the public affairs of the new nation. The city of Washington was from its inception a slaveholding community, and it remained so by the express volition of Congress, which in 1801 decreed that the laws of Virginia and Maryland should continue in force within the District of Columbia. Thus the only sizable area of the country exclusively and permanently under United States jurisdiction acquired its own slave code, established and enforced by federal authority. One finds a federal judge in 1807 sentencing a slave convicted of robbery to be "burnt in the hand and whipped with one hundred stripes." Of course the fact that many early presidents, cabinet members, and congressmen were owners of slaves likewise tended to normalize and legitimate the institution on a national basis.

Federal jurisdiction over western territories also helped implicate the United States government in the maintenance and promotion of slavery. To be sure, the first Congress did re-enact the Northwest Ordinance with its famous antislavery article, but in 1790 Congress endorsed the expansion of slavery into the Southwest. There, as in the District of Columbia, slave codes adopted under federal authority were enforced by federally appointed officers.

The conduct of foreign affairs was still another realm of responsibility that involved the federal government in the protection of slavery. For example, American slaves carried off by British forces during the Revolution and the War of 1812 were the subject of prolonged diplomatic negotiations between the two governments. To demand recompense for the slave-owners was obviously to affirm that slaves were property, and yet men of antislavery sentiment like John Jay and John Quincy Adams allowed themselves to be enlisted in the enterprise. Adams was especially successful. He played a major part in securing indemnities that totaled over a million dollars.

Slave ships on the high seas could also spell trouble for the United States government in its relations with foreign powers. During the 1830s, slaves from several distressed or shipwrecked coasting vessels were rescued in British West Indian waters and promptly set free. The Jackson and Van Buren administrations repeatedly demanded compensation for the slave-owners, insisting that slaves were property under American law. The British government eventually agreed to make payment in certain cases.

Anglo-American relations were further embittered in 1841 when slaves aboard the *Creole*, en route from Virginia to Louisiana, staged a mutiny and took the ship to Nassau in the Bahamas. Daniel Webster, secretary of state in the Tyler administration, insisted that the slaves must be returned to the United States. But the British stood firm, though a claims commission many years later awarded a small indemnity to the American owners.

The case of the *Amistad* was substantially different, involving a Cuban ship taken over in 1839 by mutinuous slaves and eventually brought into an American port. It soon came to light that most of the slaves had been carried off from Africa in violation of treaties suppressing the international slave trade. The Spanish government nevertheless demanded return of the slaves, and the Van Buren administration tried earnestly to comply. Because of salvage claims, however, the issue went to trial in a federal district court and reached the Supreme Court in 1841. With only one justice dissenting, the Court declared the Negroes to be free men. Yet the executive branch of the federal government refused to accept the Court decision as final. Presidents Tyler, Polk, Pierce, and Buchanan all recommended payment of reparations, but Congress never made the appropriation. These presidential efforts to appease Spain were probably not unconnected with the chronic presidential desire for annexation of Cuba.

Thus the regular duties of office—indeed, the very structure of government—brought federal officials frequently into association with slavery. It is unlikely that a complete detachment, if attempted, could have been achieved; but at the same time it appears that the federal government consistently gave slavery more support than law or circumstances required.

A further case in point is the act of Congress usually referred to as the Fugitive Slave Act of 1793. The relevant clause in the Constitution, as we have seen, was rather vaguely phrased and located elsewhere than among the powers delegated to Congress. A person "held to service or labor" in one state and escaping into another, it said, must be "delivered up" when claimed by the party to whom the service or labor was due. That the clause necessitated or even authorized congressional implementation is open to question. Enforcement might have been left to interstate comity or to the federal judicial process.

The first session of the first Congress apparently saw no pressing need in 1789 to include a fugitive-slave law in the great body of fundamental legislation with which it was then setting the federal government in motion. Not until four years later did the second session of the second Congress take action on the subject, and it did so more or less gratuitously.

The act of 1793 resulted from a quarrel between Maryland and Virginia over criminal extradition. But since fugitives from justice and fugitives from service had been dealt with side by side in the Constitution, it seemed logical to do so again in implemental legislation. And so Congress passed "An Act respecting fugitives from justice, and persons escaping from the service of their masters." The first half of the law, dealing with criminal extradition, proved to be essentially declaratory. Whenever the governor of a state demanded the return of a fugitive from justice who had fled into another state, it was to be the "duty" of the governor of the second state to comply. The law provided no means of compelling a governor to perform his duty. Interstate extradition thus remained a matter of interstate comity.

The second half of the law had more teeth in it and was much less deferential to state sovereignty. It authorized a slaveowner or his agent to cross a state line, seize an alleged fugitive slave, take the slave before any federal judge or local magistrate, and there, upon proof of ownership, receive a certificate entitling him to return home with his captive. Financial penalties were provided for interfering in any way with the recovery of a fugitive. The act as a whole passed in the Senate without recorded opposition and in the House by the overwhelming majority of 48 to 7.

And so, with scarcely a serious thought about the implications of its action, Congress voted to invade state sovereignty for the benefit of the slaveholder, issuing him a kind of vigilante's license to enforce his rights himself with a minimum of formality. The law set aside normal legal process, such as the writ of habeas corpus and trial by jury. It gave the alleged fugitive no protection against self-incrimination and no assurance that he could testify in his own behalf. It specified no time limitation; so an alleged slave could be claimed many years after his alleged escape. Furthermore, there was nothing in the text of the law to discourage a pursuer from taking his captive back home without bothering to obtain a certificate. The act was in fact an invitation to kidnapping, whether as a result of honest error or deliberate fraud.

The early "personal liberty laws" enacted by many northern states were primarily anti-kidnapping laws and often so entitled. Their purpose was not to flout the federal law of 1793 but rather to strike a balance between the rights of slaveholders and the rights of free Negroes threatened by the law. Meanwhile, certain federal and state courts, in the process of enforcing the act of 1793, were turning aside challenges to its constitutionality and contributing to the myth that the fugitive-slave clause had been indispensable to the success of the Constitutional Convention. By 1842 the "historical-necessity thesis" had become so well accepted in high judicial circles that five out of seven Supreme Court justices reiterated it in the single case of *Prigg v. Pennsylvania*. Joseph Story, for instance, said that the fugitive-slave clause unquestionably "constituted a fundamental article without the adoption of which the Union could not have been formed." Thus the clause, by reason of its supposed indispensability, was elevated into a special category as a kind of higher law *within* the Constitution.

Among Supreme Court decisions dealing with slavery, *Prigg v. Pennsylvania* rivals *Dred Scott v. Sandford* in historical impor-

tance. The opinion of the Court, delivered by Justice Story, had
the antislavery effect of releasing state governments from any
obligation to enforce the fugitive-slave law of 1793. What has received too little attention, however, is the extent to which the
decision also carried forward the involvement of the federal government in the protection of slavery.

Edward Prigg had been convicted on kidnapping charges in
Pennsylvania for taking a recaptured fugitive slave back to Maryland without obtaining the required certificate. Story reversed
the judgment and invalidated the Pennsylvania statute under
which Prigg had been indicted, finding it in conflict with the federal law of 1793 and with the Constitution. In the course of reasoning his way to this conclusion, he laid down a number of
weighty rulings:

1. *Slavery was entirely a creation of municipal* (*domestic*)
*law and could claim no recognition within another jurisdiction as
a matter of right.* This part of Story's opinion won applause in
certain antislavery circles; yet it had the effect of concentrating
in the federal government total responsibility for enforcement of
the allegedly indispensable fugitive-slave clause.

2. *The fugitive-slave clause of the Constitution, aside from
any implemental legislation, was self-executing.* That is, it gave
every slaveholder the "positive, unqualified right" to recapture a
slave by private effort anywhere in the Union, and to do so without interference from any quarter, provided that no breach of
the peace were committed. The slaveholder, in short, carried the
law of his own state with him when he pursued a fugitive into a
free state. The implications of such extraterritoriality were startling, though Story left them unexplored. His ruling had the effect, for instance, of compelling free states to accept the slave-
state principle that a black or mulatto was a slave unless he
could prove otherwise. One-half of the nation must sacrifice its
presumption of freedom to the other half's presumption of
slavery.

3. *The fugitive-slave law of 1793 was constitutional.* Here,
Story merely demonstrated that congressional power to enact
such legislation could reasonably be inferred from the fugitive-
slave clause. For every act of Congress, however, there are two

constitutional tests. The first is whether the Constitution autho-
rizes it; the second is whether the Constitution forbids it. What
Story coolly ignored was the argument of counsel for Pennsylvania that the law of 1793, in certain of its provisions, violated
the constitutional rights of free Negroes wrongfully or dubiously
claimed as slaves.

4. *The power to legislate for enforcement of the slaveholder's
right of recovery was vested exclusively in Congress.* Nothing in
the nature of the *Prigg* case necessitated such a pronouncement,
and nothing in the text of the fugitive-slave clause justified it.
Furthermore, the principle of federal exclusiveness could obviously cut either way in the slavery controversy, depending upon
how vigorously Congress exercised its exclusive power. Chief
Justice Taney, who concurred in the decision, dissented at this
point. State governments, he insisted, were constitutionally re-
strained only from legislation and other action *interfering* with
a slaveholder's property rights in his slave; they had the power
and even the obligation to assist in *protecting* those rights.
Fifteen years later, Taney would come to a similar conclusion
regarding federal power over slavery in the territories.

The fundamental racism in the *Prigg* decision was relatively
inconspicuous. It consisted in the Court's silent refusal to pay
any attention to the kidnapping problem—a refusal that would
have been inconceivable if the victims had been white. Similarly, the proslavery nationalist tendencies of the decision were
obscured by the fact that for a time it worked the other way, as
various northern legislatures enacted laws forbidding state officials to participate in the recovery of fugitive slaves. Despite
these antislavery consequences, the *Prigg* decision, enunciated
by an avowedly antislavery New Englander, was another major
indication of the extent to which the United States government
had voluntarily become the guardian of slaveholding rights everywhere outside the territorial limits of slaveholding law.

The fugitive-slave clause, implemented in the law of 1793
and given added force and meaning in court decisions, came to
have a significance that transcended the problem to which it was
addressed. In the long-running debate between the enemies of
slavery and its defenders, neither side maintained a consistent

position on the question of national power versus state sovereignty. Both shifted ground whenever it suited their purposes to do so. For southerners especially the issue was critical and delicate. At times driven by circumstances to invoke federal protection of their slaveholding rights, they were nevertheless extremely reluctant to endorse any increase in federal authority over slavery, fearing that the power to protect could too easily be converted into the power to destroy. Even the Fugitive Slave Act of 1850, although passed in response to southern demands, made some southerners uneasy because of its expansion of federal authority. Yet the federal fugitive-slave complex as a whole (that is, the clause, the legislation of Congress, and the judicial enforcement) provided the South with the basic formula for claiming federal protection of slavery while denying federal power to interfere with slavery.

Federal enforcement of the fugitive-slave clause treated slaves as property and thus constituted federal acquiescence in the southern definition of slaveholding as a form of property-holding. This acquiescence proved highly advantageous to the South in the constitutional debates on slavery in the territories. In addition, the federal fugitive-slave complex gave the southern law of slavery an imperial, extrajurisdictional force within the free states, thereby furnishing a precedent for similar claims to extrajurisdictional rights within the federal territories. The effect was to make slaveholding rights national in scope.

Whether so much federal intervention in behalf of slavery accorded with the letter and spirit of the Constitution was a matter of disagreement even among abolitionists, some of whom insisted that the Convention of 1787 had sold the nation's soul to the slaveholder, while others maintained that it had written an essentially antislavery document. What seems worth stressing, however, is the extent to which the framers were indeterminate in their treatment of slavery, leaving Congress and the other branches of government much freedom of choice as a consequence. That federal power should have become in many ways a bulwark of slavery was a development permitted but not required by the Constitution. It reflected not only the day-to-day advantage of interest over sentiment and the predominance of southern leadership in the federal government, but also the waning of the liberal idealism of the Revolution.

3

Aside from the fugitive's hazardous road to an uncertain future, there were various legal ways for a slave to escape into freedom. The pale southern counterpart of northern emancipation in the aftermath of the Revolution was a substantial increase of individual manumissions. Indeed, it appears that during those early decades of the Republic, more slaves may have been freed in the South than in the North. One piece of evidence supporting such an estimate is the fact that the free black population of the South grew at a faster rate than the free black population of the North.

Manumission, being an exercise of the property-holder's inherent right to renounce ownership of his property, presumably needed no express sanction of law, but like all property rights it was subject to regulation in the public interest. Substantial legislative restrictions had been laid on private emancipation in colonial times. Then, in 1782, with the spirit of the Revolution triumphant, Virginia removed her principal barriers to manumission, and most of the other southern states followed suit. Thousands of slaves were liberated in the next two decades, and during that time the free black population of the South grew three times as fast as the white and slave populations.

But a reaction soon set in. Free Negroes were, after all, an anomaly in a slaveholding society. Their presence in increasing numbers seemed likely to cause dissatisfaction in slave quarters and perhaps inspire slave resistance. The black rebellion on the island of Santo Domingo was a frightening spectacle for southerners in the 1790s, and its leaders were recently freed slaves. The shadow of Santo Domingo fell across Virginia in 1800 with the discovery of Gabriel Prosser's plot to lead a band of fellow slaves in an insurrectionary attack on Richmond. Apparently no free blacks were involved in the conspiracy, and yet Virginians

in 1806 passed a law requiring that manumitted slaves leave the
state within twelve months.

Several other southern legislatures had already begun to restrict manumission in one way or another, and this became the
dominant trend of the next half-century. Many states eventually
followed Virginia's example in requiring removal of liberated
slaves. Some states canceled the slaveholder's right to free his
slaves privately, making manumission instead a public act that
could be performed only by a court or by means of special legislation. More and more states also prohibited slaves from hiring
out their own time, thereby discouraging the practice of achieving freedom through self-purchase. Hostility to manumission
grew even stronger as the sectional conflict entered its final
stages in the 1850s. Louisiana and Tennessee required guarantees
that freed slaves would be sent out of the United States, and by
the end of the decade, several states had forbidden manumission
absolutely.

Yet, despite all efforts at curtailment, manumissions continued. They reportedly numbered some three thousand in the
year 1860, for example. This does not mean that a significant
abolitionist tradition persisted in the South, for antislavery conviction seldom appeared to be the reason for manumission.
Rather, freedom was often given as a reward for faithful service.
Even more often, perhaps, the slaveholder was simply freeing
his own children born to a slave concubine. Many of the southern laws aimed at restricting manumissions were poorly enforced
and could be circumvented in several ways. A slaveholder might
take his slaves into a free state and liberate them there. More
common was the practice of simply turning a slave loose to fend
for himself without the formality of manumission. Such quasi-
free slaves became fairly numerous in the urban South, and by
the 1850s their number in St. Louis may have included Dred
Scott.

Unintentional manumission was also possible. It could occur
as a result of a slave's merely being moved from one slaveholding state to another in violation of law. More significant, however, were the claims to freedom that sometimes arose when
slaves were taken into states or territories where slavery was pro-

hibited. What happened to the legal condition of a slave entering a nonslaveholding jurisdiction? And if he later returned to a slaveholding state, what counter-effect did that return have upon whatever change of condition had been wrought by his stay in the free state or territory? By the early decades of the nineteenth century, this problem of the status of slaves residing or once resident on free soil had already become one of the classic issues in the legal history of slavery.

Actually, it was not just a single issue but rather a cluster of issues, including the substantive question of which law should prevail and the jurisdictional question of who had the final word about which law should prevail.

To the substantive question there were three basic answers: (1) The law of slavery remained attached to a slave when he entered a free state; his status did not change. (2) The slave taken by his master into a free state became a free man and remained so permanently, wherever he might go thereafter. (3) The slave taken into a free state became free in the sense that his master lost the power to control him, but upon his returning to a slaveholding state, the status of slave reattached to him.

The jurisdictional question was essentially whether, in a suit for freedom, the forum state had an uninhibited right to apply its own law or whether it was under obligation or compulsion to apply the law of another state. Usually, the question arose in a suit brought by a slave who had been taken into a free state and then returned to a slaveholding state. The specific issue then presented was whether the emancipatory effect of the free state's law would be enforced extraterritorially, or whether the slave in returning to the slaveholding state *reverted* totally to its jurisdiction.

The jurisdictional principle of *reversion* was often linked with the substantive principle of *reattachment* (number 3 above). It is nevertheless important to maintain the distinction between the two. Without using the terms, Taney did so plainly in his *Dred Scott* opinion. Even if the principle of reversion were confirmed, a slaveholding state might embrace or reject the principle of reattachment.

Underlying the specific substantive question of which law

should prevail was the more general problem of the legal and philosophical character of slavery. Discussion of the subject usually led beyond the American constitutional system to English common law and the law of nature. Underlying the specific jurisdictional question of who had the final word was the more general problem of interstate relationships. Discussion led by analogy to the law of nations and the branch of that jurisprudence known as the conflict of laws.

Still another question of crucial importance was whether the purpose and duration of the slave's residence on free soil made any significant difference in its effect on his status. The primary distinction recognized was between residence temporary enough to be classified as "sojourning" and residence permanent enough to constitute "domicile." The dividing line could be difficult to draw in particular cases, but the distinction, as we shall see, provided the basis for a tacit sectional compromise of some duration.

The problem of the extraterritorial status of slavery had arisen several times in eighteenth-century England, eventually drawing forth the famous decision of Lord Mansfield in *Somerset v. Stewart* (1772). Somerset, a slave taken from Virginia to England and later consigned to a ship's captain for sale in Jamaica, was ordered released on the ground that nothing in the law of the realm authorized his imprisonment aboard the departing ship. Slavery, Mansfield is reported to have said, was "so odious" that it could be given legal status only by the positive law of the country in which it was used. Over the next half-century there developed an extravagant tradition that the decision had outlawed slavery in Britain, and that, accordingly, any slave brought into the country became free the moment he set foot on English soil.

In America, *Somerset* and its legend contributed significantly to the antislavery tendencies of the Revolutionary era. It became a major weapon in the arsenal of abolitionism, lending support to the argument that slavery was contrary to natural law and without legal status beyond the boundaries of the jurisdiction establishing it by positive law. Yet the *Somerset* doctrine, with one simple adjustment, also fitted into a formula of sectional accommodation. Southerners, for the most part, were willing to accept the doctrine in so far as it applied to slaves *domiciled* by their masters on free soil; northerners, in turn, generally agreed that it should not apply to instances of transit, sojourn, or temporary residence.

In some northern states, such as Pennsylvania and New York, sojourning rights were acknowledged and specified by statute; in others, such as Ohio and Illinois, the same effect was achieved by implicit understanding. Northern state judiciaries offered no serious challenge to sojourning during the early decades of the Republic. Southern courts, for their part, consistently ruled that a slave taken to live permanently in a free state or territory was thereby emancipated. More than that, they consistently held that such freedom vested in the former slave and could not be rendered void by his return to a slaveholding state. That is, the southern courts did not invoke the principle of reattachment and embraced instead the principle of "once free, forever free." This pattern of southern liberalism was developed within an explicitly restricted context. Court decisions in favor of freedom were limited almost entirely to instances of permanent slaveholding residence on free soil in defiance of state or federal law. Often the court expressly discriminated between sojourning and domicile, making it plain that only the latter worked emancipation.

The sectional accommodation thus incorporated two of the three possible answers to the question of which law should prevail. In the case of sojourning, the law of slavery remained attached to a slave when he entered a free state; in the case of domicile, the law of the free state emancipated him and irreversibly so. Within this formula of compromise there was no place or need for the third answer—the principle of reattachment.

Certain northern states were the first to breach the tacit understanding. They began to do so in the 1830s at a time when antislavery sentiment was crystallizing into a sustained antislavery movement. In 1836 the Supreme Judicial Court of Massachusetts freed a six-year-old slave girl who had been brought into the state by her mistress on a visit. Chief Justice Lemuel Shaw rejected an appeal to interstate comity, declaring that slavery was contrary to natural right and dependent upon local law for its existence. To extend comity in such cases, he said, would

mean permitting any amount of slaveholding residence short of
outright domicile, and that, being repugnant to state policy, was
"inadmissible." Thus sojourning had been pronounced illegal in
Massachusetts. One year later, a slave held "temporarily" in Connecticut for some twenty-four months was awarded her freedom
by the supreme court of the state. In the 1840s, New York and
Pennsylvania repealed their laws permitting sojourners to remain
for nine and six months respectively.

Southerners bitterly resented these demeaning barriers being
raised against slaveholding travel into the free states, and they set
about defending themselves against what a Georgia judge called
"the foul . . . spirit of modern fanaticism." Lending strength to
their defense was a fairly recent English court decision that
trimmed back the more extravagant ramifications of the *Somerset* tradition. The case of *The Slave Grace* (1827) involved a
slave who had accompanied her mistress on a one-year visit to
England and then returned willingly to Antigua. More clearly
than with *Somerset*, this was a case of sojourning instead of domicile. In the Court of Admiralty, Lord Stowell ruled that Grace,
although free in England, had resumed her status as a slave once
she was back in Antigua. Stowell thus rejected the idea that
emancipation was irreversible, enunciating instead the principle of reattachment as a restrictive corollary to the *Somerset*
doctrine.

Southerners, as we have seen, had no need for the principle
of reattachment so long as northern states agreed that temporary residence in a free state did not change a slave's legal status. When northern courts and legislatures began to outlaw sojourning, however, southern judges began to make use of Stowell's
formulation, but only as a defense against the new northern
doctrine of immediate, foot-on-the-soil-of-freedom emancipation.
Except in Missouri as a result of the Dred Scott case, there appears to have been no decision of a southern appellate court that
denied a suit for freedom in a clear-cut case of permanent residence on free soil. Such cases, to be sure, were unlikely to arise
in the later antebellum period; for few slaveholders were willing
to risk losing their property in this manner, and any Negro who
did gain a claim to freedom by virtue of longtime residence on

free soil was not likely to risk it by returning to the hostile legal environment of a slaveholding state. The fact remains, however, that there was no sweeping repudiation by southern judiciaries of the old tacit sectional accommodation on the status of slavery in nonslaveholding jurisdictions.

The northern assault on sojourning privileges reached its climax in a half-forgotten New York case of the 1850s that caused much excitement at the time. In *Lemmon v. The People* (1860), first decided in the trial court in 1852, the state freed a number of slaves that were merely in transit from Virginia to Texas by coastal vessels. "It marked," says one legal scholar, "the uttermost expansion of the libertarian implications of *Somerset*." To southerners it seemed that they were being treated more and more like lepers, and their resentment soon found expression in the documents of secession. The Mississippi resolutions of November 30, 1860, for example, declared that the northern states had "insulted and outraged our citizens when travelling among them for pleasure, health or business, by taking their servants and liberating the same . . . and subjecting their owners to degrading and ignominious punishment."

Although manumission was prohibited or severely restricted in much of the South by the late antebellum period, suits for freedom were still generally permitted and often carefully provided for by statute. The number of such suits prosecuted in trial courts is unknown, but according to one tabulation, state supreme courts heard 670 appeals during the entire slaveholding era. Decisions were rendered in 575 of these cases, with blacks winning their suits 57 per cent of the time.

Black "freedom" in a slaveholding state, however, was in many respects little more than a special category of slavery. The southern free Negro lived in a precarious world cramped between two boundaries—the line of slavery separating him from the great mass of blacks and the color line separating him from the great mass of free men. More often than not, it was the color line that determined his status and treatment.

At the end of the Revolution, free Negroes probably constituted less than 1.5 per cent of the South's total population and less than 4 per cent of its black population. By law and custom in the colonial period they had been assigned an inferior social status and deprived of many rights and privileges possessed by white persons. Yet the process of exclusion and degradation had been a haphazard one, and it varied extensively from colony to colony. Of course social pressure often served as the agency of repression when the law did not, but with the exception of prohibitions against miscegenation, there was nothing approaching uniformity in southern racial policies before the Revolution. Moreover, the free Negro of colonial times, although scorned and in many ways deprived, had not yet become a serious cause for alarm and therefore enjoyed more freedom from surveillance than he did in the antebellum period.

But with the free black community growing more rapidly than other elements of the population, and with southerners becoming ever more fearful of slave revolts, the racial restraints increased in number and severity. One by one, the southern states formally disfranchised the free Negro. They excluded him from jury service, and in most of the South he could not testify against a white person. His freedom of movement came under heavy restriction as other states forbade him to immigrate and his own state required him to register, carry freedom papers, and, in the lower South especially, have a guardian appointed by law.

Increasingly, free blacks were equated with slaves in southern law. Among other things, this meant that they were subject to search without warrant and to trial without jury for all but capital offenses. They were denied the right of assembly and forbidden to own or carry arms. They were barred from professions and many trades by laws, high license fees, and extralegal pressures. They were excluded from schools, and it was a crime to teach them to read or write.

In addition, there was always a danger of slipping back into slavery. The free Negro had to be able at all times to produce proof of his status or risk losing it, and in most southern states he could be reduced to temporary or permanent servitude for a variety of offenses. Georgia law required that tax-delinquent Negroes be hired out "from year to year," during which time their status would be the same as that of slaves. The state code also declared: "The punishment of a free person of color for immigrating into this State, in violation of its laws, shall be sale into perpetual bondage."

It is true that such regulations were often ignored or evaded, but it is also true that the free Negro's legal disabilities were supplemented with a good deal of informal coercion and discrimination in his local community. Free blacks were widely regarded as a subversive influence on slaves and as potential agents of abolitionism. In the upper part of the Old South there was also much apprehension about their growing numbers. Nowhere, says Ira Berlin, was the fear of an eventual free black majority more intense than in Maryland, the home state of Roger B. Taney.

In the North, free Negroes were generally regarded as a nuisance but not as a serious menace. Freer than their southern counterparts from linkage with slavery and from the danger of re-enslavement, they nevertheless lived marginal lives as a despised and deprived minority. Some states, such as Illinois and Indiana, forbade their entry. Some forbade them to testify in cases involving white persons. Social pressure restricted them largely to menial labor. Their children either attended segregated schools or were barred entirely from public education. More than 90 per cent of them were disfranchised. The fact that these northern black laws were poorly enforced took much of the sting out of them, to be sure, but the threat of enforcement hung in the air, adding to the precariousness of life for the free Negro. In one notorious instance, a Cincinnati effort to enforce the Ohio black laws requiring registration and posting of bond drove more than a thousand Negroes into flight from the city.

The Constitution of the United States, though it provided some basis for the federal government's support of slavery, contained no authority for federal discrimination against the black race. Yet Congress in 1792 excluded Negroes from the militia and in 1810 denied them the right to work as mail carriers. By congressional action, free Negroes in Washington, D.C., were disfranchised, excluded from certain kinds of business activity, and made subject to many of the laws regulating slaves. From time to time, Congress also disfranchised blacks in the territories. The executive branch, though it never developed a consistent and comprehensive racial policy, added discriminatory edicts of various kinds, such as those excluding Negroes from the Navy and Marine Corps in 1798 and denying them pre-emption rights on public lands in 1856.

With racial discrimination so pervasive in American law and society, there inevitably arose the question whether free Negroes were citizens of the United States and of the states in which they lived. It was an issue clouded not only by the free Negro's intermediate status between slavery and freedom, and by the variations in his treatment from New England to the deep South, but also by the vague and flexible meaning of the word "citizen" itself. Adding further to the confusion was the problem of the undefined relationship between state citizenship and national citizenship in a federal republic.

No longer "subjects" of the British crown, Americans in the Revolutionary era began to speak of themselves as "citizens" of their respective states and their new nation. The term appeared in both the Articles of Confederation and the Constitution, but it was not given authoritative and precise definition until after the Civil War. In its broadest and perhaps most common usage during the early national period, "citizen" meant any domiciled inhabitant except an alien or a slave. Sometimes, however, the word was used to designate only those active partners in a sovereign community who possessed all its civil and political privileges, including suffrage and eligibility to hold public office. This definition, strictly applied in the early nineteenth century, would have excluded not only women, children, and most free blacks, but also many white male adults who could not meet religious and property-holding qualifications for voting.

It is easy enough to demonstrate that the stricter definition did not universally prevail. Women, for example, although not allowed to vote, were recognized as citizens for the purpose of bringing suit in federal courts, and foreign-born women were capable of becoming citizens of the United States through naturalization or even through marriage.

At times, free Negroes were likewise recognized in the language of the law as falling within the circle of citizenship, broadly defined, and this was especially true during the early decades of national independence. For one thing, the fourth article of the Articles of Confederation, approved by the Continental Congress in 1778, treated the word "citizens" as interchangeable with the word "inhabitants." It declared that the "free inhabitants" of each state should be entitled to "all the privileges and immunities of free citizens in the several States." A proposal from South Carolina that the word "white" be inserted in this clause was defeated by a vote of eight states to two. Five years later, in the abortive amendment on apportionment of taxes that first introduced the three-fifths ratio, Congress referred to "white and other free citizens." At about the same time, the Virginia legislature repealed an earlier law limiting citizenship to white persons and provided instead that "all free persons born within the territory of this commonwealth" should be entitled to all the rights, privileges, and advantages of citizenship. Moving into the nineteenth century, one finds a resolution of the House of Representatives in 1803 referring to "such American seamen, citizens of the United States, as are free persons of color."

Evidence of this kind is by no means consistent, and it can too easily be mistaken for proof of a racial equalitarianism that did not exist. The Revolutionary generation's disposition to view the Negro as racially inferior and unassimilable was plainly exhibited—for instance, in the federal statute of 1790 that limited naturalization to "free white persons." Yet the crucial question that later arose was not what the founding fathers had thought of the free Negro as an element in the American population, but rather what status they had actually accorded him in American law. And the evidence is that by implication, sufferance, and inadvertence they often classified him as a citizen. For example, neither the Ordinance of 1787 nor the first constitutions of Kentucky (1792) and Tennessee (1796) discriminated against blacks in civil rights or suffrage, and citizenship could reasonably be inferred from the failure to do so.

Whatever such permissiveness may have owed to the liberalizing influence of the Revolution, it primarily reflected the fact that free Negroes were at first too insignificant in number to be taken separately into account every time a constitution or statute

was drafted. As we have seen, however, the rapid growth of the
free black population during the post-Revolutionary period inspired the legal imposition of many new racial restraints and disabilities. This increase of racial repression in turn raised perplexing questions about the status of free Negroes and the meaning
of citizenship.

Southern appellate courts wrestled occasionally with the problem and returned a variety of answers. In general, they agreed
that the free Negro possessed some fundamental rights but not
all the rights of a white man. They disagreed as to whether persons thus occupying an intermediate position between slavery and
freedom could be considered citizens of a sort. Justice Frederick
Nash of North Carolina expressed some of the judicial uncertainty in 1844 when he declared: "The free people of color cannot be considered as citizens in the largest sense of the term, or,
if they are, they occupy such a position in society as justifies the
legislature in adopting a course of policy in its acts peculiar to
them."

If the issue had been strictly a matter of *state* law and *state*
citizenship, it would have amounted to little more than a dispute
over terminology. But any use of the word "citizen" in connection with free blacks provided the basis for a claim that they
were protected by the first paragraph of Article Four, Section
Two, of the Constitution: "The citizens of each State shall be
entitled to all privileges and immunities of citizens in the several
States." Plainly, recognition of the free Negro as a citizen within
the meaning of this clause would have been incompatible with racial policies established throughout most of the country and with
southern efforts to fortify the slave system against subversion. It
is therefore not surprising that most of the prominent judicial
rulings *against* Negro citizenship were made in cases involving
rights claimed under the privileges-and-immunities clause.

For one thing, if the clause did protect free blacks, then state
laws prohibiting or severely restricting their immigration were
constitutionally indefensible. A number of states had enacted
such legislation, beginning in 1793, but the issue did not capture
national attention until the final stage of the Missouri controversy

in 1821. As authorized in the famous compromise of the preceding year, a Missouri convention drafted a state constitution, and it put in a clause calling for prohibition of Negro immigration. With the sectional struggle fiercely renewed as a consequence, antislavery leaders used the issue of Negro citizenship as the basis for one last effort to prevent the admission of Missouri. They failed, however, and had to settle for a meaningless compromise drafted by Henry Clay, which left unresolved the question of whether free blacks were included in the citizenry protected by the privileges-and-immunities clause. Rarely, in the decades that followed, did the subject again provoke serious debate in Congress.

Late in that same year, 1821, two members of the Monroe cabinet took up the question. Secretary of the Treasury William H. Crawford, a Georgian, wrote to Attorney General William Wirt, a Virginian, asking whether a free Negro could command an ocean-going vessel operating out of Norfolk, given the requirement that such commanders must be citizens of the United States. Wirt answered in the negative. "No person," he said, "is included in the description of citizen of the United States who has not the full rights of a citizen in the State of his residence." Therefore, free Negroes living in Virginia were not citizens of the United States. Thus Wirt subscribed to the principle that federal citizenship depended on state citizenship and also to the hard-line view that only persons enjoying complete civil and political equality could be regarded as state citizens. By discussing just the status of Virginia Negroes, Wirt left open the possibility that blacks in several New England states could qualify for national citizenship, but even so, his criterion excluded at least 95 per cent of the free black population of the country.

About six months after Wirt presented his opinion, the insurrectionary plot of Denmark Vesey, a former slave who had freed himself by self-purchase, was discovered and crushed in Charleston. The South Carolina legislature responded by tightening its restrictions on free Negroes. One of the new security measures required that black crew members of any ship coming into port must be arrested and held in jail until their vessel departed. This policy, eventually adopted with variations by a half-dozen other southern states, affected black British sailors as well as Americans and caused friction in Anglo-American relations until the coming of the Civil War.

In 1823, Justice William Johnson of the United States Supreme Court, while on circuit court duty in his home state of South Carolina, ruled that its Negro seamen law was unconstitutional. Attorney General Wirt came to the same conclusion in an official opinion written the following year. Both men, however, regarded the law as an invasion of federal authority. Neither gave any consideration to the rights of free Negroes under the federal Constitution.

Despite these rulings, South Carolina retained and enforced the Negro seamen law. The nationalism expressed by Johnson and Wirt was in any case already losing ground throughout much of the South. In 1831, Attorney General John M. Berrien, whose home state of Georgia now had a Negro seamen law of its own, presented an opinion overruling Wirt and pronouncing the South Carolina statute constitutional. In effect, Berrien held that state police powers, protected in the Tenth Amendment, took precedence over federal power to regulate commerce. He too ignored the question of the rights of free American Negroes.

Soon Roger B. Taney replaced Berrien as Jackson's attorney general. Further trouble with Britain, this time over a North Carolina Negro seamen law, elicited a lengthy opinion from him. Taney, unlike Wirt and Berrien, took up the subject of free American Negroes and concluded that they had no rights under the Constitution at all:

> The African race in the United States even when free, are everywhere a degraded class, and exercise no political influence. The privileges they are allowed to enjoy, are accorded to them as a matter of kindness and benevolence rather than of right. They are the only class of persons who can be held as mere property, as slaves. . . . They were not looked upon as citizens by the contracting parties who formed the Constitution. . . . And were not intended to be embraced in any of the provisions of that Constitution but those which point to them in terms not to be mistaken.

Thus Taney, in 1832, formulated the same harsh racial doctrine that he would proclaim from the bench twenty-five years later. But his opinion had little influence at the time, because for some reason it was not published along with other opinions of the attorney general.

The Berrien and Taney opinions placed the Jackson administration firmly on the side of the South in defense of the Negro seamen laws, and subsequent British protests were met with the reply that the matter was "beyond the reach of any power vested in the President." James Buchanan, as Polk's secretary of state, not only reiterated the assertion of executive impotence but also threatened abrogation of the commercial convention of 1815 unless the British ceased to make demands which, if complied with, said Buchanan, would result in a dissolution of the Union.

The nature of citizenship, state and national, and whether it included free Negroes, remained unsettled issues when the Dred Scott case reached the Supreme Court in the 1850s. Although certain abolitionist theorists had developed a doctrine of paramount national citizenship, the general tendency was to regard state citizenship as primary, with United States citizenship deriving from it. This made it reasonable to maintain that at least *some* free Negroes, being recognized as citizens in their own states, were entitled to protection under the privileges-and-immunities clause. Yet no federal court or high state court had expressly endorsed the claim, and several state courts had expressly rejected it.

Meanwhile, the increasing use of the corporate form of business organization was opening up the question of whether a corporation, as an "artificial being," had the legal status of a citizen. In 1839, the Supreme Court, with Taney delivering the decision, rejected the contention of counsel that a corporation was a citizen within the meaning and protection of the privileges-and-immunities clause. Five years later, however, the Court upheld a claim that corporations were citizens within the meaning of the diverse-citizenship clause of Article Three, Section Two, and thus capable of being litigants in the federal courts. Taken together, these two decisions had the effect of declaring that a corporation was a citizen in one respect but not in another.

Perhaps, then, the same could be said minimally about Negro citizenship. That is, since free blacks had access to the courts in their own states, were they not citizens at least to the extent of having access, like corporations, to the federal courts under the diverse-citizenship clause? It would have been reasonable to think so. There are indications that free Negroes did sometimes appear as parties in federal suits without being challenged on racial grounds. Indeed, the leading attorney in one such case was Roger B. Taney.

Yet southerners, always hostile to any influence that might weaken their system of racial control, were generally unwilling to allow any linkage between the word "Negro" and the word "citizen." Thus, the Georgia legislature by unanimous resolution in 1842 declared that free Negroes were not citizens of the United States and that Georgia would "never recognize such citizenship." Two years later, the South Carolina legislature empowered the governor to use the militia, if necessary, to prevent the release by writ of habeas corpus of any person imprisoned under the Negro seamen act. This meant that South Carolina was prepared to invoke military force to prevent federal judicial intervention in behalf of Negro seamen claiming the protection of the privileges-and-immunities clause. No northern state ever went that far in resisting enforcement of the fugitive-slave laws.

2

Expansion and Slavery
in National Politics

The problem of territorial government and its relationship to slavery arose in the 1780s, when the first state cessions of western lands made it clear that the new United States was about to take on certain attributes of an empire. In 1784, a congressional committee headed by Thomas Jefferson presented an ambitious plan dividing the entire transappalachian West into at least fourteen states, each to be virtually self-governing from the start. To this liberal design Jefferson added several restrictions, one of which declared: "That after the year 1800 of the Christian era, there shall be neither slavery nor involuntary servitude in any of the said states, otherwise than in punishment of crimes." The clause was deleted, however, upon the motion of a North Carolina delegate. The Ordinance of 1784, as finally enacted, therefore contained no reference to slavery. But then the Ordinance proved so impractical that it was never put into operation.

Instead, another committee drafted a new and much different plan of government for the West. After considerable debate and revision, it won the approval of Congress in July 1787. The measure included a repeal of the Ordinance of 1784, and a change of title made it explicitly applicable only to "the territory of the United States North West of the river Ohio." At almost the last moment before passage, a Massachusetts delegate moved an addition to the five "articles of compact between the original States and the people and States in the said Territory." This sixth article read:

> There shall be neither Slavery nor involuntary Servitude in the said territory otherwise than in the punishment of crimes, whereof the party shall have been duly convicted; provided always that any person escaping into the same, from whom labor or service is lawfully claimed in any one of the original States, such fugitive may be lawfully reclaimed and conveyed to the person claiming his or her labor or service as aforesaid.

Surprisingly, this antislavery amendment won prompt approval, and the ordinance as a whole was then passed by a unanimous vote of the eight states present. Only three of those states were northern; only one (Massachusetts) had itself actually abolished slavery. In short, the first legislation discriminating against slavery in the West was the work of a predominantly southern Congress. To be sure, the ordinance laid no restrictions on slavery in the still unceded lands of the Southwest, and the fugitive slave provision may have won some southern support. Most important of all, perhaps, is the simple fact that the southern outlook in 1787 was much different from what it would be in the 1850s. The geographical line between slavery and freedom was still not clearly drawn. The South was not then obviously destined to be a minority section. Criticism of slavery, pitched well below the Garrisonian level of fury, carried less of the menace associated with it in later years, and southerners accordingly were less worried about their political strength within the Union. In short, the morally vulnerable section had not yet become the politically vulnerable section of the Union.

Another mystery about the ordinance is why no one at the time challenged the power of Congress to enact it. James Madison in *Federalist* 38 said that the measure was passed "without the least color of constitutional authority," a view subsequently echoed by Taney in the Dred Scott decision. It is by no means certain that Madison was right, for one could argue that the authority to administer ceded western lands had become, by common consent, a part of the Articles of Confederation. But at any rate, the most striking thing is Madison's comment that this alleged usurpation went unnoticed. "No blame has been whispered," he wrote, "no alarm has been sounded." Whether legal or extralegal, the power of Congress to take action in the matter seems to have been universally conceded.

Unlike Jefferson's earlier plan, the Ordinance of 1787 allowed only partial self-government and amounted to a strong assertion of congressional control over the West in its pre-statehood phase. At Philadelphia, meanwhile, the Constitutional Convention was giving somewhat belated attention to the problem of the West. Provision for the admission of new states had been included from the beginning, but nothing was done about territorial government or western lands until Madison proposed a number of additions to the power of Congress, the first two of which were:

> To dispose of the unappropriated lands of the U. States.
> To institute temporary Governments for New States arising
> therein.

It would be difficult to believe that Madison, in drafting these proposals, did not have in mind the equivalent legislation of the Confederation Congress—that is, the Land Ordinance of 1785 and the Northwest Ordinance of 1787, enacted just five weeks earlier.

Much subsequent controversy would have been avoided if Madison's phrasing had been retained, but the Convention telescoped his two propositions into one ambiguous clause: "The Legislature shall have power to dispose of and make all needful rules and regulations respecting the territory or other property belonging to the United States." The question that later arose was whether the rule-making authority applied only to the disposal of public land or whether it included the power to establish territorial government. Everything in the record supports the latter interpretation. The Convention approved the clause without debate and probably without dissent. There is no evidence that any delegate thought a major alteration had been made in the substance of Madison's proposals, and a decision *against* granting Congress the power to provide temporary government would surely have inspired discussion, especially in view of the recent passage of the Northwest Ordinance.

The territory clause does not appear to have been a matter of controversy during the process of ratification. On August 7, 1789, the first Congress under the Constitution, without any challenge to its authority, re-enacted the Northwest Ordinance, making some necessary modifications, but including the antislavery provision. Nineteen members of the Constitutional Convention were sitting in this Congress, and a twentieth, George Washington, signed the law as President. It seems clear enough that no one then doubted the power of Congress to govern the West and prohibit slavery there.

The head start thus apparently given to antislavery in the West was soon offset in several ways. For one thing, in spite of the plain language of the Ordinance, slaves already held within the Northwest Territory were exempted from the legislative prohibition by executive interpretation of the territorial governor, Arthur St. Clair. This high-handed action converted an abolition measure into a mere ban on further importation of slaves, but it won silent acquiescence from Congress and the President. More flagrant violations of the Ordinance naturally followed. Both Indiana and Illinois territories established indenture systems that differed little from chattel slavery, and in Illinois especially, vestiges of indenturing survived until the 1840s.

Meanwhile, Congress was also using the Northwest Ordinance as a model for territorial government in the region south of the Ohio River, but with a crucial difference. By 1789, slavery had already emplanted itself firmly in the transappalachian districts of Virginia and North Carolina that would soon become the states of Kentucky and Tennessee. Accordingly, when North Carolina ceded its western land in December of that year, it did so on the condition that "no regulation made or to be made shall tend to emancipate slaves." Congress accepted the cession with the condition attached. Shortly thereafter, Southwest Territory was organized along the same lines as the Northwest, but with the antislavery clause explicitly deleted. In the circumstances, it would have been difficult for Congress to do otherwise. There were strong reasons for avoiding delay in the completion of North Carolina's cession, and the well-established presence of slavery in Kentucky, beyond the reach of federal authority, no doubt militated against the possibility of prohibiting it farther south.

Thus, with very little controversy, the first Congress voted in effect to extend the Mason and Dixon line westward along the Ohio River. Without being entirely conscious of doing so, perhaps, it officially adopted a policy of having two policies regarding slavery in the western territories. North of the Ohio, slavery was forbidden by federal authority in a way that prefigured the Wilmot Proviso and the platform of the Republican party. South of the Ohio, Congress did *not* establish or protect slavery in federal territory. It merely refrained from prohibiting the institution. This omission had the effect of leaving decisions about slavery to the local population. In later years, such restraint on the part of the federal government would be called "nonintervention," and its implied corollary would be made explicit as "popular sovereignty."

For all practical purposes, the short history of Southwest Territory came to an end with the admission of Tennessee in 1796. But at about the same time Spain relinquished its claim to the Yazoo strip, extending across what is now southern Mississippi and Alabama. Congress in 1798 therefore proceeded to organize Mississippi Territory. Again, as in 1790, the legislation followed the form of the Northwest Ordinance, with the antislavery provision deleted. A motion to strike out the deletion, offered by George Thacher of Massachusetts in the House of Representatives, set off the first recorded congressional debate of any significance on the subject of slavery in the territories. Much of the argument was in terms that would later become tediously familiar, but in two important respects it differed markedly from that of the antebellum years. First, many southerners were then still speaking of slavery as a national misfortune which, though presently ineradicable, would surely disappear in some far-off, better future. Second, Thacher's proposal to prohibit slavery in Mississippi Territory was denounced as unwise, unjust, and impracticable, but not as unconstitutional. The amendment in any case had no chance of passing. When the vote was taken, only eleven of Thacher's colleagues supported him in this last effort to delimit slavery east of the Mississippi River.

Georgia, meanwhile, continued to claim the Yazoo strip along with the rest of her western lands, all of which the state finally ceded in 1802. The articles of agreement and cession included an anti-antislavery provision similar to that extracted by North Carolina. Acceptance of Georgia's terms amounted to a final stamp of defeat on Jefferson's plan of 1784, which would have excluded slavery from the entire transappalachian region. Instead, the West, like the East, was to be partly free and partly slaveholding. All of this had been effectively determined before Jefferson entered the White House, and it was probably beyond his power to cancel the arrangement, even if he had wanted to.

In 1803, the whole question was opened up again with the purchase of Louisiana. The long struggle over slavery in the territories now entered the second of its three major phases. Jefferson could now try, if he wished, to prevent the institution from becoming permanently established west of the Mississippi River. He had the advantage of his presidential authority and prestige; settlement of the vast region had barely begun; and there were no state claims to be used as leverage against a federal antislavery policy.

Yet Jefferson in power did nothing to advance the antislavery cause, except in the matter of terminating the African slave trade, and he seems to have had no qualms of conscience about signing a law that made Louisiana a slaveholding territory. Himself an owner of more than a hundred slaves, he had for many years been publicly silent on the question of abolition. A quarter of a century had passed since his assertion in the Declaration of Independence that all men are created equal, and a middle-aged Jefferson, shocked by the excesses of the black revolution in Santo Domingo, had allowed racial preconceptions and fears to blunt his lifelong hatred of slavery as the greatest of all injustices. Furthermore, he headed a political party of predominantly southern interest, but one that needed northern allies and thus had good reason to muffle the sectionally divisive issue of slavery. By the time of his inauguration, he had settled into the not uncomfortable conclusion that the enormous problem was beyond the power of his own generation to solve and must be left to the indefinite future—to the stream of human progress. In the midst of the Jeffersonian silence, then, the principal antislavery voices in national politics during the first decades of the nineteenth century were certain northern Federalists—men no doubt motivated in part by moral imperatives but also fully aware that they were probing a weak spot in the armor of the enemy.

Previous legislation had already established the rule that slavery could go anywhere in federal territories where it was not positively forbidden by federal law. This was doubly true of Louisiana, where the institution had been legal under both French and Spanish rule. The Jefferson administration could therefore erect Louisiana as a slaveholding territory simply by passing an organic act that contained no prohibition against slavery. Such a measure was introduced late in 1803 by a Jeffersonian senator. As finally passed, it organized only the area south of the thirty-third parallel (substantially, the later state of Louisiana) into "Orleans Territory." The remainder of the vast region, containing few settlers, was designated the "District of Louisiana."

Before passage of the act, however, a Connecticut Federalist named James Hillhouse offered several antislavery amendments that stirred up heated debate. He failed in his effort to secure eventual emancipation of all slaves taken into the territory after a certain date, but among his successful amendments was one outlawing the domestic slave trade as a commercial enterprise. It prohibited the introduction of slaves into Louisiana by anyone except a citizen who was their bona fide owner and was taking them there for his own use. This was the strongest antislavery restriction imposed on any portion of the lower South between 1733 and 1865. But it proved to be temporary.

In 1805, without significant debate, Congress passed a bill authorizing a representative assembly for Orleans. It also provided that the inhabitants were to enjoy all the rights guaranteed by the Northwest Ordinance and enjoyed by the people of Mississippi Territory, specifically exempting Orleans from the antislavery article of the Ordinance. Territorial officials were not slow to conclude that these clauses wiped out the Hillhouse ban on domestic slavetrading. Thus Orleans was fully assimilated to the rest of the slaveholding South.

At the same time, Congress enacted legislation converting the "district" of Louisiana into a full-fledged territory, but this measure omitted all reference to the Northwest Ordinance. It neither authorized nor prohibited slaveholding, thus leaving the institution, presumably, still legal under previous French and Spanish law. Surprisingly, no northern senator or representative tried to obtain restrictions on slavery in Louisiana Territory in exchange for surrendering the antislavery restriction previously imposed on Orleans Territory. Most of the slaves within the Louisiana Purchase were concentrated in Orleans, and prohibition of slavery north of the thirty-third parallel might well have won majority support, especially if linked with acquiescence in slavery south of that line. Perhaps the reason for the omission must be sought in the desultory, uncrystallized nature of the antislavery sentiment itself, but it also appears that the solution of the dividing-line—the policy of having two policies—had not yet fully impressed itself on the American consciousness. The consequences of the omission were in any case immense; for the whole west bank of the Mississippi had been opened to slavery.

In 1812, having admitted Orleans Territory as the state of Louisiana, Congress enacted legislation changing the name of Louisiana Territory to Missouri Territory. A motion in the House to prohibit the admission of slaves was defeated emphatically. The act contained no reference to the Northwest Ordinance or its antislavery article. Four years later, amendatory legislation raised Missouri to a higher territorial grade, but no effort was made either to inhibit or to sanction slavery. Missouri remained slaveholding territory by virtue of congressional default.

Thus, territorial legislation for the Louisiana Purchase between 1803 and 1819, as it affected the problem of slavery, is difficult to fathom. By far the strongest efforts to discourage slavery were made in the organization of Orleans Territory at the southern tip, where the institution was already firmly implanted; while for the remainder of the region, stretching northward to the Canadian border, only one slight antislavery gesture appears on the record. Moreover, all other territories of the period were ex-

pressly assimilated to the Northwest Ordinance, with the antislavery article either reaffirmed (Indiana, Michigan, and Illinois
territories) or excluded (Southwest, Mississippi, and Orleans territories). But the organic acts of 1805 and 1812 for Louisiana-
Missouri Territory, while using the Ordinance as a model,
carefully omitted all reference to it. The effect was to establish
in its purest form the policy that would later be called "nonintervention."

Antislavery sentiment of the kind manifested in support for
the Hillhouse amendments probably became increasingly difficult to sustain during the long crisis in foreign relations that cul-
minated in the War of 1812. The ending of the war did not bring
an immediate resurgence of antislavery effort, but early in 1819,
certain northern members of Congress, trying to recover some of
the ground passively yielded during the preceding fifteen years,
provoked the first major sectional conflict over the expansion of
slavery. They did so by opposing the admission of Missouri as a
slaveholding state.

The great constitutional issue that the Supreme Court tried
to settle in the Dred Scott decision was whether Congress had
the power to prohibit slavery in the territories. Throughout the
Missouri controversy of 1819-21, however, the crucial issue was
whether Congress could place perpetually binding conditions on
the admission of a new state. The territorial question was not
critically important and arose when it did primarily in connection with Arkansas rather than Missouri itself. Since the proposed
admission of Missouri necessitated establishing a new territory
farther south in the less populated region centering on the Arkansas River, bills authorizing statehood for Missouri and creating Arkansas Territory proceeded almost side by side through
Congress in 1819. Discussion of the two measures tended frequently to intermingle.

The House of Representatives passed the Missouri enabling
bill on February 17, having added an amendment proposed by
James Tallmadge, Jr., a New York Republican of the disaffected
Clintonian faction. It prohibited the further introduction of slavery into Missouri and provided that slave children born after the
date of admission should be free at the age of twenty-five. Al-

though the amendment did not affect the ten thousand slaves already held in Missouri, it amounted to a long-term plan of gradual abolition. Southerners were angry and virtually unanimous in their opposition. Three days later, the House passed the Arkansas bill, but in this case, similar antislavery efforts were defeated.

In previous debates on slavery in the territories, the constitutional power of Congress had scarcely come into question. But the Tallmadge amendment was more difficult to justify in constitutional terms because it proposed to place on one state a disability not placed on all states. The amendment thus tended to turn the Missouri struggle into a constitutional debate, and the close association between the Missouri and Arkansas bills apparently encouraged some members of Congress to consider also the constitutional aspects of the problem of slavery in the federal territories.

No doubt there were other reasons for the shift of emphasis. For example, the Supreme Court in 1819 handed down a series of decisions that provoked widespread public discussion of a constitutional nature. Most notably, *McCulloch v. Maryland,* in which John Marshall presented his classic statement of the case for broad construction of congressional power, was argued at the very time that the Arkansas and Missouri bills were being considered in the Senate. But then it was perhaps inevitable that once the Constitution had been written and generally accepted, the political theorizing of the founders' generation should give way to the narrower activity of constitutional exegesis in the age of Webster, Clay, and Calhoun. From the beginning, moreover, there had been a tendency on the part of any party or element finding itself in the minority to convert political issues into constitutional issues. The Jeffersonians had done so repeatedly in the 1790s, and New England Federalists followed their example after 1800. Southern members of Congress in 1819, after many years of suffering only occasional antislavery reproach, were shocked at the amount of support given the Tallmadge amendment. Accordingly, they began to talk more than ever before about limitations on congressional authority to interfere with the expansion of slavery.

Not that debate on the Arkansas bill was cast exclusively or even primarily in constitutional terms, but it did contain rudiments of argument that would one day appear in the Dred Scott decision. That is, several southerners insisted that Congress lacked the power to prohibit slavery in the Louisiana Purchase. One or more of them maintained that such prohibition would violate the treaty with France, that it would deny inhabitants the right of self-government, and that it would constitute an illegal seizure of property.

The voting on the Tallmadge amendment seemed to indicate the sudden emergence of an antislavery majority in the House of Representatives. Yet when the House then turned to the Arkansas bill, where restrictionism stood on firmer constitutional ground, the antislavery advantage melted away. It appears that the determination of some northerners may have been weakened by the fierceness of the southern response. For instance, Thomas W. Cobb of Georgia talked of disunion, saying, "We have kindled a fire which . . . seas of blood can only extinguish."

By failing to attach antislavery amendments to both measures, the House gave up any possibility of using one as leverage to elicit senatorial approval of the other. The Senate simply passed the Arkansas bill (which was then signed into law by President James Monroe), while refusing to accept the Missouri bill unless the Tallmadge amendment were deleted. The House, in turn, refused to allow the deletion. On this note of sharp sectional division, Congress adjourned, and the issue went to the country.

That first flurry of excitement over Arkansas and Missouri lasted scarcely three weeks and was confined largely to the halls of Congress. In those days of slow communication it took much longer to awaken popular interest nationwide. But by December 1819, when the next Congress assembled, an antislavery crusade had taken shape in many northern states, and the demand for exclusion of slavery from Missouri echoed in mass meetings, pamphlets, editorials, and legislative resolutions. From Missouri, meanwhile, came angry protests against the efforts at restriction and the resulting delay of admission. The strength of proslavery sentiment there must have made it obvious that no one could turn Missouri into a free state. The work of salvation had begun much too late, and the best that the antislavery forces could hope for was some kind of *quid pro quo*.

At this point, the incipient state of Maine entered the scene and promptly became a sectional hostage. Maine had long been a part of Massachusetts and, with the latter's consent, now applied for admission. The House passed a bill for that purpose on January 3, 1820. The Senate amended it by adding a Missouri enabling act unencumbered with restrictions on slavery. The object, plainly, was coercion of the House, and in order to make the yoking of the two measures more acceptable there, the Senate added another amendment offered by Jesse B. Thomas of Illinois, a native Virginian. It declared slavery to be "forever prohibited" in the remainder of the Louisiana cession lying north of 36° 30'. The House responded by twice refusing to accept the Senate's package but in the end retreated and approved the compromise. The critical vote, on deletion of the antislavery clause, was 90 to 87. Fourteen of the majority's votes came from northerners.

The Thomas amendment, a grossly uneven division of the remaining federal territory, was a southern concession to northern antislavery sentiment. Northern members of Congress voted for it 115 to 7 (Senate: 20 to 2; House: 95 to 5). As a separate measure, it would have been opposed by southerners with similar solidarity, but proslavery strategists brought it forward as an offer of part of the price to be paid for the admission of Missouri as a slave state. The question of making this concession divided the southern membership in Congress, a membership that had otherwise displayed a high degree of unity wherever slavery was concerned. Southerners voted for the Thomas amendment, 53 to 45 (Senate: 14 to 8; House: 39 to 37). This was, in a sense, a measure of southern willingness to compromise. The northern membership, on the other hand, voted overwhelmingly against the compromise package of Missouri, Maine, and the Thomas amendment, 105 to 18 (Senate: 18 to 4; House: 87 to 14).

Neither house engaged in extensive discussion of the 36° 30' amendment. Yet, during the long and wide-ranging debate, there were frequent references to the territorial aspect of the slavery issue, and a number of southerners either denied or at least questioned congressional power to forbid slavery in the territories. Among those who did so were Charles Pinckney of South Carolina, one of the framers of the Constitution, and John Tyler of Virginia, a future President. A leading authority on the Missouri controversy has concluded that "almost half" of the southern membership was unwilling to acknowledge the power as a matter of principle, although "somewhat more than half would vote for it in the form of a 'hoss trade' compromise."

When the Missouri enabling act came to President Monroe for his signature, that strict constructionist consulted his cabinet about the Thomas amendment. According to John Quincy Adams, then secretary of state, there was general agreement that Congress had the power to impose the 36° 30′ restriction, though several, including John C. Calhoun, could not find explicit authority for it in the Constitution. With Adams alone dissenting, the cabinet also agreed that the phrase "forever forbidden" actually meant only for the duration of the territorial period. It is astonishing that southerners should have permitted the word *forever* to be used in the Thomas amendment; for it seemed to mean literally that the antislavery restriction would carry over after each territory north of 36° 30′ became a state. Southerners thus virtually surrendered the very principle for which they were fighting so desperately in opposing antislavery restrictions on Missouri—namely, the principle of state equality. One can only conclude that Thomas, in phrasing his amendment, drew somewhat thoughtlessly on the tradition of the Northwest Ordinance.

The strongest opposition to the 36° 30′ restriction came from the state of Virginia. Both Virginia senators voted against it, and, in the House of Representatives, eighteen Virginians contributed almost half of all the negative votes. They received emphatic support from the two greatest living Virginians. Jefferson, who had practically invented the idea of prohibiting slavery in the American West, now embraced the "diffusion" argument that the expansion of slavery would ameliorate the condition of the slave. Madison wholeheartedly sided with the South and questioned the constitutionality of the Thomas amendment. These attitudes can be explained in various ways—as manifesting the conservatism of the elderly, for instance; or as resulting from the strong suspicion (which Monroe shared) that the Missouri agitation was essentially a Federalist scheme to split the Republican party; or as reflecting the economic interest of Virginia, a slave-surplus state, in the continuing expansion of the peculiar institution. But in addition, the proslavery attitudes of Jefferson and Madison signalized the depth and unity of southern commitment to slavery by 1820. The Missouri crisis had strikingly revealed just how solid the South could be on this issue.

Most southerners in Congress, and Jefferson too, continued to go through the motions of deprecating slavery, but their words over the years had come to sound increasingly hollow, especially when they insisted that nothing could be done about the problem and that it was dangerous to try or even talk of trying. The Missouri crisis apparently came at a time of internal crisis for many southerners who had begun half-consciously to readjust their conceptions of the future of slavery in the United States. Many simply set the great day of ultimate extinction infinitely far ahead in time, but a few took the logical step of praising as a public good what so many were already defending as a necessity. Some were obviously in transit, such as the future vice president Richard M. Johnson of Kentucky, who said that slavery was a "necessary evil . . . not incompatible with true religion." Various speakers insisted that slaves were generally a happy breed; several took their listeners back to ancient Greece and Rome in defense of slavery on historical grounds; and a number turned to the Bible for testimony that the institution was part of God's plan.

Missouri's struggle for admission did not end with passage of the enabling act in March 1820, but the second crisis and compromise that followed a year later involved the status of free Negroes rather than the expansion of slavery. The latter question had been settled by drawing the 36° 30′ line, a solution that would presumably also be suitable for any additional territory that might be acquired. Politically and constitutionally, slavery in the territories became more or less a moot issue, and sectional hostility found other avenues of expression.

2

The success of the Missouri Compromise resulted primarily from its having left no sectional borderland of undetermined status, together with the fact that neither northerners nor southerners were at this point prepared to insist, on moral or constitutional grounds, that all federal territory should be uniformly closed or uniformly open to slavery. The 36° 30′ line had little to do with the success of the Compromise, for it merely stipulated realities that everyone acknowledged. Iowa Territory, created in 1838 with slavery forbidden, was too far north to provoke southern opposition. Florida, acquired by treaty from Spain in 1821, was too far south to invite a serious antislavery effort. Arkansas Territory, bounded on three sides by slave states, had already been conceded to slavery. Yet, even in these conditions, some controversy arose. For instance, framers of the bill for the organization of Florida Territory in 1822 copied it from the Orleans act of 1804, including the Hillhouse provision that no slaves could be taken into the territory except by bona fide owners. Southerners in the Senate managed to get this clause deleted, but only by a vote of 23 to 20.

With the subsidence of the territorial issue after 1820, the history of the slavery controversy tends to move away from Congress for a time, but not entirely so. There was a long running debate on proposals for federal assistance to the African Colonization Society. In 1824, the Senate, after heated argument, emasculated a convention signed with Great Britain for stricter enforcement of laws prohibiting the international slave trade. The year following, Rufus King of New York proposed to the Senate that proceeds from the sales of public lands be used to finance a program of emancipation and colonization. Senator Robert Y. Hayne of South Carolina in a vehement response denied that Congress had power to create such a fund, which would constitute a threat, he said, to the "peace and harmony of the Union." In 1828, the House of Representatives spent an extraordinary amount of time on a private bill remunerating the owner of a slave impressed into federal service during the War of 1812 and wounded as a consequence. Was this the same as having one's property damaged? No, replied a number of northerners, for under the Constitution slaves were persons, not property. This stirred the wrath of Edward Livingston of Louisiana, the transplanted New Yorker who would soon become Andrew Jackson's secretary of state. "Slaves not property!" he exclaimed. "What are they then? If they are not property, then they are free."

Slavery remained a haunting presence in national politics, unmentioned much of the time, but inspiring many apprehensive glances over the shoulder. Behind the emerging partisan alignments and behind many issues of the period were strong sectional purposes, and the core of sectional consciousness, especially in the South, was the problem of slavery. Still, if partisanship often masked sectional motives, it also discouraged sectional excess. Like its Jeffersonian predecessor, the triumphant Jacksonian coalition of 1828 was essentially a southern-based party—proslavery at heart, but quietly so in order to accommodate its robust northern wing. The opposition, developing into the Whig party with a somewhat more northerly center of gravity, likewise found it expedient to repress the slavery issue in the interest of building a southern constituency. Thus the exigencies of party formation in the Jacksonian period tended to push slavery out of national politics. Yet certain external forces already at work would eventually produce a stronger counter-pressure.

The most striking development, of course, was the rise of radical abolitionism as exemplified in the person of William Lloyd Garrison and in his newspaper *The Liberator*, which he launched on New Year's Day, 1831. As a matter of conviction, but also as a choice of strategy, Garrison and the new abolitionists set out to destroy slavery by direct, personal attack upon everyone associated with the institution and everyone who temporized with it. Their inflammatory style won some converts but made many enemies, in the North as well as in the South. The effect was to intensify greatly the antagonism over slavery that had never been entirely absent from the American nation.

Zealotry was nothing new among opponents of slavery, however, and although radical abolitionists grew steadily in numbers after 1830, they continued to be a very small part of the total population. It was by rising to a new level of dedication and organization that they managed to become a dynamic, disruptive element in American society. Except among the Quakers, earlier antislavery activity had often been a secondary concern of busy men of affairs and therefore not entirely free of dilettantism. The new, Garrisonian breed made the war on slavery the central factor in their lives. They thus professionalized the movement, and, in spite of their alleged anti-institutional bias, they institutionalized it. Opposition to slavery for the first time became an interest as well as a sentiment, and the slaveholding interest felt the difference immediately.

Furthermore, the racial equalitarianism openly embraced by Garrison and many other abolitionists after 1830 added a provocative new element to the slavery controversy. It intensified the fury of southern reaction and was apparently the principal stimulus to an outburst of violent anti-abolitionist activity in the North. All antislavery men, however moderate, thereafter became vulnerable to the charge of being "Negro-worshippers"—a charge that few politicans could afford to leave undenied.

"Abolition and the Union cannot coexist," said Calhoun. After Nat Turner's rebellion in 1831, southerners tended to view all abolitionist propaganda as incendiary in purpose. By a combination of state laws and connivance of federal officials, they achieved substantial success in closing down mail circulation of objectionable publications. The South also tightened its system of control over slaves and free Negroes. It treated peddlers and other travelers from the North with increasing suspicion and sometimes with harassment. Some states, such as Virginia, passed severe laws punishing advocacy of abolition. Vigilance committees ferreted out subversives, administering whippings and other chastisements. By 1837, no southern abolition societies remained in existence, and the defense of slavery as a positive good was replacing the old argument that it was an unfortunate but inescapable legacy. More and more, southerners regarded every attack on the institution as an impeachment of their decency, virtue, and honor.

It was the swelling volume of antislavery petitions and the notorious "gag rule" imposed in 1836 that brought slavery to the center of congressional politics for the first time since the Missouri crisis. Southerners demanding outright rejection of all such petitions argued that no one had a right to petition Congress for legislation not within its delegated authority. The primary target of petitioners in 1836, however, was slavery in the District of Columbia, and there the Constitution empowered Congress "to exercise exclusive legislation in all cases whatsoever." These words seemed clearly to invest Congress with the power to establish or prohibit slavery in the District. Yet Calhoun, among other southerners, denied it. In a notable anticipation of Taney's Dred Scott opinion, he invoked the Fifth Amendment provision against deprivation of life, liberty, or property without due process of law. Due process, he declared, meant jury trial, and "were not the slaves of this District property?"

In a series of resolutions introduced December 27, 1837, Calhoun also set forth his theory that the federal government was created as the "common agent" of the sovereign states with the duty of "strengthening and upholding" the domestic institutions of those states. Slavery, he said in a speech, was actually "as much under the protection of the Constitution" in the District of Columbia and in the territories as it was "in the states themselves." In this manner Calhoun laid the basis for that convenient contradiction whereby southerners, especially in the late 1850s, were able to maintain that slavery was a local institution beyond the power of Congress to restrain in any way, and yet at the same time deserving full protection in the territories by direct force of the Constitution itself. Thus "nonintervention" could be converted at will to mean intervention.

With each new Congress after 1836, northern support for the gag rule diminished; yet it continued in effect for eight years. The growing intensity of the slavery controversy was offset for a time by the growing tensile strength of party allegiance. No political leader was more determined to keep the lid on the slavery issue than Martin Van Buren, elected President as Andrew Jackson's successor in 1836, the very year in which the gag rule was first imposed. But in that year another outside force began to broaden the base of the antislavery movement and intensify sectional antagonism in Congress—namely, the renewal of American territorial expansion.

A dubious American claim to Texas as part of the Louisiana Purchase had been relinquished in the Florida treaty of 1819-21. Nevertheless, American settlers had begun to enter Texas in the 1820s, drawn there by generous Mexican land grants. Predominantly southerners, they took their slaves along and kept them even after Mexico formally abolished slavery in 1829. So when Texas, after fighting and winning a war for independence in 1836, requested annexation to the United States, it did so as a slaveholding republic. But antislavery spokesmen in and outside of Congress had already launched a fierce campaign against annexation, charging that the revolution in Texas was part of a slaveholders' plot to enlarge the domain of their peculiar institution. The threat to Democratic party unity in the abolitionist crusade, together with the danger of driving Mexico to a declaration of war, induced Jackson and Van Buren to deal cautiously with the Texas question. Annexation, as a consequence, was postponed for nearly a decade.

Public attention turned to other problems, but interest in the annexation of Texas never entirely subsided, and by 1844 it had been emphatically revived. Sam Houston, having returned to the presidency of Texas, was able to exploit a growing American concern about British designs on Texas. There was also a new enthusiasm for territorial expansion, soon to be associated with the phrase "manifest destiny." The overland movement of settlers to Oregon and California had begun, and the whole North American continent suddenly seemed barely large enough domain for the American eagle.

No less important were the vagaries of politics. John Tyler, a pseudo-Whig who succeeded to the presidency in 1841 after the death of William Henry Harrison, broke with Henry Clay and other party leaders over the issue of re-establishing a national bank. In the hope of gaining some measure of glory for his administration and perhaps gathering a new political following, Tyler set out to acquire Texas. Negotiations at last produced a treaty of annexation laid before the Senate in April 1844. By that time, Americans were in the midst of a presidential campaign, with Texas as the central issue. Both of the expected nominees, Clay and Van Buren, promptly published letters opposing immediate annexation. Calhoun, now secretary of state, killed whatever hope there may have been for the treaty by defending annexation on proslavery grounds in an imprudent letter to the British minister in Washington. As a consequence, the treaty was soundly defeated on June 8 by a vote of 35 to 16.

The Texas question decisively altered the course of American history in 1844 because of its influence on one of the most crucial of all presidential elections. Hostility to annexation probably cost Van Buren the Democratic nomination and may very well have made the difference in Clay's narrow defeat by James K. Polk. At any rate, contrary to all expectations when the year began, an enthusiastic expansionist was elected President. Tyler, interpreting the outcome as a referendum in favor of his policy, recommended annexation of Texas by joint resolution instead of treaty. This maneuver circumvented the need for a two-thirds majority in the Senate. In spite of strong opposition from Whigs and some antislavery Democrats, the desired resolution passed both houses of Congress at the end of February 1845, just in time for Tyler to sign it triumphantly before he left office.

One significant feature of the resolution, in view of the fact that it received the support of all southern Democrats voting on it in the House and Senate, was that it included a reaffirmation of the Missouri Compromise restriction. Texas claimed an enormous area, and a small part of that claim extended north of 36° 30'. The annexation measure provided that as many as four additional states might, with its consent, be formed from Texas. Any such states lying south of the Missouri Compromise line must be "admitted into the Union with or without slavery, as the people . . . may desire." But in any state or states formed north of the line, slavery was prohibited. Since nearly all of Texas lay south of 36° 30', the essential purpose of reaffirming the Missouri Compromise line was to make sure that any subdivision of the state would leave slavery secure. Yet, in accomplishing their purpose, southerners theoretically acknowledged the power of Congress to exclude slavery, not merely from a federal territory, but from a new state entering the Union. The latter was the very power that southerners had denied so vehemently during the Missouri struggle.

The two major historical consequences of the Texas question were these, however: it brought Polk to the presidency and brought Mexico and the United States into conflict. Given the brute force of American expansionism, the extravagance of Texan boundary claims, and the imprudence of Mexican policy, the war may have been unavoidable no matter who occupied the White House. But a war merely to hold all the land claimed by Texas would not have necessitated the conquest of California or the capture of Mexico City. Polk, whatever his responsibility for making the war, was certainly responsible for turning it into a war of territorial aggrandizement. His purposes were clearly revealed in the prompt dispatch of General Stephen W. Kearny to Santa Fe and Los Angeles. Kearny's force was entering New Mexico when David Wilmot of Pennsylvania rose in the House of Representatives on August 8, 1846, to introduce his famous Proviso.

Offered as an amendment to a special appropriation of $2 million requested by Polk, the Proviso forbade slavery in any territory that might be acquired from Mexico. Wilmot acted for a group of northern Democrats inspired by other motives besides their dislike of slavery. For various reasons, they shared a growing animosity toward Polk and the South. Some resented the Oregon Treaty, signed with Great Britain in June, and some were angry about the President's recent veto of a rivers-and-harbors appropriation. In each of these two cases, the blow had fallen most heavily on the Northwest, and in each the heavy hand of southern influence seemed all too visible. But the center of disaffection was New York, where Van Buren Democrats were still unhappy about the defeat of their leader in the national convention of 1844. They regarded themselves as mistreated by Polk and feared that they were losing ground to the Whigs in state politics because national party policies compelled them to carry too much proslavery weight.

However, the reasons why certain northern Democrats decided to introduce the Proviso will by no means suffice as an explanation of why nearly all northern votes in the House of Representatives were cast in its favor. The distinction is important and seldom made. Whatever one may say about its origins, the Wilmot Proviso was essentially what it appeared to be—a remarkably strong effort to terminate completely the expansion of slavery.

This first skirmish over the issue was exceedingly brief. It came at the very end of a session of Congress that had lasted eight months. On a hot Saturday evening, the House voted 83 to 64 for the Wilmot amendment and 86 to 64 for the $2 million bill to which it was attached. In neither instance was there a roll call, but on the intervening motion for engrossment of the bill, the *ayes* and *nays* were recorded. They showed southerners opposed, 67 to 2, and northerners in favor, 83 to 12, with 8 of those 12 negative votes cast by unyielding anti-expansionist Whigs. Thus it can be said that of 164 congressmen only six really crossed sectional lines in the voting.

The measure did not reach the Senate until the final hour of the session on August 10. There it died at the hands of John Davis, a Massachusetts Whig, who filibustered until the hour of adjournment arrived. Apparently he did so to prevent the Senate from striking out the Proviso and returning it to the House in time for the latter to acquiesce under pressure. The notion that Davis made an enormous blunder, preventing an antislavery triumph, seems unfounded. The bill, as long as it included the Proviso, had little chance of passing the Senate in the few minutes available, and beyond that barrier lay the presidential veto power.

During the next session of Congress, the House again attached the Proviso to a special appropriation bill, and the Senate again refused to accept it. Calhoun at this time introduced a set of resolutions in which he spelled out his "common-property" doctrine: Congress as the "joint agent" of the sovereign states, had no power to prevent the citizens of any states from "emigrating with their property" (i.e., slaves) into the territories, which were the "common property" of all the states. In his accompanying remarks, the South Carolinian declared that the Proviso, if enacted, would ultimately give the free states an overwhelming preponderance in the Union. Such a destruction of sectional balance, he warned, would mean "political revolution, anarchy, civil war, and widespread disaster."

Concurrently, there was also a furious struggle over a bill for the organization of Oregon Territory, with slavery duly prohibited. Southerners in the House hoped to use Oregon as a sectional hostage in their fight against the Proviso. They accordingly proposed adding the words, "inasmuch as the whole of the said territory lies north of 36° 30′ north latitude," thus by implication extending the Missouri Compromise line to the Pacific. Few northerners would vote for the amendment, and it was soundly defeated, after which the Oregon bill, with its antislavery clause intact, passed in the House and died in the Senate. Congress adjourned in March 1847, with American power extending to the Pacific, but with the status of slavery in New Mexico, California, and Oregon still undetermined.

3

The Wilmot Proviso transformed American politics, and, together with the doctrine articulated by Calhoun, it constituted the "territorial shears" that would one day sever the Union. At the same time, there were influences tending to counteract the divisive effects of the slavery controversy. For one thing, between the extremes represented by Wilmot and Calhoun stood many men temperamentally disposed to be peacemakers, mediating differences and drafting programs of compromise. In addition, the party system had its own imperatives which continued to moderate sectional passions, as both Democratic and Whig organizations struggled to hold themselves together and retain their bisectional constituencies. In the approaching presidential campaign, victory seemed to depend upon finding some formula of compromise or evasion with which to bridge the sectional rift.

The Whig solution proved to be nothing more than the nomination of General Zachary Taylor—a slaveholding southerner to counterbalance the party's northward leaning, and a military hero who presumably transcended the political conflict over

slavery. The Democrats, on the other hand, embraced two compromise formulas and for a time were divided over which one was
better. Polk's secretary of state, James Buchanan, tied his presidential aspirations to advocacy of the Missouri Compromise line.
But that was a somewhat threadbare solution, already rejected
emphatically on several occasions by the House of Representatives. Many Democrats therefore became increasingly receptive
to a solution that had the double advantage of being conveniently
ambiguous and of seeming more innovative than it really was.
Vice President George M. Dallas was the first candidate who
proposed "leaving to the people of the territory . . . the business
of settling the matter for themselves." But it was Lewis Cass who
made the doctrine of popular sovereignty peculiarly his own in
a public letter addressed to A. O. P. Nicholson of Tennessee. The
Democratic nomination of Cass in May 1848 signified an informal
endorsement of the doctrine, even though it was not at this time
incorporated into the party platform.

With Martin Van Buren heading the ticket of the new Free
Soil party, slavery for the first time in American history became
the leading issue of a presidential contest. The results of the
election scarcely constituted a mandate, however. The voters, by
a relatively narrow margin, elected Zachary Taylor, the one candidate not committed to any of the four solutions to the territorial problem—not the Proviso, or the Calhoun doctrine, or popular sovereignty, or extension of the Missouri Compromise line.
The voice of the people had been heard, but the message was
Delphic.

The Proviso controversy turned American history into a new
channel, but the extent to which it inspired a new set of political
principles about slavery has been overstated. One historian says,
for instance, that "in the 1840's three virtually new views of the
powers of Congress as to slavery in territories were presented to
the public"—namely, the "free-soil doctrine," the "Calhoun doctrine," and the "Cass doctrine." Yet the cluster of doctrines that
seemed to emerge in the 1840s was actually a blending of old
and new, and it is important to understand the nature of that
blend.

Generally speaking, practice had preceded theory, and as a

matter of practice, Congress from the beginning had had three functional choices. It could prohibit slavery in federal territory; it could establish and protect slavery; or it could refrain from laying down any rules regarding slavery. In practice, the third option meant leaving the decision to the persons settling a territory. They did so, informally at first, simply by bringing or not bringing slaves with them, and then officially, through the action of their territorial government. In short, the practical effect of nonintervention by Congress was popular sovereignty in the territories; they were national and local aspects of the same policy. Along with these three functional alternatives, Congress had the further option of making different provisions for different territories. That is, it could adopt a policy of having more than one policy.

Not until 1861 did Congress ever seriously consider legislation establishing and protecting slavery in a federal territory. During the preceding three-quarters of a century it employed the other two alternatives in rather haphazard combination. By 1790, as we have seen, Congress had settled for a policy of prohibition north of the Ohio and nonintervention to the south. In the case of the Louisiana Purchase, however, this precedent was followed only with respect to Orleans Territory. A policy of nonintervention silently prevailed in Louisiana-Missouri Territory until 1820. Then antislavery sentiment forced a westward extension of the dual system, with slavery expressly forbidden north of 36° 30′ and nonintervention silently continued south of that line. The Missouri Compromise thus renewed and formalized the policy of having two policies, but one of them—nonintervention—remained largely a matter of implication. In annexing Texas twenty-five years later, Congress reaffirmed the 36° 30′ restriction and for the first time said something definite about the rights of persons south of the line. The joint resolution, in providing that any additional states formed from the region were to be admitted "with or without slavery," as the people might desire, offered confirmation that popular sovereignty had always been understood to prevail in territories where slavery was not prohibited.

If such a "compromise" seems lopsided in favor of the North, with slavery forbidden on one side of the line and merely per-

mitted on the other, it was all the South wanted or needed in the
early decades of the Republic; for the westward movement during those years was lopsided in favor of the South. The outpour-
ing of southern settlers nearly made slave states of Indiana and
Illinois in spite of the Northwest Ordinance. Texas was settled
and independent a year before Michigan entered the Union.
Down until 1861, no free state was ever formed out of territory
in which nonintervention had been the rule. In practical terms,
nonintervention had meant popular sovereignty, and popular
sovereignty had always meant slavery.

Three of the four doctrines current in the 1840s had already
been put into practice by 1790, but what little debate they
aroused during the early years was over considerations other
than their constitutionality. It seems to have been generally assumed that Congress possessed the authority to do virtually anything it wished concerning slavery in the territories. Principles
were appealed to along with expedience, but not constitutional
principles. The policy of prohibiting slavery naturally received
much support on moral grounds; nonintervention could be justified as a recognition of the right of local self-government; and
the policy of having two policies sprang from the dictates of
intersectional equity.

Congressional power over slavery in the territories first came
under challenge in a significant way during the Missouri controversy. Relatively few voices were raised on the subject, since it
was not the central constitutional issue of the crisis. Nevertheless,
one finds here and there the rudiments of the subsequent "Calhoun doctrine," although Calhoun at the time endorsed the constitutionality of the Thomas amendment prohibiting slavery north
of 36° 30'.

The great change in Calhoun's thought and feeling about the
future of the slaveholding South occurred in the 1820s. His theory of the nature of the Union, conceived no later than 1828 and
matured during the nullification crisis of 1832-33, was ready for
use shortly thereafter when slavery once again became a burning
issue in Congress. By 1837, as we have seen, he and a number of
other southerners were prepared to deny federal power to prohibit slavery, not only in the territories but even in the District

of Columbia. The "Calhoun doctrine" and the cluster of attitudes associated with it emerged in response to the abolitionist crusade of the 1830s, although its full articulation was not called for until the expansionism of the following decade revived the dormant territorial issue.

So none of the four principal solutions to the territorial problem offered in 1847-48 were innovations. The Calhoun doctrine, to be sure, was much newer than the other three, and, significantly, it alone originated in constitutional theory and had never been put into practice. The other three solutions had begun as political policies, implemented with scarcely any overt attention to the constitutional implications. But by the 1840s, partly as a result of the Calhoun example, it had become the fashion to justify any sectionally controversial proposal in constitutional terms. The crucial change in the slavery controversy occurring during the 1840s was therefore not the introduction of new principles or formulas, but rather the constitutionalizing of the argument. Once that process was completed, a long step would have been taken toward the Dred Scott decision.

The ultimate purpose of such argument, moreover, was not merely to claim constitutional sanction but to impose a constitutional imperative—that is, to demonstrate that only one proposed course of action was permitted by the Constitution, or better yet, that it was virtually compelled by the Constitution. According to the Calhoun doctrine, for instance, the other three options were all unconstitutional, and more than that, the Constitution *required* the federal government to protect the property (including slaves) of state citizens everywhere within its exclusive jurisdiction. The effect was to make slavery national except where interdicted by the sovereign power of a state.

The policy of prohibition, originating in the Northwest Ordinance, was at first adopted as a matter of legislative discretion. It rested on the assumption that Congress had the power to prohibit and *ought* to exercise it. In the late 1840s, however, the Wilmot Proviso became a constitutional imperative proceeding from the argument that the Constitution itself *forbade* the establishment of slavery in the territories.

The principal antislavery imperatives were proslavery argu-

ments turned upside down. Thus, the due-process clause of the
Fifth Amendment, to which southerners occasionally appealed,
with emphasis on the word *property*, could be invoked by northern radicals, with emphasis on the word *liberty*. "Slavery," wrote
Salmon P. Chase in 1844, "never has lawfully existed in any territory of the United States since the adoption of that amendment
which declares that no person shall be deprived of liberty without due process of law." This argument was incorporated into the
platforms of the Liberty party in 1844, the Free Soil party in
1848, and the Republican party in 1856 and 1860. Also, southern
insistence that the Constitution, with two very specific exceptions, delegated Congress no power to legislate concerning slavery (an argument that had proved especially serviceable during
the controversy over the admission of Missouri) could be turned
to northern advantage with the proposition that Congress had
been delegated no authority to introduce or permit slavery where
it did not previously exist. This had the effect of making freedom
national and slavery exclusively the creature of state law. The
argument was especially relevant to the Mexican Cession, where,
unlike Louisiana and Florida, slavery had been abolished by the
previous regime.

Nonintervention, which in practice meant popular sovereignty, had been installed in 1790 as a proslavery policy for the
Southwest. Southerners from time to time had defended it as a
matter of intersectional equity and territorial self-government,
but no elaborate constitutional justification seemed necessary for
a policy of abstention. In the fashion of the 1840s, however,
Lewis Cass did his best to infuse a measure of constitutional compulsion into the principle of nonintervention. He did so by
adopting a line of argument that some southerners had taken as
early as 1820, and that Roger B. Taney would follow in 1857—
that is, a very narrow interpretation of the territory clause as
referring only to property and not to jurisdiction. According to
this theory, any general legislative power exercised by Congress
in the territories derived from the clause providing for the admission of new states. Such power could not be extended beyond
the "creation of proper governments for new countries," together
with "the necessary provision for their eventual admission into

the union, leaving, in the meantime, to the people inhabiting them, to regulate their internal concerns in their own way." The Wilmot Proviso, Cass maintained, was therefore unconstitutional.

Popular sovereignty as a discretionary congressional policy had been simple enough, but as a constitutional doctrine it proved to be elusive and equivocal. In addition to certain logical shortcomings, it went against a strong grain of precedent and gave rise to conflicting corollaries. Cass, himself a territorial governor for eighteen years, ignored the virtually unlimited control that Congress had regularly exercised over the territories. Although the structure of territorial government had been substantially democratized by the 1840s, this trend was offset in organic acts and other legislation that imposed increasingly detailed congressional supervision and restraint. The Cass doctrine also ignored the fact that in every organic act Congress reserved the right to disallow any territorial law. By this legislative veto alone, it possessed the means to sponsor or prevent the establishment of slavery in a territory. And if Cass was right, scores of federal territorial laws having nothing to do with slavery were unconstitutional.

The Cass argument was also in conflict with what appeared to be the most relevant judicial precedent. Chief Justice John Marshall, in *American Insurance Company v. Canter* (1828), had designated the territory clause as the most likely among several possible sources of "unquestioned" congressional authority over the territories. "In legislating for them," he added, "Congress exercises the combined powers of the general and of a State government."

In practice, nonintervention on the part of Congress had meant popular sovereignty for the territory, but this was not necessarily true of nonintervention as a constitutional principle. For if Congress merely *withheld* its authority to prohibit or establish slavery, that implied an intention to leave the decision in the hands of the territorial population. But if Congress *lacked* such authority, how could it be exercised by a subordinate government which Congress had created? Cass, Stephen A. Douglas, and other advocates of popular sovereignty would struggle for years with this difficult question.

To the constitutionalized version of nonintervention (that is, the principle that Congress lacked the constitutional authority to legislate concerning slavery in the territories) popular sovereignty was therefore a possible, but by no means a necessary corollary. Beginning with the same principle, some antislavery men reached the conclusion that the Constitution, of its own force, excluded slavery from the territories. Historically more significant, however, was John C. Calhoun's use of the principle to reach the opposite conclusion that the Constitution, of its own force, *protected* slavery in the territories. This was the South Carolinian's response to the northern argument that slavery, having been abolished by Mexico, could not be re-established in ceded Mexican territory except by positive legislative enactment. In effect, he was asserting not only that slavery automatically followed the Constitution, but also that the Constitution automatically followed the flag.

It is a matter of some importance that the Calhoun and Cass doctrines went a certain distance together before diverging; for northern and southern Democrats could talk about "nonintervention" and have different corollaries in mind. This was the first of two ambiguities with which the party would hold itself together until shortly before the Civil War. Eventually, the party did more or less endorse the Cass corollary, popular sovereignty, whereupon that term suddenly acquired a convenient doubleness of meaning. This second ambiguity was associated with the question of *when* the people of a territory could begin to exercise their popular sovereignty. Cass had obviously intended that the decision concerning slavery might be made by a territorial legislature as soon as it came into existence. This was the orthodox northern version for which Stephen A. Douglas later became the pre-eminent spokesman. The southern interpretation, camouflaged until the 1850s, held that the territorial decision could be made only at the time of admission to statehood. Before that time, accordingly, no authority could prohibit slavery in the territories. This version made a mockery of the phrase "popular sovereignty."

Of the four major territorial formulas under discussion in 1847-48, the one that could not be erected into a constitutional doctrine was the proposal to extend the Missouri Compromise line to the Pacific coast. Because of its biform nature, there was no way of making such an extension constitutionally imperative; for if the Compromise-line formula was constitutional, so too must be the two policies that it combined. Perhaps this theoretical deficiency is one reason the idea of extending the 36° 30′ line faded away as a serious alternative in the sectional conflict.

Of course a great deal of the debate over slavery in the territories was conducted at the level of interest and expediency, rather than at the level of constitutional theory. To many politicians favoring sectional conciliation, extension of the 36° 30′ line seemed the obvious solution at first. Douglas, a political pragmatist, turned to popular sovereignty only after failing in several attempts to get the Missouri Compromise solution accepted. But popular sovereignty was not in itself a substantive compromise; for it simply transferred the decision-making responsibility from Congress to the territorial legislatures. It dealt with the vexed issue by banishing it to the wilderness. The hard-headed expediency of the strategy was what appealed to realists like Douglas, who had little interest in the labyrinthine paths of constitutional argumentation.

Yet, constitutional questions, once raised, had a logical priority and often seemed to become psychologically compulsive for men in public life. Even Douglas in the end would succumb to the pressure and write a long, tedious article defending the constitutionality of popular sovereignty. Furthermore, the progressive constitutionalization of the debate tended to make popular sovereignty seem absurd. For, even if the territorial inhabitants were indeed the persons best qualified to choose between slavery and antislavery as a matter of practical local considerations, they were undoubtedly little qualified to decide questions of high constitutionality for the nation. The next inference was soon reached—that Congress should transfer the vexed issue, not to the territorial legislatures, but to the federal judiciary.

≈ 3 ≈

Toward Judicial Resolution

When Cass, Taylor, and Van Buren were nominated for the presidency by their respective parties in May and June 1848, the Treaty of Guadalupe Hidalgo had confirmed Mexico's cession of the Southwest, and gold had been discovered in California. In Congress, the principal territorial problem continued to be Oregon, where American settlers were still living under an extra-legal provisional government that they themselves had established five years earlier. Southerners persisted in the strategy of holding Oregon as a hostage until the status of slavery in the Mexican Cession had been determined. Debate accordingly ranged over the whole embittered subject of congressional power and territorial policy.

Douglas, now chairman of the committee on territories in the Senate, introduced a new Oregon bill on January 10, 1848. One section declared that the existing laws of the provisional government (which included a ban on slavery) would remain in force until altered or repealed by the territorial legislature. The effect was to establish popular sovereignty, with every indication that it would mean the continued prohibition of slavery. This satisfied neither the vehemently antislavery senators, who wanted the prohibition made explicit in terms of the Northwest Ordinance, nor the militantly proslavery senators, who were unwilling to let

Oregon become a territory without at the same time settling the issue of California and New Mexico.

On June 27, at the urging of President Polk, administration spokesmen launched another effort to link the Oregon bill with extension of the 36° 30′ line. But the proposal made little headway against strong opposition from both sections and the knowledge that it had slight chance of success in the House.

With all progress seemingly halted, the Senate accepted a proposal from John M. Clayton of Delaware for reference of the Oregon bill to a select committee. Under Clayton's leadership, the committee labored and brought forth a substitute measure called a "compromise," although there was much justice in the complaint of one northern senator who said, "This bill is no compromise; it is no compromise at all." In dealing with Oregon, the committee simply followed the original Douglas bill, validating the provisional laws already in effect and confirming the power of the territorial legislature to amend or repeal them. The later sections of the measure established territorial organizations in New Mexico and California. There, the legislatures were *forbidden* to pass any law "respecting the prohibition or establishment of African slavery." At the same time, the Constitution was extended to the two territories and special provisions were made for review by the Supreme Court of any lawsuit testing the status of slavery in either of them. Thus, popular sovereignty was to be explicitly conferred on Oregon, but explicitly denied to New Mexico and California.

What the committee had sought and found, in dealing with the Southwest, was a new formula of sectional compromise—one which, like popular sovereignty, transferred the substantive problem to other hands. "The bill," said Clayton, "leaves the entire question which is in dispute to the Judiciary." Constitutionalization of the struggle over slavery in the territories had at last been pursued to its logical conclusion, but the motives for doing so were primarily opportunistic. In their theoretical foundations there was a vast difference between leaving the question to the territorial legislature elected by the local population, and leaving it to nine judges in Washington, elected by, and responsible to, no one. Yet, as political expedients for evading a troublesome congressional responsibility, the two formulas had much in common, and this was not the last time they would appear together in the same legislation.

But exactly *what* question did the Clayton bill leave to the judiciary? Not, as one is led to believe by most historical accounts, *not* the classic question of whether Congress had the power to prohibit slavery in the territories. That could be tested judicially only with an act providing such prohibition.* What the Clayton bill in effect submitted to judicial disposition was the question of the status of slavery throughout the Mexican Cession *in the absence of* congressional and territorial legislation on the subject. The answer, presumably, would be in terms satisfactory either to Wilmot or to Calhoun. Either Mexican antislavery law remained in effect until superseded by positive legislation; or the Constitution, *proprio vigore,* superseded Mexican law and carried with it the right to hold slaves in the conquered territory.

The thought of putting so much at risk in a single court action inspired considerable apprehension. Many northerners believed that the southern majority on the Supreme Court would close ranks and hand down a proslavery decision. But there were also southerners who feared that, as a matter of law, the antislavery cause might prove to be the stronger. Some realists, moreover, challenged Clayton's sanguine prediction that "the people, being law-abiding," would submit to the decision of the Court because it occupied "the highest place in their confidence." Instead, said a North Carolina Democrat, "the moral influence of the Court must be forever destroyed in one section or other of the Union."

Consideration of the Clayton bill took place during the heat of the presidential campaign, and there was much calculation of its potential effect on party fortunes as well as on sectional discord. The Senate passed the measure on July 27 by a vote of 33 to 22, with the majority overwhelmingly Democratic and southern. But any senators who expected the House to endorse their

---

* It is conceivable, to be sure, that the Court might have invalidated the provision forbidding the territorial legislature to take any action, giving as its reason the lack of congressional power over any aspect of slavery in the territories. That was not what the Clayton committee had in mind, however.

"compromise" were quickly disabused. With scant courtesy it was laid on the table the very next day. Then the House took up and passed its own Oregon bill, with the provisions of the Northwest Ordinance included.

Many senators were furious at this cavalier treatment. Andrew P. Butler of South Carolina called the House bill "a masked battery, from behind which the institutions of the South were to be assailed." His advice to his own constituents, he said, "would be to go to these new Territories with arms in their hands . . . and take possession of the lands which they had helped to acquire." The Senate majority, still unwilling to give in, passed the House bill only after amending it to include extension of the Missouri Compromise line. Every southerner present voted for that amendment, which, according to prevailing southern theory, was unconstitutional. But the House remained firm, promptly rejecting the 36° 30′ amendment. On August 12, the Senate receded by a vote of 29 to 25, and Polk reluctantly signed the measure, explaining at length that he did so only because the area concerned lay north of the compromise line. Oregon Territory had at last been organized, and with slavery prohibited there, but the festering problem of the Southwest remained unsolved.

2

The presidential campaign of 1848 was in certain respects a very strange contest. It took place while Congress was engaged in a sustained and bitter struggle over the extension of slavery; yet both major parties did all they could to smother or evade the issue in their platforms and nominations. Efforts to play down the territorial question nevertheless proved futile, and the campaign resolved itself into an odd combination of partisan and sectional advocacy. Each of the two major parties claimed in each section that its own candidate was the more reliably proslavery or antislavery, as the case required. Their success in this strategy of dualism was roughly equal. The Democrats carried eight northern and seven southern states; the Whigs carried seven northern and eight southern states; but Zachary Taylor received the larger number of electoral votes.

Congress assembled for its short session in December 1848, and from the opening day it was clear that the deadlock between House and Senate remained unbroken. On December 11, Douglas introduced a bill to organize the whole Mexican Cession as one huge state, with the provision that Congress might later create additional states out of the area lying east of the Sierra Nevada. When this inventive but unrealistic proposal got nowhere, Douglas suggested admitting only California. Then, as chairman of a select committee, he presented still a third plan, creating two states, with California to be admitted immediately and New Mexico when it had sufficient population. Frustrated at every turn, the Little Giant would soon find his direct-admission approach to the problem taken over by the Whigs and their new President.

Meanwhile, passage of a House resolution calling for abolition of the slave trade in the District of Columbia inspired a caucus of the more militant southerners, from which there emerged Calhoun's famous manifesto, the "Southern Address." An eloquent document saying nothing really new, the "Address" adhered closely to Calhoun's doctrine of nonintervention as a constitutional imperative. "The Federal Government," he declared, "has no right to extend or restrict slavery, no more to establish or abolish it . . . What then we do insist on, is, not to extend slavery, but that we shall not be prohibited from immigrating with our property, into the Territories of the United States, because we are slaveholders."

The distinction drawn by Calhoun was extremely subtle, and in the end it would prove impossible to maintain. If a person's right to "immigrate" with his "property" were interfered with, where would he find protection? Congress could scarcely enact protective legislation without thereby tending to "extend" or "establish" slavery. Territorial legislatures, according to the Calhoun view, had no powers greater than those of Congress in this respect. Self-protection by force of arms, as suggested by Senator Butler, was the kind of lawless solution that would prevail for a time in Kansas. The only other conceivable alternative was protection through the courts of law. Thus, by its very nature, the Calhoun doctrine generated pressure toward a judicial disposition of the territorial question.

Reference to the judiciary was regarded sympathetically by many congressional moderates who did not embrace the Calhoun doctrine. But antislavery men, with a few exceptions, remained suspicious of such proposals. In fact, they grew increasingly fearful that slavery might be slipped into the territories through some constitutional back door. It is against this background that one must place the furor produced near the end of the session by the "Walker amendment."

During consideration of a major appropriation bill, Senator Isaac P. Walker of Wisconsin offered an extraneous amendment extending the Constitution and applicable laws of the United States over the territory acquired from Mexico and authorizing the President to establish temporary means of government there. Young and inexperienced, Walker was apparently acting under southern influence. At the very least, his proposal would abrogate the antislavery law of Mexico in the Southwest, and it would provide a statutory basis for promotion of the Calhoun doctrine that slavery in the territories was under the direct protection of the Constitution.

There resulted a long, confused debate in which Daniel Webster, among others, argued that the Constitution was made for the states alone and could not be extended wholesale to the territories, while Calhoun insisted that the Constitution followed the flag. Antislavery senators opposing the Walker amendment placed themselves in a vulnerable position, for, as Calhoun gleefully pointed out, their opposition seemed to acknowledge his major contention that the Constitution was a "shield to the South," protecting the expansion of slavery. Northerners denied that any such concession had been made, but they were probably unwise in allowing the discussion to be shifted from the status of slavery in the territories to the status of the Constitution in the territories.

The Walker amendment passed the Senate by a narrow margin, and the appropriation bill to which it was attached reached the House of Representatives just two days before adjournment.

From that moment until a few hours before Zachary Taylor took the presidential oath, the Capitol was a scene of turmoil, as tempers flared, insults flew, blows were exchanged, and gavels pounded away futilely in both chambers. The House predictably rejected the amendment, and the appropriation measure was eventually passed with no territorial rider attached. Meanwhile, the House had approved its own bill organizing California as a territory, with slavery forbidden, but the Senate, by a vote of 28 to 25, refused to take it up. An angry, exhausted Congress adjourned at 7:00 a.m. on March 4, leaving the embittered question to its successor.

During the next nine months, the sectional quarrel over slavery reached the level of a national crisis. Trouble was brewing over the extravagant boundary claims of Texas, which extended as far west as Santa Fe, and the Gold Rush made California's need for stable government more desperate every day. Zachary Taylor, who came increasingly under the antislavery influence of William H. Seward, adopted as administration policy Douglas's idea of by-passing the territorial issue by admitting California and New Mexico directly to statehood. Californians, however, were already taking matters into their own hands. Without congressional authorization, a constitutional convention met at Monterey in September 1849 and drafted a state constitution with slavery prohibited. By virtue of this document, voters went to the polls in November and elected a governor, a state legislature, and two congressmen. The legislature, convening in December, elected two United States senators. Thus, when the new Congress met that same month, it was confronted with a *fait accompli* on the Pacific coast.

Southerners were unhappy at this turn of events and alarmed by the behavior of President Taylor, who told a Pennsylvania audience, for instance, that "the people of the North need have no apprehension of the further extension of slavery." The natural results were a weakening of the Whig party in the South and a strengthening of the movement for southern unity. The North, Calhoun asserted, must be presented with "the alternative of dissolving the partnership or of ceasing on their part to violate our rights."

Along with sectional antagonism, there was the added disadvantage that neither major party had full charge of the government. A Whig occupied the presidency, and the Democrats retained control of the Senate. In the House of Representatives, no party could claim a majority, and a dozen or so Free Soilers held the partisan balance of power. A bitter contest over the election of a Speaker lasted nearly three weeks, and the House at times, according to its reporter, was "like a heaving billow." Then, with Democrat Howell Cobb finally installed in the chair by a plurality vote, members spent another full month wrangling over rules and other officers. Meanwhile, the sectional crisis deepened.

With the House in such disarray, there was all the more reason for the Senate, which had always been the more compromise-minded of the two, to take the lead in formulating a plan for sectional conciliation. The senatorial membership provided an illustrious cast for what was to be the most famous legislative event in American history, and it was altogether fitting that Henry Clay should be the one to lead the way. In a set of resolutions introduced on January 29, 1850, he advocated admission of California with its antislavery constitution, and, as counterbalance, the organization of Utah and New Mexico Territories without restrictions on slavery. Similarly, reduction of the area of Texas would be balanced by federal assumption of the Texas debt, and prohibition of the domestic slave trade in the District of Columbia would be balanced by passage of a more effective fugitive-slave law.

After many weeks of debate, the resolutions were referred to a select committee headed by Clay, which reported on May 8, lumping the California, territorial, and Texas proposals together in one "omnibus bill," while dealing with the fugitive slave and slave trade problems in separate measures. The omnibus proved to be mistaken strategy, and at the end of July, it was knocked to pieces on the Senate floor. An exhausted Clay went off to rest, and Douglas assumed the leadership of the compromise effort. The sudden death of Taylor on July 9 had removed a major obstacle; for his successor, Millard Fillmore, was entirely in sympathy with Clay and Douglas. Furthermore, a surge of support for compromise throughout the country could be felt in the halls of Congress. Between July 31 and September 16, the Senate passed the compromise in six separate measures embodying the principal features of the original Clay resolutions. In no instance was the voting really close. The overall total of *yeas* was nearly double that of *nays*.

In the House it was not so easy, of course. There, the New Mexico bill and the Texas boundary and debt bill were joined together in a "little omnibus," which became the critical test. From September 4 to September 6, the chamber was in an uproar. Some of the roll-call votes were "perilously close," and on one occasion the Speaker broke a 103-103 tie. Efforts to attach the Wilmot Proviso proved fruitless, and at last the measure passed, 108 to 98. Everything that followed was anticlimax. The House took only eleven more days to pass the other four bills admitting California, organizing Utah Territory, prohibiting the slave trade in the District of Columbia, and providing a new system for the recovery of fugitive slaves.

Only a minority of the members of Congress voted for the Compromise of 1850, but by joining forces with the sectional supporters of each bill, they assembled the necessary majority six times in the Senate and five times in the House—not to mention all the preliminary votes taken. If one defines a supporter of compromise as a member who voted for at least four of the five measures related to the slavery question (that is, omitting the Texas bill in the Senate) and who opposed none of them, then there were 47 compromisers in the House and 14 in the Senate. Of these 61 men (constituting about 21 per cent of the entire membership), 38 were northern Democrats, and 11 were southern Whigs. Just 17 compromisers were southerners, and only 4 came from the eleven states of the future Confederacy. It has been well called "the Armistice of 1850."

The antislavery strategy that failed even in the House, despite presidential support until Taylor died, had been to push through a separate bill for the admission of California. From the beginning of the session, California assumed a place similar to the one previously occupied by Oregon in the sectional conflict—that is, admittedly closed to slaveholding, but held as a hostage to prevent further success of the Wilmot Proviso. Thus the territorial issue remained alive only in regard to the predominantly arid region then called New Mexico, but including present-day Utah and Nevada, most of Arizona, and parts of Colorado and Wyoming. In this context, it is not surprising to find some realists like Webster concluding that the Proviso game had ceased to be worth the candle. The law of nature, he declared, "settles forever, with a strength beyond all terms of human enactment, that slavery cannot exist in California or New Mexico." This was a line of argument frequently used by supporters of compromise, and it may have weakened resistance in some moderate antislavery circles.

What southerners wanted, fundamentally, was an end to agitation of the slavery question. Their absolute minimum was repudiation of the proscriptive principle embodied in the Wilmot Proviso. The Proviso meant disunion. Southerners had begun saying so even during the speakership contest in December, and the threat echoed and re-echoed through the many months of debate that followed. If disunion in turn meant war, then, as a Virginia congressman put it, the fighting would be "between men contending for their firesides, and the robbers who are seeking to despoil them of their rights, and degrade them before the world."

Quite clearly, then, successful compromise required a non-Proviso settlement of the territorial question to balance the admission of California as a free state. Yet the anti-Proviso elements in Congress could not agree upon an alternative. Neither the Calhoun doctrine, nor the Missouri Compromise line, nor popular sovereignty could command sufficient support. Henry Clay realized from the beginning that the only possible solution was nonintervention, pure and simple—that is, the organization of New Mexico and Utah territories without any mention of slavery whatsoever. Now, nonintervention, being actually just a half-doctrine, had a splendid elusiveness about it. The meaning of the term seemed to vary, said Jefferson Davis, "as often as the light and shade of every fleeting cloud." According to the southern version of nonintervention, slaveholders could enter a territory without interference throughout the territorial period; then, at the time of admission to statehood, a constitutional convention

would make the choice between establishing and prohibiting
slavery. To Cass and Douglas, on the other hand, nonintervention meant that the territorial legislature, as soon as it was organized, could establish or prohibit slavery. To Clay himself,
nonintervention in New Mexico and Utah meant that the antislavery laws of Mexico would remain in effect, thus reinforcing
the climatic barrier to slavery and making the Proviso doubly
unnecessary.

Ultimately, of course, nonintervention by Congress meant
that some other authority would have to intervene. That authority, in Clay's view, was the federal judiciary. Did Mexican law
continue in force until explicitly superseded? Did a territorial
legislature have the power to establish or prohibit slavery? Did
the Constitution protect slaveholding in the territories as a matter of property right? Such questions, being essentially legal in
nature, should be left to "the proper and competent tribunal—
the Supreme Court of the United States." Clay's solution to the
territorial problem, like that offered by Clayton two years earlier, was to convert a political issue into a constitutional case at
law. Accordingly, the Utah and New Mexico acts, as finally
passed, included provisions facilitating the appeal of slavery
cases to the Supreme Court.

There was only one other direct reference to slavery in the
text of the two acts. Proposed by Senator Pierre Soulé of Louisiana and derived from the joint resolution for the annexation of
Texas in 1845, the passage read: "And, when admitted as a State,
the said Territory, or any portion of the same, shall be received
into the Union, with or without slavery, as their constitution may
prescribe at the time of their admission." This clause, approved
after extensive debate by the overwhelming vote of 38 to 12, is
the one most often quoted by historians summarizing the Compromise of 1850. But precisely what did it signify?

Many northern senators, including some who voted with the
majority, regarded the amendment as superfluous, in that it affirmed a right already generally acknowledged, and as useless, in
that it was essentially an attempt to bind the action of a future
Congress. Yet Alexander H. Stephens later called the Soulé
amendment "the turning point" upon which "everything de-

pended" in the compromise effort. The news of its adoption, he added, was "well calculated to make a nation leap with joy." And, indeed, one finds in the pages of debate a curious intensity of feeling about this declaratory clause.

Soulé himself explained that his purpose was to "feel the pulse of the Senate" on the question of whether any more slaveholding states were ever to be admitted to the Union. Like the rest of the compromise, he said, the clause would be a compact, "binding *in future*." He meant binding, not in law but as a pledge of honor, with the threat of disunion serving as the sanctional force. Here, in fact, one gets a preview of sectional politics in the next decade, with southerners forever calculating the value of the Union and testing it, like ice on a river in early spring, to see how much proslavery weight it would still bear. Here, also, was a view of the compromise legislation as a set of pledges negotiated like an international treaty, the violation of which would lead to sovereign reprisals.

Certainly, the Utah and New Mexico acts did not expressly install popular sovereignty, though they may perhaps be regarded as silently permitting it. Southerners, however, were generally insistent that slavery was subject to prohibition by territorial action only at the time of admission to statehood, and they could point to the Soulé amendment as explicit confirmation. The amendment, as a Connecticut senator had pointed out in opposing it, assumed the nullity of Mexican antislavery law and the validity of the Calhoun doctrine that slavery followed the Constitution, which in turn followed the flag. For how else could slavery enter the territories and necessitate the eventual choice provided for in that amendment? Thus it appears that the territorial legislation of 1850 was open-ended—adaptable either to popular sovereignty or to the Calhoun property-rights doctrine, but legitimizing neither on an exclusive basis.

The effect of the Compromise of 1850, taken together with the act creating Oregon Territory in 1848, was to continue the policy of having two territorial policies, with the new dividing line extending westward along the 42nd parallel to the Pacific, but with California, south of that line, admitted as a free state. On one side of 42° slavery was prohibited, and on the other side it was permitted, just as in the Missouri Compromise. The South, unable to secure the extension of the 36° 30′ line to the Pacific, had, in effect, traded off the loss of southern California for the opening of Utah to slavery.

The problem of slavery in Utah and New Mexico ceased to be significant, however, as soon as the Compromise of 1850 was passed. Slaveholders simply did not migrate to either territory. The census of 1860 reported no slaves in New Mexico and twenty-nine in Utah. New Mexico nevertheless perversely became the only jurisdiction in American history to enact a slave code for a slaveless society. This action was taken in 1859 as a response to the Dred Scott decision, and it reflected the growing southern influence in New Mexico as a consequence of the territorial appointments made by Presidents Pierce and Buchanan. The territorial acts of 1850 did have an important indirect effect on the sectional conflict over slavery, but it was felt in Kansas rather than in Utah or New Mexico.

3

The Compromise of 1850 inspired sighs of relief throughout the country and was grudgingly welcomed even by many men who disliked some of its provisions. The resounding victory of Franklin Pierce in the presidential election of 1852 was to some extent a measure of popular support for the principle of "finality"— which meant that the last word had been said about slavery as a national issue.

Yet it quickly became apparent that in some northern states, militant minorities were determined to resist enforcement of the Fugitive Slave Act. Equally clear and ominous was the fact that in much of the South, "conditional Unionism" had more or less officially emerged as a majoritarian sentiment. Southerners, as David M. Potter has observed, rejected secession itself for the time being but embraced the principle of secessionism. The "Georgia platform," drafted by a state convention in December

1850, became the sectional credo of the next decade. Accepting the Compromise (without fully approving of it) as "a permanent adjustment," the platform then listed the conceivable northern aggressions, any one of which would justify southern resistance, even to the point of disrupting the Union. The principal ones were: legislation abolishing slavery in the District of Columbia or forbidding slavery in the territories of New Mexico and Utah, or suppressing the interstate slave trade; repeal, substantial modification, or nonenforcement of the Fugitive Slave Act; and refusal to admit a new state because of the existence of slavery therein.

Stephen A. Douglas was nevertheless convinced that the settlement would endure. Douglas firmly believed that the Compromise of 1850 had installed the principle of popular sovereignty—a principle which he did not yet regard as a constitutional imperative. That is, he did not agree with Lewis Cass that Congress *lacked the power* to establish or prohibit slavery in the territories. Instead, he gave essentially three reasons why the question *ought* to be left "to the decision of the people themselves." Popular sovereignty, he maintained, was the wisest public policy in view of sectional rivalries; it was in accord with democratic principles; and it was a recognition of the inevitable. Douglas was therefore temperamentally and ideologically ready, when pressed by circumstances, to replace the old Missouri Compromise restriction with the principle of popular sovereignty.

With the movement of settlers across the Missouri River into what had so recently been called "permanent Indian country," there was considerable local agitation for territorial organization. A bill creating Nebraska Territory, passed by the House of Representatives early in 1853, contained no mention of slavery, but everyone assumed that the institution was still forbidden north of 36° 30′. The Senate refused to pass the measure, and southerners conspicuously provided most of the opposition. Thus a new sectional barrier to westward expansion had been raised, and it amounted to the Wilmot Proviso in reverse. Southerners, many of whom insisted that a policy of "no more slave states" would mean disunion, were now seemingly committed to a pol-

icy of "no more antislavery territories." They wanted erasure of
the 36° 30′ line because they had come to regard any overt federal prohibition of slavery as an unbearable moral reproach.

According to the "railroad interpretation" of the Kansas-
Nebraska Act, Douglas wanted immediate territorial organization in order to strengthen the hand of those supporting a central
route for the proposed Pacific railway, and so he resolved to
bring in a bill more attractive to southerners in its treatment of
the slavery problem. The neatness of this explanation may have
lent it more credibility over the years than it really deserves; for
the absence of territorial organization was only a technical objection to the central route as far as the southern argument was
concerned. The real objection, as Douglas and everyone else
knew well, was that southerners wanted a southern route, and
there is not the slightest evidence that passage of the Kansas-
Nebraska Act altered that objection. Certainly, if the act was
visualized as the preliminary step in the authorization of a Pacific railroad, it proved to be a great miscalculation. Seven years
later, little progress had been made toward realization of the
project.

Railroad considerations were in fact just one of a number of
pressures, local and national, for territorial organization of the
Nebraska region. Perhaps the most important factor of all was
the very existence of the anomaly, conspicuous on any map, of a
great region in the heart of the continent, possessed by the nation for a half-century, but still ungoverned.

At any rate, on January 4, 1854, Douglas reported a bill for
the organization of Nebraska as one big territory stretching from
36° 30′ to the Canadian boundary. The measure incorporated the
slavery provisions of the Utah and New Mexico acts while
making no reference to the Missouri Compromise restriction,
which was presumably still in force. The familiar Soulé clause
declared that "when admitted as a state or states, the said territory . . . shall be received into the Union, with or without slavery as their constitutions may prescribe." There was also the
same provision for easy access to the Supreme Court in slavery
cases. The effect was similar to that achieved four years earlier:
Popular sovereignty was apparently permitted but not plainly es-

tablished, and the status of the Missouri Compromise restriction, like the status of Mexican antislavery law in 1850, was left undefined and to be determined either by the territorial legislature or by judicial process.

In thus attempting to neutralize the Missouri Compromise restriction without formally repealing it, Douglas awakened the anger of antislavery men and yet fell short of satisfying many southerners. After various negotiations and conferences in which President Pierce assumed an important role, the Illinois senator on January 23 presented a new bill establishing two territories instead of one and declaring the slavery restriction to be "inoperative and void." It was to this measure that Salmon P. Chase and other antislavery radicals responded with the denunciatory "Appeal of the Independent Democrats," which set the tone of bitterness for the long struggle that followed.

One clause in the Kansas-Nebraska bill justified voiding the Missouri Compromise restriction on the grounds that it was "inconsistent with the principle of non-intervention by Congress with slavery in the territories" as embodied in the Compromise of 1850. During the legislative debate, Douglas went even further to argue that the Compromise of 1850 had legally "superseded" the Missouri Compromise in respect to slavery in the territories.

The foundations of this argument were very weak. For one thing, it assumed a uniformity of principles in the government of territories that had never existed in American history. During the Jefferson administration, for example, slavery had been expressly forbidden in Indiana Territory, expressly unforbidden in Orleans Territory, and totally unmentioned in the organization of Louisiana Territory. Even more conclusive is the complete lack of evidence that any members of Congress in 1850 thought that the Utah and New Mexico acts would have any effect on the status of slavery in Nebraska country. But perhaps the most fundamental weakness of the "supersession" argument is one that has gone largely unnoticed—namely, the falsity of the assumption that there was something new in the principle of nonintervention as it appeared in the territorial acts of 1850. In fact, as we have seen, the Far West, like all earlier American Wests, had been divided in 1848 and 1850 between the policy of prohibition and the policy of nonintervention.

The Kansas-Nebraska Act, to be sure, went beyond the Compromise of 1850 in attempting to establish popular sovereignty as a corollary to nonintervention. One clause declared that the "true intent and meaning" of the act as a whole was "not to legislate slavery into any Territory or State, nor to exclude it therefrom, but to leave the people thereof perfectly free to form and regulate their domestic institutions in their own way, subject only to the Constitution of the United States." But what, precisely, did this passage mean? Did it authorize the territorial legislatures to establish, recognize, or prohibit slavery, as Douglas believed? Southerners would later find it easy to argue that the "people" of a territory could take action only through a constitutional convention called to prepare for statehood. Before that time, according to this southern version, pure nonintervention would prevail, with slaveholders free to enter the territory at will.

Equivocal, then, at best, in the degree to which it established popular sovereignty, the Kansas-Nebraska Act, like the Utah and New Mexico acts which it imitated, also looked toward a judicial settlement of the slavery controversy. Addition of the superfluous phrase, "subject only to the Constitution," was a reminder of the fact that beyond the uncertain authority of the territorial legislature stood the certain authority of the Supreme Court. Vagueness in legislation is a kind of delegation of power, and the very vagueness of the Kansas-Nebraska Act invited, if it did not authorize, an eventual judicial disposition of a difficult issue. During the debates, there was considerable speculation about the outcome of the expected Court decision. Under the Kansas-Nebraska Act, however, it would not have been possible to secure a judicial test of the power of *Congress* over slavery in the territories; for the act renounced the use of that power. Instead, it was the power of the *territorial legislature*, the principle of popular sovereignty, and perhaps the validity of the Calhoun doctrine that would have been tested in the envisioned court case. The power of Congress could be tested only where it could be challenged—that is, where it was operative.

The debates on the Kansas-Nebraska bill ranged over the whole of the slavery controversy—its history, moral conflict, and constitutional theory. Southerners frequently justified their support of the measure by arguing that the Missouri Compromise restriction was unconstitutional. These were in many cases the same men who, as recently as 1850, had urged extension of the 36° 30′ line as the best means of resolving the sectional conflict. Yet perhaps even more anomalous was the spectacle of radical antislavery men appealing to the sanctity of the venerable Missouri Compromise, which they had consistently rejected as a basis for further conciliation.

Southerners in Congress voted 92 to 11 in favor of the Kansas-Nebraska bill; northerners opposed it, 103 to 58. One can easily forget, however, that the measure was a partisan as well as a sectional issue, receiving the official support of a Democratic administration and the approval of a heavily Democratic Congress. The bill passed the Senate easily in March 1854, but in the House of Representatives it took nearly three months for administration forces to whip enough northern Democrats into line. On May 22, the effort succeeded, 113 to 110, and Franklin Pierce signed the measure eight days later, thereby writing the label on his entire presidency. The two major consequences were a revolution in the party system and a civil war in Kansas.

4

The angry reaction against the Kansas-Nebraska Act throughout the North spelled disaster for the Democratic party in a midterm election year. Its huge majority in the House of Representatives melted like snow during a sudden thaw. More than 70 per cent of the party's free-state seats were lost. Only seven of the forty-four northern Democrats who had voted for the bill won re-election. The fate of the Whig party in the North is more difficult to fathom; for it suffered curiously from having been on the right side of the issue. Tainted with nativism and already in partial dissolution, it seemed to have been given, in the Kansas-

Nebraska Act, a last chance to survive—not as a national party any longer, but as the antislavery party of the North. Whiggery, however, proved unable to turn the party revolution to its own advantage, partly because the "anti-Nebraska" movement included many Democrats and thus could not maximize its strength under the Whig banner.

Conversion of the spontaneous, loosely organized anti-Nebraska movement of 1854 into the new and permanent Republican party proceeded at different speeds in the various free states and was not entirely completed even by 1860. The virtually simultaneous national emergence of political nativism in the form of Know-Nothingism (officially, the "American party") further complicated an already confused situation and enabled the Democracy, in spite of its weakened condition, to capture the presidency one more time.

The Republican party should not be viewed simply as the Free Soil party writ large; for it became a *major* party, and that made a critical difference in the nature of the antislavery movement. On an earlier page it has been suggested that antislavery for a long time was primarily a sentiment, whereas proslavery from the beginning was a powerful interest. The abolitionist organizations on a small scale constituted an antislavery interest, but not in the same sense as the Republican party after 1854. For the Republicans began immediately to capture statehouses and legislatures, not to mention making a strong run for the presidency as early as 1856. In the process, the party drew support, not only from all kinds of antislavery men, but also from many men who cared less about slavery than about winning elections and distributing patronage. Diffuse antislavery sentiment had at last been converted into a major, organized political interest, with its own self-sufficient reasons for survival and growth.

Moreover, because of its utterly sectional nature, Republicanism differed from other major parties in its attitude toward agitation of the slavery question. For the Federalist, Jeffersonian, Democratic, and Whig organizations, all aspiring to be national in scope, there had always been good reason to reduce sectional tension; but Republicanism, as the very circumstances of its birth testified, had a stake in the continuance of the slavery controversy. That is one of the central facts in the history of "bleeding Kansas."

Before 1850, a congressional policy of nonintervention, whenever adopted, had always led to the establishment of slavery in the respective territories and states because the policy had been generally limited to regions lying across the path of southern migration that were more or less suitable for plantation agriculture. By 1854 it could already be seen that the effect of such a policy in Utah and New Mexico would probably be different, and nobody seriously expected slavery to take root in Nebraska. Kansas, however, was plainly a borderline case, unlikely to become the goal of a large-scale migration of slaveholders, and yet almost certain to be heavily influenced for a time by the adjacent proslavery population of western Missouri.

The troubles began with the first territorial elections. There had been a widely publicized movement in the Northeast to organize "emigrant aid societies" and save Kansas from slavery. This provided the excuse for an invasion of illegal voters from Missouri, who secured the election of a proslavery legislature. At its first session in the summer of 1855, the legislature enacted a severe slave code. By then, however, a considerable number of *bona fide* settlers had arrived from nearby free states. The militants among them repudiated the "bogus legislature" and in the autumn organized their own rival government at Topeka. Thereafter, Kansas suffered under the rule of two governments, each in its own way illegitimate.

President Pierce supported the official, proslavery government in Kansas. He denounced the Topeka government as "revolutionary" but took no decisive action to suppress it, and neither he nor the federal authorities in the territory seemed capable of ending the intermittent violence that reached its peak in May 1856 with the "sack" of Lawrence and John Brown's retaliatory murders at Pottawatomie Creek. Sensationalized Kansas news filled the Republican press, to the increasing embarrassment and anger of the Democrats. With each party in effect supporting its own faction in the bedeviled territory, Kansas became a kind of violent extension of the approaching contest for the presidency.

The thirty-fourth Congress, elected in the aftermath of the

struggle over the Kansas-Nebraska bill, assembled in December 1855, with Kansas and presidential politics very much on its mind. The Democratic party had lost control of the House of Representatives, which, as in 1849-50, entered upon a long, tiresome contest over the choice of a Speaker. After two months and 133 ballots, the members finally elected Nathaniel P. Banks of Massachusetts, a Know-Nothing recently turned Republican.

It was just at this time that the case of *Dred Scott v. Sandford,* which had been on the docket for more than a year, finally came before the Supreme Court. Oral argument began on February 11, nine days after the election of Banks as Speaker. The Court held a number of conferences on the case during the next several months, while members of Congress were engaging in still another fierce oratorical battle over the question of slavery in the territories. The justices, all political men in some degree, read their newspapers and probably followed the legislative debate in the *Congressional Globe.* Most of them mingled freely with political leaders in Washington and privately exchanged opinions on the issues of the day. With the territorial question now laid squarely before them, it seems likely that they paid very close attention to the proceedings of Congress in 1856.

The debate was launched by Franklin Pierce in his annual message to Congress of December 31, 1855. Embittered by the ruinous effect of the Kansas controversy on his administration and his personal popularity, Pierce closed the message with a harangue placing the entire blame for the sectional conflict on the critics of slavery. The President acknowledged no merit in the moral opposition to the institution, which he described as a "passionate rage of fanaticism and partisan spirit." He offered his own emphatically pro-southern history of the territorial issue, during the course of which he pronounced the Missouri Compromise restriction of doubtful legality. It was, he said, "in the estimation of many thoughtful men, null from the beginning, unauthorized by the Constitution, contrary to the treaty stipulations for the cession of Louisiana, and inconsistent with the equality of these States." Pierce had thus provided the Supreme Court with a presidential opinion on the central constitutional issue of the Dred Scott case.

Several weeks later, the President sent to Congress a special message on Kansas, taking the proslavery side, denouncing the Topeka government again, and recommending legislation that would authorize Kansas to prepare for statehood in the near future. The Senate referred the recommendation to its committee on territories, still presided over by Douglas, who responded on March 12, 1856, with a report of forty-one printed pages. In it, significantly, for the first time, he undertook to provide a constitutional imperative for his principle of popular sovereignty.

Douglas followed the example of many southerners, and of Lewis Cass as well, in maintaining that the territory clause of the Constitution referred only to property and therefore conferred no power of government. Anticipating Taney's reasoning in the Dred Scott decision, he concluded that the authority must be implied instead from the delegated power to admit new states. But to Douglas this meant that territories were essentially incipient states, to which the rule of state equality fully applied. The organic act for a territory, he declared, "must contain no provision or restriction which would destroy or impair the equality of the proposed State with the original States, or impose any limitation upon its sovereignty which the constitution has not placed on all the States." More specifically, the organic act "must leave the people entirely free to form and regulate their domestic institutions and internal concerns in their own way, subject only to the constitution of the United States."

The latter passage was taken, of course, from the text of the Kansas-Nebraska Act, with the notable addition of the word "must." What had been set forth in 1854 as "the true intent and meaning of this act" now became the true intent and meaning of the Constitution itself. In other words, Douglas now maintained that the repeal of the Missouri Compromise restriction in 1854 had been dictated by constitutional necessity, joining southerners in the conviction that Congress possessed no authority to enact such a restriction. Thus, one full year before the Dred Scott decision, its most important conclusion had already been reached by Democratic leaders of both sections.

That Douglas, a man for whom theory had always been secondary to practical achievement, should now find it expedient to

constitutionalize the principle of popular sovereignty is a striking
indication of the increasing formalism and casuistry in the public
debate over slavery. "The constitution," said one editor, "threat-
ens to be a subject of infinite sects, like the Bible." The effect of
Douglas's new argument was to convert *popular sovereignty,*
with its theoretical roots in the Lockean individualism of the
Revolution, into *territorial sovereignty,* a constitutional theory
stressing the corporate rights of an organized territory and, in
effect, wiping out the distinction between territories and states.
In this respect, Douglas was returning to the outlook of Jefferson in 1784, but ignoring the history of territorial legislation over
the intervening seventy years.

By 1856, as compared with the years of the Wilmot Proviso,
the question of congressional power over slavery in the territories had lost some of its relevance. Having become essentially
a partisan issue between Democrats and Republicans, it inspired
much debate and editorial exchange but was no longer an urgent
public problem. The Proviso principle, after all, had been rejected by Congress in 1850 and then rolled back from Kansas
and Nebraska in 1854. For southerners, accordingly, there was
no reason to press the matter, and for Republicans there was little use in doing so until restriction again became politically
feasible.

The paramount public issue of 1856 was the turmoil in Kansas, involving primarily questions of fact and policy, rather than
constitutional law. The only constitutional question of any urgency did not arise between Democrats and Republicans, but,
instead, between the northern and southern wings of the Democratic party. First, there was a preliminary problem of statutory
construction—namely, whether the Kansas-Nebraska Act authorized the territorial legislatures to establish or prohibit slavery.
If it did, then there followed the question of whether the territorial legislatures could constitutionally exercise such authority.
For Democrats, trying to maintain a semblance of party unity in
an election year, this was a touchy subject which they would
have preferred not to talk about. But Republicans could readily
see the advantage of forcing the Democrats to confess their sec-

tional disagreement on the issue. So the Douglas version of popular sovereignty replaced Provisoism as the focus of constitutional argument.

What *was* the "true intent and meaning" of the Kansas-Nebraska Act regarding the power of the territorial legislature over slavery? The senator who pursued Douglas most relentlessly with this question was his new Illinois colleague, Lyman Trumbull, an anti-Nebraska Democrat turned Republican. Douglas detested Trumbull as a party renegade, and Trumbull fully returned his enmity. On March 12, Douglas read his Kansas report, concluding with the announcement that he would soon bring in a bill to prepare Kansas for statehood. Two days later, Trumbull attacked the report in a lengthy speech, giving considerable attention to Douglas's constitutional argument. He ridiculed the idea that the Kansas-Nebraska Act and all previous territorial legislation had been based entirely, as Douglas now maintained, on congressional power to admit new states. He also pointed out that the report, like the Kansas-Nebraska Act, did not say precisely *when* the people of a territory could make the decision about slavery. Had the territorial legislature been empowered to do so, or did the authority rest solely with a constitutional convention on the eve of statehood, as most southerners maintained?

Douglas reported his promised bill for Kansas statehood on March 17 and opened debate on the measure three days later. For two and one-half hours he held the attention of a full chamber and crowded gallery, but during that time he said nothing in response to Trumbull's question about the ambiguity of the Kansas-Nebraska Act. As his biographer notes, "He wisely avoided being drawn into a constitutional discussion by making no further mention of his attempt to base popular sovereignty on legal and constitutional grounds."

The Douglas bill furnished the basis for senatorial debate on Kansas during the next three months. On May 2, Judah P. Benjamin of Louisiana delivered a speech in the course of which he took up the question that Trumbull had posed. Supporters of the Kansas-Nebraska Act, he declared, were in agreement about how to handle their one point of disagreement:

All agreed that, whether Congress had the power or not to ex-clude slavery from the Territories, it ought not to exercise it. All agreed that, if that power was owned by us, we ought to delegate it to the people whose interests were to be affected by the institutions established at home. We therefore put that into the bill.

Then came the point upon which we disagreed. Some said, as I say, Congress has no power to exclude slavery from the common territory; it cannot delegate it, and the people in the Territory cannot exercise it except at the time when they form their constitution. Others said, Congress has the power; Con-gress can delegate it, and the people can exercise it. . . . On this proposition we disagreed; and to what conclusion did we come? We said, in this bill, that we transferred to the people of that Territory the entire power to control, by their own legis-lation, their own domestic institutions, subject only to the pro-visions of the Constitution; that we would not interfere with them; that they might do as they pleased on the subject; that the Constitution alone should govern. And then, in order to provide a means by which the Constitution could govern, by which that single undecided question could be determined, we of the South, conscious that we were right, the North asserting the same confidence in its own doctrines, agreed that every question touching human slavery, or human freedom, should be appealable to the Supreme Court of the United States for its decision.

Of course, no such agreement had ever been formally con-cluded. Benjamin's account was a mixture of fact and fiction—a prescription for 1856, rather than an accurate historical recon-struction of what had happened in 1854. Not surprisingly, both Douglas and Cass promptly praised the speech, the latter calling it "magnificent and patriotic." The Benjamin formula incorpo-rated the northern statutory construction of the Kansas-Nebraska Act, while leaving the constitutional construction to the Supreme Court. This meant that the territorial legislature did possess the power to prohibit slavery, *if that power could be constitutionally given*. The qualification, it should be noted, had always existed, whether stated or not. What the South gained was added empha-sis upon it. Not all southern Democrats were willing to accept the Benjamin formula with its substantial concession to northern sentiment. Nevertheless, most members of the party could readily see the political advantages of adhering to the formula, and Republicans could readily see the necessity of demolishing it.

Ten days after the Benjamin speech, the Supreme Court ordered a re-argument of the Dred Scott case, thereby postponing its decision until the next term, after the presidential election. Soon public attention was diverted by the Preston Brooks assault on Charles Sumner and by renewed violence in Kansas, including the attack on Lawrence and John Brown's retaliation at Pottawatomie Creek. These events were still fresh when the national party conventions assembled in June.

The Know-Nothings had already nominated Millard Fillmore for President in February, but the party had been split by the slavery question, and a substantial portion of its northern members would soon join the Republicans. At Cincinnati, in early June, the Democratic convention nominated James Buchanan. This was not a victory for the South, which preferred Pierce or Douglas. The party platform, on the other hand, embodied the southern interpretation of the Kansas-Nebraska Act by stressing "nonintervention" and the right of a territorial population to accept or reject slavery at the time of framing a constitution for statehood. Later events tend to cloud the fact that the Cincinnati convention produced a northern candidate on a southern platform. Buchanan, however, was a political trimmer without strong antislavery conviction and would take the southern side when it seemed safe to do so.

Two weeks later at Philadelphia, the Republicans nominated the explorer John C. Frémont but defined their party more clearly in framing the platform. It declared that the Constitution conferred upon Congress "sovereign powers over the Territories of the United States for their government," and that in the exercise of those powers it was both the right and duty of Congress "to prohibit in the Territories those twin relics of barbarism—Polygamy and Slavery." This presented the orthodox free-soil doctrine in the tradition of the Northwest Ordinance— that is, Congress possessed the power of exclusion and, as a matter of good policy, ought to exercise it. The reference to polygamy was, of course, a sly thrust at popular sovereignty and the Kansas-Nebraska Act, with its declared intention of leaving the territorial population (including, presumably, the Mormons of Utah) "perfectly free to form and regulate their domestic institutions in their own way."

But the Republicans, like Douglas, felt the constitutionalizing pressure of the times and the consequent need to convert their political policy into a constitutional imperative. They accordingly adopted also the argument of Salmon P. Chase and certain other party radicals that slavery was illegal in the federal territories by virtue of the due-process clause of the Fifth Amendment. This formulation ruled out popular sovereignty and lent reinforcement to the expectation that the fundamental sectional differences over slavery would ultimately have to be settled in the courts. There is, moreover, some minor historical irony in the fact that the due-process clause, which would soon figure prominently in Taney's Dred Scott decision, received mention only from the Republicans in the platform-writing of 1856.

The threat of Republicanism convinced even militant southern leaders that Kansas must somehow be pacified before the presidential election in November. Robert Toombs of Georgia came forward in late June with a plan for Kansas statehood that seemed fairer than anything either side had previously supported. Under the supervision of five commissioners appointed by the President, there was to be a new census of the territory and a new registration of voters. A convention elected in November would meet in December to draft a state constitution. Admission could presumably be consummated before the adjournment of Congress in March 1857. Thus Toombs proposed to wipe the slate clean and begin anew in Kansas. The measure truly deserved to be called a compromise.

Republicans nevertheless greeted the bill with suspicion and hostility. Nothing in Pierce's record encouraged the belief that he would in fact administer the law impartially, and the conclusive test of fairness would not come until after the presidential contest had been decided. Many Republicans agreed sincerely with Henry Wilson of Massachusetts when he insisted that the bill was intended to make Kansas a slaveholding state. Yet Republicans were also fully aware of the partisan advantage to be gained from a continuation of the turmoil in Kansas, and their opposition to the Toombs compromise left them vulnerable to the charge of playing politics with the lives of settlers in Kansas. "An angel from heaven," Douglas exclaimed, "could not write a bill to restore peace in Kansas that would be acceptable to the Abolition Republican party previous to the presidential election." These words received loud applause from the Senate gallery, and the Democrats did have the better of the controversy, even though their legislation failed. No less politically motivated than their opponents, they had nevertheless made the right gesture. The Toombs bill seemed fair, and the opposition to it seemed unreasonable. After passing the Senate easily enough, it was turned aside contemptuously in the House, but one suspects that it won some votes for Buchanan in the fall.

Congress had scarcely reconvened after the Cincinnati convention before Trumbull resumed his pestering of Douglas about whether the territorial legislature of Kansas had the power to exclude slavery. Douglas and several other northern Democrats responded by reciting the Benjamin formula. The Kansas legislature, they said, had been invested with all the power over domestic territorial affairs that Congress could rightfully confer. Whether that included the power to prohibit slavery was a constitutional question, which Douglas solemnly refused to answer on the ground that it belonged exclusively to the Supreme Court. Congress, he said, ought not to "coerce and dragoon that court" in the performance of its duty. He himself had too much respect for the Court to discuss judicial questions in the Senate.

As a political expedient, the argument was clever enough, but Trumbull quickly exposed its logical absurdities. "Every law which we pass," he said, "is subject to the scrutiny of the Supreme Court of the United States, whenever a case properly arises." Why, then, was it a legislative function to declare that the people of Kansas Territory were "perfectly free to form and regulate their domestic institutions in their own way," but not a legislative function to say more precisely that the territorial legislature might establish or prohibit slavery? Were not both equally subject to judicial review?

My colleague can spend days in arguing the power of Congress to establish a territorial government; he can study the Constitution until he derives that power from the clause authorizing the admission of new states into the Union. . . . He has no trouble in deciding that constitutional point. . . . How is it that he can give a judgment here on all these constitutional questions; but when he comes to the very one about which one opinion is proclaimed in the North, and another in the South, he says he has no opinion.

Trumbull pressed the issue again during the debate on the Toombs bill in early July. He offered one amendment and then another interpreting the Kansas-Nebraska Act as endowing the territorial legislatures with the authority to regulate slavery. But Cass, Douglas, and other northern Democrats rejected this confirmation of their own version of popular sovereignty. The Trumbull amendments, they rightly observed, were irrelevant to a bill that dealt with statehood rather than with territorial government. In any case, the extent of territorial power over slavery was a judicial question, Douglas reiterated. Cass and others echoed him— "a judicial question, a judicial question," and the phrase became a kind of political incantation for warding off the curse of Republicanism. The Trumbull amendments were defeated, 34 to 9 and 34 to 11, with not a single Democrat voting in the affirmative.

It should be borne in mind that the "judicial question" talked about so much in Congress at this time was not the same as the question before the Supreme Court. What the Court was about to pass judgment on in the Dred Scott case was the power of *Congress* to prohibit slavery in the territories. What Democrats with their Benjamin formula were turning over to the Court was the task of defining popular sovereignty—that is, of saying whether a *territorial legislature* had the power to prohibit slavery.

Most southerners, to be sure, assumed that the two questions were intimately related. They insisted that if Congress lacked the power to prohibit slavery in the territories, it certainly could not delegate that power to a territorial legislature. But Cass and Douglas obviously did not accept this inference, and no northern Democrat could do so without finding himself in trouble with his constituents. In fact, neither sectional wing of the Democratic party could accept the other's definition of popular sovereignty. This meant that the Benjamin formula would work just so long as it was not carried to execution. Talk of referring the question of territorial power to the Supreme Court might promote Democratic unity for the presidential campaign, but an actual Court decision on the subject was likely to have the opposite effect and redound to the advantage of the Republicans.

It therefore appears that the political need for a judicial pronouncement on slavery in the territories was to some extent an illusion. Kansas, the principal danger area in 1856, would be little affected by such a pronouncement; for the troubles there were not essentially constitutional, and Kansas, in any case, had by general consent become a state-making problem rather than a territorial problem. Exclusion of slavery by congressional authority, prevailing only in Minnesota Territory and the Pacific Northwest, was not a concrete issue of any significance in 1856. Exclusion of slavery by territorial authority prevailed nowhere at all in 1856, and any judicial ruling on the subject would therefore be premature at best, aside from its destructive effect on Democratic unity.

Still, the pressures for judicial intervention in the mounting sectional conflict over slavery, though somewhat illogical, were nevertheless very strong. As we have seen, the tendency to constitutionalize the territorial issue dated back many years. It was reinforced in 1856 by the peculiar needs of the Democratic party and especially by the strategy of unity through evasion, as embodied in the Benjamin formula, with a consequent increase in talk about "leaving it to the Supreme Court." The Court, furthermore, was the one major agency of government that had not yet tried its hand at resolving the conflict. More than a few Americans apparently believed that at its command, agitation of the slavery question would subside and the years of crisis would come to an end. Indeed, some members of the Court itself seem to have harbored the belief that it possessed some such extraordinary power.

4

The Taney Court
and Judicial Power

Years of political pressure for a judicial settlement of the slavery
controversy undoubtedly had their effect on the collective judgment of the Supreme Court in its handling of the Dred Scott
case. But the boldness with which it acted also reflected public
understanding of the nature of judicial power and the Court's
own sense of strategic responsibility in the American constitutional system.

There is no simple historical explanation for the extraordinary
power of the judiciary in the government of the United States.
One can find its sources, for instance, in the system of English
law transplanted to the colonies, in the constitutional nature of
the British colonial empire as perceived by eighteenth-century
Americans, in certain aspects of pre-Revolutionary argumentation over colonial rights, and in the formal structure of the federal republic created between 1776 and 1789.

The place to begin, perhaps, is with the English common-law
tradition, which crossed the Atlantic with every shipload of English colonists, even though the body of the common law, in all
its patchwork complexity and technical detail, was never more
than fractionally "received" by the American commonwealths.
The law of the common-law tradition was essentially judge-made
law, but not self-admittedly so. In theory, the judge was merely
the expositor of an existing body of law consisting partly of

statute but deriving largely from general custom made legitimate by its long survival. In practice, the judge relied on what other judges had decided in earlier, similar cases, sometimes making reasoned adjustments to suit new circumstances. Thus the judge followed precedent but also occasionally set precedent (that is, made law) in response to the changing legal needs of a changing social order.

Each judicial decision accordingly became one of the "building blocks of law." But in addition to the enormous accumulation of discrete cases that could be sought out and cited as precedents for other discrete cases, the process of law-building gradually produced certain basic patterns of procedural rules and general principles that formed a significant part of the "unwritten" English constitution. These general principles of common law, often identified in eighteenth-century Anglo-American thought with the first principles of natural law and natural rights, came to be regarded (in the words of John Marshall) as a great "substratum of the laws"—that is, a foundation of justice more elemental and pervasive than any enacted law, even a constitution. In the common-law tradition, then, not only was the judicial power of central importance, but also, much of the country's fundamental law was developed by judges in the course of deciding ordinary legal disputes between private individuals.

The common-law tradition did not, however, include a functioning system of judicial review. That is, neither in England nor in colonial America did courts make a practice of invalidating legislation on the ground of its repugnance to fundamental law. In England, where the concept of separation of powers was never institutionalized, judicial review would have been incompatible with the principle of parliamentary supremacy as it became established after 1688. In America, the colonials themselves had only occasional reason to want restraint placed on the power of their provincial assemblies, and imperial officials had other, more effective means of imposing or securing such restraint.

At the same time, certain features of the British colonial system no doubt helped to prepare American ground for the introduction of judicial review. The colonial charters served as prototypes of written constitutions, conferring and limiting governmental power. The British empire, moreover, was in some respects a functioning federal system, and colonials became accustomed to having their local laws subject to disallowance by the central authority of the Privy Council. In its judicial capacity, the Privy Council also heard appeals from colonial courts and upon a number of occasions took the validity of colonial legislation under advisement. In the most notable of these cases, the Council voided a Connecticut intestacy act on the grounds that it violated the law of England and the colony's charter as well.

It was in the polemics of pre-Revolutionary resistance to British authority that Americans, invoking both natural law and the principles of English common law, developed a coherent theory of constitutional limitations on legislative power. To be sure, much of the argument proved at first to be mere rhetoric sent into battle against Parliament. When the Revolution began, its circumstances tended generally to enhance legislative supremacy in the various colonies. The tendency was reflected in most of the first state constitutions, even though they paid lip service to the principles of constitutionalism and separation of powers. With but few exceptions, the executive authority in these constitutions was weak, and the judiciary was subject in some degree to legislative domination. This concentration of power in the legislative branch was inconsistent with the trend of American political theory and proved highly unpopular in practice. James Madison joined in the outcry against it. "The legislative department," he wrote in *Federalist* 48, "is everywhere extending the sphere of its activity and drawing all power into its impetuous vortex. . . . it is against the enterprising ambition of this department that the people ought to indulge all their jealousy and exhaust all their precautions."

By the middle of the 1780s, there was a growing conviction among thoughtful Americans that if their constitutions were to have effective force as restraints on government, they would have to make the theory of separation of powers more of a reality by strengthening the executive and judicial departments. The judiciary benefited especially from this gradual change in the climate of opinion, and judges in several states during the decade even ventured tentatively onto the ground of judicial review by holding statutes, or parts of statutes, to be unconstitutional and unenforceable.

It was in this context of disillusionment with legislative supremacy and of renewed commitment to separation of powers that the men of 1787 assembled at Philadelphia to write a new federal constitution. The resulting document, emphatically declaring itself to be the "supreme law of the land," enlarged the powers of the national government and established within it a strong executive and an independent judiciary. According to the theory of separation of powers, each department should be, not only independent, but capable of protecting itself against encroachments by the other departments. This, in the view of Alexander Hamilton, was a major purpose of the presidential veto and the legislative power of impeachment. The judiciary was not expressly provided with any such weapon of self-defense. But in the Constitutional Convention there appears to have been some agreement with the observation of Elbridge Gerry that the judiciary would have "a sufficient check against encroachments on their own department by their exposition of the laws, which involved a power of deciding on their constitutionality."

Beyond this narrow conception of judicial review as an instrument of self-defense, there were the more expansive views of men like Hamilton, who assumed from the beginning that the courts of justice must be the principal guardians, not only of their own independence, but also of the integrity of the Constitution—especially against legislative excesses. Judicial review so broadly defined could not have been introduced into the text of the Constitution without considerable resistance. Instead, the idea was left to be developed by inference and practice until it became, in the end, the most remarkable of all the "implied powers" of the Constitution.

All American constitutions, state and national, incorporate the principle of limited government called "constitutionalism." In each instance they create a government, describe its working parts, and define the relationship between government and people. But the Constitution of the United States is more complex in that it also incorporates the principle of partly decentralized gov-

ernment called "federalism." It defines the political relationship
between the nation and the states. The contours of federalism,
like those of constitutionalism, are indicated in both positive and
negative clauses of the Constitution. Least ambiguous are certain
powers expressly delegated to the federal government and expressly forbidden to the states, such as coinage of money. In a
number of important instances, however, the framers neglected
to draw the line between state and federal authority with any
precision. For example, one clause empowered Congress to establish "uniform laws on the subject of bankruptcies throughout
the United States." But was this power intended to be exclusive,
or, in the absence of congressional action, could the states enact
bankruptcy legislation of their own? Many such questions arose
in the early decades of the Republic, testifying to the fact that in
the work of defining the federal relationship, the Constitution itself was only a beginning.

The core of the federal problem for the framers at Philadelphia was finding an appropriate means of sanctional control in a
country where loyalty to one's state commonly remained the
highest form of patriotism. How were the various constitutional
restrictions on state power to be made effective, and how was
federal law generally to be enforced, without serious impairment
of state sovereignty? The critical operational question in this respect was whether the central government should continue to
function through the agency of the state governments. Experience had already shown that it could not do so effectively without some kind of coercive control. Madison and the other authors
of the "Virginia plan" accordingly proposed that Congress be
empowered to disallow state laws and, more than that, "to call
forth the force of the Union against any member of the Union
failing to fulfill its duty under the articles thereof." But the Convention rejected this solution, with its unpleasant echoes of British coercive policy on the eve of the Revolution. Instead, the
delegates chose to create a federal government that would have
its own agencies of enforcement, thus by-passing the states and
operating directly upon the people. State government and federal government would consequently function side by side, in-

dependent of one another, and each supreme within its own designated sphere of power.

Yet, even if that proved sufficient as the means of compelling individual obedience to federal law, there remained the problem of how, without direct coercion, the state governments could be held faithful to the Constitution of the United States. The solution eventually adopted by the Convention was a clause that had, in fact, been brought forward by anti-nationalists, who obviously did not realize the amplitude of its potential force:

> This Constitution and the laws of the United States which shall be made in pursuance thereof; and all treaties made, or which shall be made, under the authority of the United States, shall be the supreme law of the land, and the judges in every State shall be bound thereby, anything in the constitution or laws of any State to the contrary notwithstanding.

By itself, this "supremacy clause" could be read as relying upon *state judges* to uphold the federal Constitution against the legislatures of their own states, simply because they were bound by oath to do so. Elsewhere, however, the framers provided that the power of the *federal judiciary* should extend to all cases in law and equity arising under the Constitution, laws, and treaties of the United States. This seemed to mean that the Supreme Court would have authority to review state court decisions involving the federal relationship, and in the Judiciary Act of 1789, Congress expressly invested the Court with such authority. As a consequence, the American judicial system assumed a pyramidal shape that was more or less inconsistent with the design of dual federalism, in which state and federal governments functioned independently. State legislatures were not accountable to Congress; governors were not accountable to the President; but state courts were, in certain crucial respects, accountable to the federal Supreme Court.

So the foundation of American judicial power was well and truly laid in 1787. The Constitution, to begin with, was itself *law* to be enforced. Its negative provisions, such as the clauses forbidding *ex post facto* laws, were enforceable directly by the courts and perhaps in no other way. The framers had left primarily to the judiciary the task of protecting the Constitution against encroachment by Congress, the President, and the state governments. They had done so more by default than as an act of crystallized volition. In fact, judicial responsibility resulted almost automatically from their having created a *hierarchical* order of law, in which the federal Constitution was superior to federal legislation, and both took precedence over state legislation. That is, in any ordinary case at law, a court might be called upon to say whether a right claimed under a statute must give way to a right claimed under a constitution or other superior law. To accept the responsibility of making such a decision was in itself an exercise of judicial review, no matter how the court should eventually rule.

From all this it should be clear that "judicial review" is a term of complex meaning used to designate an institutional pattern of complex origin. In its most familiar usage, the phrase signifies a decision of the federal Supreme Court declaring an act of Congress to be unconstitutional and therefore void. Such "coordinate" judicial review at the national level has its counterpart at the state level in state court decisions invalidating state laws as contrary to state constitutions. Perhaps most important historically, however, is "federal" judicial review, in which a state law may be set aside on the ground that it violates the federal Constitution or conflicts with a federal law or a treaty. A court decision *upholding* the constitutionality of a law is likewise an instance of judicial review, and it illustrates the important point that the institution has been a legitimating as well as a curbing influence in American political development. In other words, the full significance of judicial review cannot be calculated from the sum total of those court decisions invalidating legislation. And neither, it should be added, can the dimensions of judicial power be measured exclusively in terms of judicial review. In the process of statutory construction, judges shape much of the law into its final form. Without any question of constitutionality arising, a court may divert legislation far from its original intent and even render it virtually inoperative.

The frequency and scope of judicial review have depended

largely upon the will of the judiciary itself—that is, upon the extent to which, through the years, it chose to embrace activism or self-restraint. But the force or effect of judicial review has always depended in addition upon how much acceptance it might win and how much resistance it might encounter within the judicial system, from other departments of government, and among the people at large. Acceptance, from the beginning, implied much more than mere compliance with the judgment rendered, and it was this outward reach of judicial review that provoked strong resistance. The critical question was whether interpretation of the Constitution is pre-eminently a judicial function, in which the word of the Supreme Court is final (barring constitutional amendment) and binding on all other public officials in the country. Thus it was a question, and nothing less, of who possessed the ultimate power to determine the fundamental structure of the Republic.

2

The Supreme Court at first heard no more than a handful of cases each year, and few of these were in any way historically significant. The first two chief justices, John Jay and Oliver Ellsworth, went off to Europe on diplomatic missions while continuing to hold their judicial posts. Jay, during his six-year tenure, also sought the governorship of New York on two occasions and resigned from the Court when his second effort proved successful. All of this tended to bear out Hamilton's prediction that the federal judiciary would be "beyond comparison the weakest of the three departments of power." Yet Alexis de Tocqueville in the 1830s concluded that the Supreme Court was "placed higher than any other known tribunal." No nation in history, he said, had "ever constituted so great a judicial power as the Americans."

What the early Court needed most of all was a clearer vision of its essential role in the constitutional system and a firmer hold on its bases of power. That required the seasoning of time, as well as the genius of John Marshall. For one thing, it took time to achieve a sufficient measure of aloofness from current party politics, and the appointment of Marshall, an intense partisan, did not make the matter any easier. The problem down until 1801 was that the members of the Court were too cosily a part of the Federalist regime, but the election of Jefferson put an end to that and placed the Court squarely in the path of Jeffersonian hostility. Judicial independence, which had been yielding to seduction, now seemed more in danger of outright destruction; for the threat of impeachment and other reprisals hung heavy in the air. Yet it was during those years of peril that Marshall, with his most famous constitutional pronouncement, laid out the classic rationale for judicial review of federal legislation. His argument came down to the twofold assertion that the Constitution, being law, must be interpreted by the judiciary, and, being supreme law, must prevail over statute whenever the two were in conflict.

The bold words of *Marbury v. Madison* (1803) were strictly declaratory, however. In practical terms, the decision settled no important point of law. It was essentially a brilliant political maneuver, combining ingenuity and prudence in such a way as to rebuke the executive power while avoiding a direct confrontation with it. To put the matter as briefly as possible, Marshall held that the Jefferson administration was in violation of law and subject to correction by court order, *but* that the Supreme Court itself could not issue a writ of mandamus as requested, even though authorized to do so by the Judiciary Act of 1789, because that authorization was an unconstitutional expansion of the Court's original jurisdiction and therefore null and void. Thus *Marbury v. Madison*, while setting forth the doctrine of judicial review in comprehensive terms, was itself an exercise of the narrowest kind of judicial review in which the judiciary interpreted that part of the Constitution applying directly to its own duties.

Furthermore, the court over which Marshall presided for another thirty-two years never again expressly invalidated even so small a part of an act of Congress, although upon occasion it did take a question of constitutionality under review. The *Marbury* doctrine remained prominently on the record, well respected but more or less dormant. The federal government, down until the

Civil War, confined itself to a very limited range of activities, leaving most of the regulation of society to the states. Congress tended to be constitutionally conservative, only rarely enacting laws that might be open to challenge in court.

Despite the fame of *Marbury v. Madison*, the main contributions of the Marshall Court to American constitutional development were associated with the federal-state relationship. Most fundamental was the Court's successful exercise of its authority to review state court decisions, as provided in Section 25 of the Judiciary Act of 1789. By repeatedly upholding and enforcing that authority against vigorous state opposition (most notably in *Cohens v. Virginia*), it confirmed the principle and the pyramidal structure of judicial nationalism.

Meanwhile, the power to invalidate state legislation had also been asserted. In *Fletcher v. Peck* (1810), with Marshall as spokesman, the Court for the first time declared a state law to be in conflict with the federal Constitution. *Fletcher v. Peck* is thus the state-level equivalent of *Marbury v. Madison*, and the contrasts between them are worth noting. *Marbury* involved the right of one man to his commission as justice of the peace, and it resulted in the invalidation of one minor section of a federal statute. *Fletcher* intervened in the notorious Yazoo land fraud case originating in the wholesale corruption of the Georgia legislature, and it accordingly affected the financial claims of a large number of people. The decision invalidated a state law rescinding the corrupt land grants in question, and it did so by expanding the contract clause of the Constitution beyond the intent of the framers to include public grants as well as private contracts. In short, *Marbury* was a gesture that the future would invest with much greater relevance and force; *Fletcher* was a real exercise of judicial power having immediate and extensive impact.

Fletcher v. Peck proved to be a typical Marshall case; for most of the Court's other leading decisions during his tenure involved judicial review of state laws. The list includes *McCulloch v. Maryland, Dartmouth College v. Woodward, Gibbons v. Ogden, Sturges v. Crowninshield,* and *Craig v. Missouri.* We are speaking here of the triumph of judicial nationalism—that is, the Court's effective assertion of the power to review decisions rendered by state courts and to review laws passed by state legislatures. While the right of review was consistently maintained, the substance of review did not always run against state authority. Sometimes the Marshall Court upheld the constitutionality of state legislation. But the general tendency of its principal state-federal decisions was to expand the range of national power while restricting the power of the states. Marshall himself was not only a judicial nationalist but also a political nationalist in the manner of Hamilton, Webster, and Clay. These two kinds of nationalism were not necessarily inseparable, however, and they have sometimes been confused in discussions of the Supreme Court. Judicial nationalism was in fact an independent force that could be brought to bear in support of particularism or sectionalism.

A high percentage of the great Marshall decisions were concentrated in the period from 1819 to 1824. Those were the Court's years of maximum cohesion and power, when its nationalism briefly suited the national mood. Soon, the political environment became more hostile, and new appointments eroded the internal unity that Marshall had so carefully nourished. The Court, during his last years as chief justice, spoke with less authority and gave ground before the dynamic forces of Jacksonianism and particularism. Most notably, it adopted a more permissive attitude toward state legislative power. Thus the transition from the Marshall Court to the Taney Court was begun before Marshall's death.

But the Supreme Court, in making such adjustments and strategic withdrawals as prudence might seem to advise, did not relinquish any part of its essential right to decide constitutional issues coming before it. In fact, the prestige and power of the Court were often fortified during relatively quiet intervals when it aroused little controversy; for then the justices best fitted their Olympian image as "keepers of the covenant, and therefore touched with its divinity." The Court's bases of power were secure when Marshall died. Over the years it had made many enemies and sustained much vigorous attack, but none of the various efforts to curb its authority ever came close to succeeding. In 1830, for instance, the House of Representatives considered a bill to repeal Section 25 of the Judiciary Act of 1789 but defeated it by a vote of 138 to 51. And, significantly, President Andrew Jackson, whose hostility to Marshall and defiance of the Court are among the authentic elements in the Jacksonian legend, gave no support to this measure or to any other aimed at weakening the institutional structure of the federal judiciary.

Roger B. Taney was already fifty-nine years old when sworn in as chief justice in March 1836, and because of chronic ill health it seemed unlikely that he would enjoy a long tenure. President after President took office with the mistaken expectation that before the end of his term he would probably have the naming of a new chief justice. Taney's ailments were real enough, but he fussed about them excessively and wore an air of invalidism that grew more pronounced with advancing age. Six feet tall, flat-chested and stooped, with homely features and irregular, tobacco-stained teeth, he was an unimpressive figure until he began to speak. Then, without oratory or gesture, he held his audience by the force of his reasoning and conviction.

Taney was provincial in his outlook and experience, never having traveled very far beyond the boundaries of Maryland. One of the friends of his youth was Francis Scott Key, whose sister he married in 1806, more than eight years before the writing of "The Star-Spangled Banner." Taney was a Roman Catholic who bitterly resented the nativism that came to flourish in his home state. He was also one of that curious breed, a former Federalist turned into a Jacksonian Democrat. From the Whig point of view, he reeked with partisanship, having served as Jackson's hatchet man in the war on the Bank of the United States. "The pure ermine of the Supreme Court is sullied by the appointment of that political hack, Roger B. Taney," said a New York newspaper. Yet Taney on the bench quickly demonstrated judicial capacities of a high order. Eventually, it is said, even his old political adversary Henry Clay acknowledged his fitness to succeed John Marshall.

Taney, like Marshall a soft-spoken man of urbane manners and simple tastes, presided gently but firmly over the Court, and his judicial opinions, written in a plain, dry style, were much praised for their lucidity and pointedness. At the same time,

Taney displayed little of his predecessor's remarkable talent for achieving consensus. Marshall, after much effort, had succeeded in replacing the custom of *seriatim* opinions with a system in which he, or another justice appointed for the task, delivered the "opinion of the Court." Often it was the only opinion presented. Dissent sometimes occurred, but it was much less frequent than in later periods of the Court's history. The semblance of internal unity undoubtedly contributed to the growth of judicial power. It was usually achieved by discussion, concession, and compromise, in which Marshall himself set an example of flexibility. The system began to disintegrate in Marshall's last years, however. Multiple opinions became more common, especially in cases of major importance. Dissent caused little confusion, but multiple concurring opinions often made it difficult to determine what part of the designated opinion of the Court had enough support from other justices to be considered *ratio decidendi,* binding as precedent in other courts.

Scholarly debate about the Taney Court has often centered upon the question of how sharply it changed the course of American constitutional development from the direction set by the Marshall Court. Three decisions rendered in 1837 seemed to signal a "judicial revolution" overturning the structure of nationalism and economic conservatism that Marshall had engineered. In each instance, the Court upheld the constitutionality of a state law, and each time it seemed to do so in contravention of one of the major Marshall decisions. Taney's opinion in *Charles River Bridge v. Warren Bridge,* for instance, narrowed the protection given corporate charters by *Dartmouth College v. Woodward.* Justice Story, now a lonely dissenter, saw the old constitutional order crumbling under revolutionary assault and viewed the future of his country with deepening despair.

But the fears of Story and other Whigs proved to have been exaggerated. The change that did occur under Taney's leadership was only partly a doctrinal repudiation of the Marshall synthesis and partly also a judicial response to accelerating social change. One ineluctable reality of the Jacksonian era was the expansion of business enterprise; another was the rising public expectation of economic intervention and social control on the part of government, especially state government. These were by no means incompatible tendencies. The Taney Court in the *Charles River Bridge* case did not simply rule in favor of state power and against corporate rights. The decision in fact upheld the claims of one corporation against those of another, and besides, state power was far from being inherently hostile to corporate enterprise. Corporations, after all, were artificial entities created and nurtured by state law; and state economic legislation was as often promotional as it was regulatory in purpose. The implicative effect of the *Charles River Bridge* decision was to allow state governments somewhat more latitude in adjusting the law to new economic realities.

During the Taney period, constitutional issues coming before the Supreme Court continued to be predominantly matters of state-federal relations, involving judicial review of state legislation rather than acts of Congress. The Court steered a middle course, often upholding the state law in question but sometimes striking one down because of its intrusion on federal authority or violation of the Constitution. Nevertheless, the general trend was toward less judicial restraint on state legislative authority than the Marshall Court had been disposed to apply.

This does not mean that the Taney Court was willing to relinquish the power of review or any part of it. On the contrary, this is where the lines of continuity with the Marshall era become most plainly visible—in the unflagging determination to exalt federal judicial power and consolidate the role of the Supreme Court as the final arbiter of constitutional issues. Indeed, the Taney Court, in certain decisions expanding its own jurisdiction, displayed a more avid judicial imperialism than its predecessor. Whenever historians present evidence to show that Taney was something of a "nationalist," much of it turns out to be evidence of his *judicial* nationalism, an outlook scarcely uncommon among Supreme Court justices at any time.

The Taney Court, then, without renouncing any of its power of review, tended to use the power sparingly where the constitutionality of state legislation was at stake. Here one recognizes in operation the principle of "judicial self-restraint" with which Taney's name is often associated. But "judicial self-restraint" is a

phrase of multiple meaning, and in Taney's case it has less to do
with presumption of constitutionality than with the doctrine of
"political questions." That doctrine, although commonly regarded
as Taney's invention in *Luther v. Borden* (1849), had been foreshadowed in a number of Marshall and earlier Taney opinions.
"The powers given to the courts of the United States by the Constitution," said Taney in 1838, "are judicial powers and extend
to those subjects only which are judicial in their character; and
not to those which are political." Accordingly, some kinds of conflict, being essentially political in nature, were beyond the capacity of the judiciary to resolve and must be dealt with by the legislative branch of government. "The overriding consideration,"
says the legal scholar Bernard Schwartz, "was to steer clear of
political involvement." Most of the time, he tells us, Taney managed to carry the Court with him in the exercise of such prudence, but there came a day when the "rule of abnegation" gave
way to stronger influences. "The *Dred Scott* case was the one occasion when Taney yielded to the temptation, always disastrous,
to save the country, and put aside the judicial self-restraint which
was one of his chief contributions to our constitutional law."

Thus the conception of Taney as a major prophet and successful practitioner of judicial self-restraint leads easily to the
view that the Dred Scott decision was an unfortunate aberration,
a false step out of character and into the political thicket. Presumably, the course of wisdom would have been to treat the issue of slavery in the territories as though it were a "political
question" and avoid rendering a decision on it.* This would have
been somewhat like returning the ball to the server's court; for
political leaders in the majority party, it will be remembered,
had been busy converting the same issue into a "judicial question." But in any case, the "aberration" theory is more catchword
than explanation, and it does not bear up well under the pressure
of facts.

For one thing, there is little evidence that the decisions of the

---

* Owing to certain technical features of the Dred Scott case, Taney and his
fellow justices, if they had so wished, could have avoided the territorial issue without formally invoking the doctrine of political questions or the principle of self-restraint in any other guise.

Taney Court were actually governed in any significant way by the principle of judicial self-restraint. As a precept formally invoked, restraint was often mere rationalization; as a pattern of judicial behavior, it was the consequence of other influences, not the prime motivational force itself. The three major decisions of 1837, all upholding the constitutionality of state laws, may be said to exemplify judicial self-restraint, but they reflected the Court's attitude toward corporations, banking, and states' rights, not a philosophy of judicial power.

The appearance of restraint also emanated in some degree from the Court's political affinity with the dominant political party. For Taney, unlike Marshall, government was more often than not in the hands of political friends. This was especially true of the national government, which the Whigs seldom controlled. And during the period of Democratic ascendancy from 1829 to 1861, the national government continued to operate within a very narrow functional range, offering little challenge to constitutional limitations. Thus the fact that the Taney Court waited twenty years before declaring an act of Congress unconstitutional must be attributed to lack of provocation rather than to judicial self-restraint. (The Chief Justice would reveal the extent to which he was a judicial activist when control of the federal government passed into hostile Republican hands in 1861.) But if coordinate judicial review was unneeded at the national level, it flourished at the state level throughout the Taney period and had long since won general public acceptance. And what the state courts were doing almost as a matter of routine, the Supreme Court would not hesitate to do when the appropriate occasion arose.

Furthermore, when the Court invoked the doctrine of political questions or otherwise embraced the principle of self-restraint, it did not do so to avoid involvement in critical public issues. The cases, by and large, were legally peculiar rather than politically sensitive. They often seemed strange beyond all precedent, or unmanageable by judicial means, or likely to involve the Court in a demeaning confrontation. *Luther v. Borden,* to be sure, was an outgrowth of an important political event, the Dorr War in Rhode Island, but the struggle had ended and lost much of its controversial edge long before the Court decided the case in 1849. Taney's opinion, moreover, was scarcely a model of judicial self-restraint. Stating the political-question doctrine in its most memorable form, he held that the Court lacked authority to dispose of the substantive issues in the case; yet at the same time he discussed those issues in such a way as to come down emphatically on the side of the victorious anti-Dorr faction in Rhode Island. *Luther v. Borden* thus illustrates the point that a judicial refusal to rule may be no less political in its purpose and impact than a vigorous exercise of jurisdiction.

A constitution is as much a political as a legal document, and every constitutional decision is therefore to some extent a political act. Members of the Taney Court were predominantly politicians, appointed for political reasons in an intensely political age, and their partisanship, though it might be muted, was never entirely smothered by the proprieties of judicial office. Justices for the most part no longer participated as actively in politics as they had during the Federalist period, but the Taney Court was nevertheless decidedly a Democratic court. Of the fourteen members appointed from 1829 to 1861, only Benjamin R. Curtis of Massachusetts was a Whig (though one of the Democrats, John McLean of Ohio, had turned Republican by 1857).

Taney himself, it is true, scrupulously avoided any appearance of involvement in politics. He never endorsed political candidates, for instance, or engaged in newspaper controversy. In this respect he stands as a contrast to McLean, whose hankering for the presidency became something of an embarrassment to the Court. Yet Taney was no less political-minded than McLean and no more disposed to hold his tongue on subjects that mattered, if he could somehow speak within the bounds of his judicial duties. In one extraordinary display of partisanship, he disqualified himself from a case involving the Bank of the United States but then wrote a long commentary, amounting to a dissenting opinion, and had it printed as an "appendix" to the official report.

Where slavery was concerned, Taney gave every indication of being an intense partisan, rather than a prophet of judicial self-restraint. In *Prigg v. Pennsylvania* and *Groves v. Slaughter*, he took positions extremely defensive of slavery, and in *Strader v. Graham* he added a proslavery dictum to a ruling that the Court lacked jurisdiction. His colleague Peter V. Daniel of Virginia was a brooding proslavery fanatic, and the other southern justices in 1857—James M. Wayne of Georgia, John Catron of Tennessee, and John A. Campbell of Alabama—were all unreserved defenders of slavery and slaveholding rights in the territories. Among the four northern justices, no one expected self-restraint from McLean on slavery or any other issue, and Curtis, though conservative in temperament and politics, was nevertheless accustomed to speaking his mind. Judicial self-restraint on slavery questions probably appealed most strongly to Samuel Nelson of New York and Robert C. Grier of Pennsylvania, because as northern Democrats they were subject to the usual cross-pressures of party and section. In their general outlook, however, both men fitted the "doughface" pattern, tending to be, if not proslavery, at least anti-antislavery.

The Taney Court, like all courts, sometimes avoided deciding an issue laid before it, but this was unlikely to occur with respect to issues of great popular concern about which the justices themselves had formed strong opinions. In dealing with slavery, Taney and his colleagues showed a consistent disposition to meet the issue head-on and settle it conclusively. Any failure to do so resulted more from the diversity and vehemence of their views than from a sense of restraint. The Dred Scott decision therefore represented no "aberration"—no sharp break with a Taney Court tradition of judicial self-restraint, because that tradition is itself largely illusive.

The Dred Scott case, when it came before the Supreme Court, presented three issues that had been much debated in courtrooms, legislative halls, political meetings, and newspapers throughout the country: 1) Negro citizenship; 2) the status of slaves who had been held on free soil; and 3) the constitutionality of federal legislation prohibiting slavery in the territories. Because of certain technical complications, the Court had an unusual number of choices. It could dispose of the case by deciding the first issue alone, the second alone, the first and second together, the second and third together, or all three together. Taney, as the

Court's official spokesman, chose to decide all three. But when people talk about the great "blunder in statecraft" or the "self-inflicted wound," they appear to mean specifically that Taney should have avoided deciding the *third* issue, and the Court, as we shall see, came close to doing just that by settling for a decision limited to the second and least controversial of the three issues.

To have followed such a strategy of "self-restraint," however, would have been inconsistent with the tradition of judicial power and with the Court's assigned role as final arbiter of constitutional questions. It would have been, in the circumstances and in short, an aberration.

≫ 5 ≪

The
Dred Scott Case
in Missouri

Gateway to the trans-Mississippi West, St. Louis in 1830 was a flourishing river port that attracted many Americans on the move. Among the newcomers that year were Peter Blow and his wife Elizabeth, together with their three daughters, four sons, and six slaves. Once the owner of many acres in his native Virginia and more recently an Alabama planter, Blow was ready to try something other than farming. He set himself up as proprietor of a boarding-house called the "Jefferson Hotel," but the venture proved less than successful. Elizabeth Blow soon fell victim to a lingering disease and died in the summer of 1831. Early the next year, Peter Blow gave up hotel-keeping. His own health began to fail, and he died on June 23, 1832.

In the records of the 1830 census, Blow appears as the owner of five male slaves and one female slave. Evidently, he sold one of the five before he died; for the inventory of his estate lists only four males and one female. After his death, and probably during the year 1833, a second slave, named Sam, was sold for $500 to meet creditors' claims against the estate. None of the other four Blow slaves were sold at this time. Meanwhile, Dr. John Emerson of St. Louis had been trying to obtain an appointment as assistant surgeon in the United States army. In December 1833, Emerson received his commission and reported for duty at Fort Armstrong in Illinois. He took with him a Negro slave who had previously been the property of Peter Blow and who is known in history as Dred Scott. But which of the two slaves had Emerson purchased—the one that Blow himself apparently sold, or the one sold after Blow's death? Was Dred Scott always so named, or did he live more than half of his life as "Sam" and then somehow acquire a new name after entering Emerson's service? Historians are divided on the subject, and so is the evidence. But the only facts that matter are indisputable: John Emerson bought one of Peter Blow's slaves, and that slave was the plaintiff in *Dred Scott v. Sandford.*

Whatever name he originally wore, Dred Scott had apparently been with the Blows since his childhood or early youth. Probably born in Virginia around the beginning of the century, he had a very dark skin and may have been no more than five feet tall. A St. Louis newspaper article, published in 1857 and evidently based on a personal interview, described him as "illiterate but not ignorant," with a "strong common sense" that had been sharpened by his many travels. Such contemporary traces of the man Dred Scott are so scarce, however, that he remains a very indistinct figure. Little if anything can be said with authority about his personality, his quality as a worker, or his relations with various owners and employers. One would especially like to know how much of the initiative was Scott's own in the eleven-year legal contest that began in 1846. He has usually been regarded as a passive figure, but there are hints of a stronger spirit, determined to be free.

Perhaps the most curious feature of Dred Scott's personal history is his close association with the Blow family long after he ceased to be in their service. The Blows and Blow in-laws were his principal supporters throughout the series of court actions from 1846 to 1857. Taylor Blow in particular continued to be Dred's benefactor after the slave was finally manumitted and until the day of his death. No strong antislavery commitment inspired this loyalty; for Blow's sympathies during the Civil War were with the South. His benevolence seems to have sprung wholly from a personal affection extending back to his boyhood, and this may reveal something of Dred Scott's character as well as Taylor Blow's.

It is uncertain how Dred felt about being sold to Dr. Emerson. According to one story, he was so unhappy that he ran away and hid for a time in a swamp near St. Louis; but according to another, he begged Emerson to buy him after having been badly whipped by Peter Blow. Nor can much be said about the slave's life with his new master in the years that followed. The details of their relationship are almost entirely lacking, and it is not even known whether they liked or disliked each other. What proved to be important, however, was where they traveled together, and of that there is some record.

John Emerson was probably a native of Pennsylvania and about as old as Dred Scott, having been born either in 1802 or in 1803. He studied medicine for two years at the University of Pennsylvania and received his degree in 1824. Of his early practice little is known, although he apparently lived for a time somewhere in the South. By 1831 he had settled in St. Louis. When the regular medical officer at nearby Jefferson Barracks became ill in the fall of 1832, Emerson was hired as his temporary replacement. The arrangement proved highly satisfactory on both sides. Emerson found military life and regular pay so congenial that he decided to apply for a commission. Not many medical officers were needed in an American army that numbered only about six thousand men, but Emerson succeeded after considerable effort and set out with his slave for Fort Armstrong.

For Dred Scott, life as a personal servant at an army post was probably not arduous, but his owner found this first assignment disillusioning. Situated in lightly settled country some two hundred miles north of St. Louis, Fort Armstrong lacked the amenities of Jefferson Barracks. Within two months of his arrival, Emerson asked for leave of absence, explaining that he needed treatment of a "syphiloid disease" contracted during a recent visit to Philadelphia. This request he subsequently canceled when his condition improved. But in 1835 he began to ask for transfer to the arsenal in St. Louis, saying that he now suffered from a "slight disease" in his left foot which prevented him from wearing a shoe and might require surgery. Unsuccessful, he tried again in January 1836, giving a quarrel with one of the company commanders as his reason for wanting to leave Fort Armstrong. His various afflictions did not prevent Emerson from taking up land speculation on a modest scale. He entered several small acreages close to the fort in Illinois and bought a claim to an entire section directly across the Mississippi near what is now Davenport, Iowa. In order to improve the claim, Emerson built a log cabin on it, with Dred probably doing much of the work.

In 1836, when the Army decided to vacate Fort Armstrong, Emerson found himself transferred at last, but to Fort Snelling on the west bank of the upper Mississippi River near the later site of St. Paul, Minnesota. Then a part of Wisconsin Territory and shifted to Iowa Territory in 1838, the region lay within the boundaries of the Louisiana Purchase. Thus Dred Scott, who had been held as a slave in a free state for more than two years, was now taken into an area where slavery was forbidden by the Missouri Compromise.

At Fort Snelling, Scott met Harriet Robinson, a slave girl of perhaps half his age who belonged to the resident Indian agent, Major Lawrence Taliaferro. The Major either sold Harriet to Emerson or gave her to Dred for a wife, and, as local justice of the peace, he himself performed the ceremony uniting them. This marriage of Dred and Harriet Scott lasted until his death more than twenty years later. Of the four children apparently born to them, two sons died in infancy, but two daughters became parties in the suit for freedom.

One winter at Fort Snelling was enough for Emerson. In the spring of 1837, he wrote to the Surgeon General complaining that the cold weather had crippled him with rheumatism and requesting transfer to St. Louis or six months' leave beginning the next autumn. This time the response from Washington was favorable. Ordered to Jefferson Barracks in October, the happy doctor hurried off on his trip down the Mississippi. He left his two slaves behind him at Fort Snelling, expecting to send for them later. Bad news greeted him at Jefferson Barracks, however. Newer orders had been prepared directing him to report for duty at Fort Jesup in western Louisiana.

Emerson reached Fort Jesup on November 22, 1837, and found it unsatisfactory. Two days later, he sent off a request for transfer back to Fort Snelling, which he now looked upon as just about the "best post" in the country. Several more importunate letters soon followed. The damp climate of Louisiana had revived an old liver disorder, he said. Rheumatism was attacking his "muscles of respiration," and he could hardly breathe. He did not have a moment free of pain. Yet somehow the invalid managed to carry on a courtship and make his way to the altar on February 6, 1838. His bride was Eliza Irene Sanford, twenty-three-year-old daughter of Alexander Sanford, a Virginia manufacturer who had moved to St. Louis. Miss Sanford, usually called Irene rather than Eliza, was described at the time of her death many years afterward as "a cultivated woman of unusual beauty." She had come to Fort Jesup for a visit with her sister, whose husband, Captain Henry Bainbridge, was stationed there. Soon after the wedding, Emerson apparently sent for Dred and Harriet Scott, who were still at Fort Snelling, hired out to one or more of its officers. That the two slaves did make the journey to Louisiana seems fairly certain. They traveled in the spring of 1838, and no doubt by steamboat, but no details of the trip are known.

Before long, Emerson resumed his pleas to the Surgeon General, who eventually proved accommodating, perhaps in the hope of reducing his correspondence. By September, Emerson was happily on his way back to Fort Snelling. Mrs. Emerson accompanied him, and so did the Scotts. Thus Dred was taken not just once but twice into territory supposedly closed to slavery by the Missouri Compromise. The travelers arrived at St. Louis on September 21, 1838, and transferred to the *Gypsy,* a small stern-wheeler of light draft that crept cautiously up the Mississippi in low water, reaching Fort Snelling on October 21.

Another man who boarded the *Gypsy* at St. Louis was the Reverend Alfred Brunson, a Methodist missionary to the Indians. In his autobiography published many years later, Brunson recalled that four-week trip upstream. "Among the passengers," he wrote, "were Dr. Emerson and his wife, having with them their servants, Dred Scott and his family, who belonged to this lady. On the upward trip one of Dred's children, a girl, was born." The Scotts gave their baby Mrs. Emerson's first name, Eliza. Her birth occurred when the *Gypsy* was north of the northern boundary of Missouri—that is, indisputably in free territory.

Immediately upon his arrival at Fort Snelling, Emerson got involved in a squabble with the medical officer whom he was replacing, the latter accusing him of using underhanded methods to obtain the transfer. A more spectacular quarrel the following year is not as well authenticated, but it may throw some light on the Doctor's second departure from the fort. According to a story told many years afterward, Emerson asked the quartermaster to provide Dred with a stove and, upon being refused, became angry and abusive. The quartermaster, a small man, struck Emerson, a large man, with enough force to bruise his nose and break his glasses. Emerson left the scene but soon returned brandishing two pistols. His adversary fled, and the post commander placed Emerson under arrest. Whether as an outgrowth of this incident or not, Fort Snelling before long had a new medical officer. In the spring of 1840, orders arrived transferring Emerson to Florida, where the Seminole War was still in progress.

The Emersons and their slaves took passage on a steamboat to St. Louis in May or early June. Mrs. Emerson did not accompany her husband when he continued on to Florida. Instead, she settled down to await his return on her father's estate near the city. The Scotts remained behind with her and may have been employed by Sanford or hired out as servants.

Emerson's tour of duty in Florida lasted more than two years. He complained frequently of illness, adding remittent fever to his list of disorders. After a while, he began writing requests for transfer again. Then, in August 1842, he dashed off an angry letter to the Surgeon General's office, protesting against a new assignment in Florida. For his long-suffering superiors, this outburst must have been the last straw. Taking advantage of an order for reduction of medical staff, they awarded him an honorable dismissal from the service. Five weeks after writing the letter, Dr. Emerson found himself suddenly returned to civilian life.

Upon arriving home in St. Louis, Emerson was soon discouraged about the prospect of building up a private practice there. In the spring of 1843, he moved to Davenport, a new town near his land claim in Iowa Territory. There he advertised his professional services, purchased two town lots, and started construction of a brick house. At this point, with his wife expecting a child, Emerson's health began to fail in earnest. He survived for only a month after the birth of his daughter, Henrietta. On December 29, 1843, he signed a will prepared to his order and then died sometime during that same night. The recorded cause of death was consumption, but this may have been a polite cover for the late stages of syphilis.

Emerson's will deserves close attention because of the confusion surrounding its later effect on the Dred Scott case. Except for one minor bequest, he left his entire estate to his wife "during the term of her natural life without impeachment of waste," and after that to his daughter. He authorized Irene Emerson to sell all or any part of his land and tenements and to use the proceeds for her own and Henrietta's maintenance. The will thus made Mrs. Emerson the holder of an estate for life, with Henrietta designated as remainderman. At law, a life estate has some characteristics of trusteeship, but it is essentially a limited inheritance, and in this instance the heiress was vested with broad authority, including the right to invade the principal of the estate.

As one of the executors of his will, Emerson named his wife's brother, John F. A. Sanford of St. Louis. Sanford was a businessman of some prominence whose marriage to Emily Chouteau had linked him with one of the city's oldest families. By neglecting to meet certain legal requirements, he failed to qualify as executor in Iowa, but it is not clear that he was ever informed of the fact. In Missouri, where the inventory of Emerson's estate listed only nineteen acres of land and some furniture, the administrator appointed by the court was Mrs. Emerson's father, Alexander Sanford. There is no evidence that John Sanford ever participated in the process of executing his brother-in-law's will. Settlement of the estate in Iowa was probably accomplished without unusual delay, since the provisions of the will were simple enough. But the elder Sanford dawdled over his responsibilities in Missouri and had not yet filed a final report when he died in 1848. No successor was appointed, and Mrs. Emerson assumed full control of her husband's property. This seems clear

from the fact that she herself sold some of his land in both
states. The estate, in short, had apparently been settled by 1850
and without any known formal assistance from John Sanford.
Thus there would appear to be no legal connection between the
provisions of Emerson's will and Sanford's later involvement in
the Dred Scott case. Still, it is possible that he *thought* himself
responsible, as executor, for supervision of the Emerson estate
during his sister's lifetime.

Emerson's slaves were not mentioned in the Missouri inventory of his estate, and the Iowa inventory has disappeared. It is
unlikely that he took the Scotts with him to Davenport in 1843;
for not only was slaveholding prohibited there, but in addition,
the Emersons had little need for servants, since they lived at a
hotel while work proceeded on their new house. At this time,
perhaps, or shortly after their owner's death, Dred and Harriet
were apparently turned over on loan to Mrs. Emerson's brother-
in-law, Captain Bainbridge, who was transferred to Jefferson
Barracks from Florida in 1843. Dred may have been in Bainbridge's service continuously until 1846. If so, he accompanied
the Captain to Fort Jesup in 1844 and then into Texas after its
annexation the following year. Whether Harriet and Eliza were
with him during this period is uncertain. Bainbridge was a grad-
uate of West Point who later received two promotions for brav-
ery in the Mexican War. Dred remembered him as a "good
man." The slender evidence suggests that Bainbridge kept Dred
with him at Corpus Christi until about February 1846 and sent
him back home after General Zachary Taylor received orders to
advance from the Nueces River to the Rio Grande. At any rate,
Dred Scott was certainly in St. Louis by March, when Mrs. Emerson hired him and Harriet out to a Samuel Russell. A few
weeks later, the Scotts took the first step in their suits for freedom.

2

On April 6, 1846, Dred and Harriet Scott filed petitions in the
Missouri circuit court at St. Louis, summarizing the circum-

stances of their residence on free soil and requesting permission
to bring suit against Irene Emerson in order to establish their
right to freedom. The judge promptly granted them leave to sue,
and on the same day the Scotts filed declarations initiating actions of trespass for assault and false imprisonment. Dred's complaint stated that on April 4, Mrs. Emerson had "beat, bruised
and ill-treated him" and then imprisoned him for twelve hours.
The declaration also averred that Dred was a "free person" held
in slavery by the defendant, and it claimed damages of ten dollars. Harriet's complaint was similar, and so, during the early
stages of the legal battle, there were two suits against Mrs. Emerson, proceeding in tandem through the Missouri courts.

A suit for freedom took the conventional form of a suit for
damages in which it was understood that the alleged acts of the
defendant were lawful chastisement of a slave by his master but
constituted assault and false imprisonment if the plaintiff were
indeed a free person. Thus, the jury could not reach a verdict
without first deciding on the validity of the plaintiff's claim to
freedom. This legal indirection meant that the suit for damages
might be brought against some person other than the actual
owner, if such person had held and treated the plaintiff as a
slave. The later confusion about who really owned the Scotts was
therefore not as important as it has sometimes been made to
seem.

Just how the Scott suits got started, and who provided the
original initiative, remains a mystery. It seems clear, however,
that the motives of the people involved were straightforward and
personal. There is no evidence of underlying political purposes,
or of an intent to contrive a test case. Besides, the central question raised in the suit—whether extended residence on free soil
liberated a slave—was not an issue in American politics and had
already been tested many times in the Missouri courts, with consistent results. The possibility that Dred Scott himself conceived
the idea of going to court should not be discounted. From his
travels he had no doubt gained some measure of self-reliance, as
well as a fund of practical knowledge, and suits for freedom occurred often enough to be common talk among St. Louis slaves.
What seems most likely is that the decision to take legal action

emerged from discussions with friends like the Blows. The number of lawyers involved in the Scott suits suggests that their services were donated or performed for nominal fees.

Anyone familiar with Missouri law could have told the Scotts that they had a strong case. Again and again, the highest court of the state had ruled that a master who took his slave to reside in a state or territory where slavery was prohibited thereby emancipated him. To be sure, military service at an army post was somewhat different from taking up residence, but the court had even disposed of that special problem in *Rachel v. Walker* (1836). Rachel had been held in slavery by an officer at Fort Snelling and at Prairie du Chien on the Wisconsin side of the Mississippi. The decision in her favor acknowledged that the defendant had been required to stay at those posts but then added: "No authority of law or the government compelled him to keep the plaintiff there as a slave." Unfortunately for Dred and Harriet Scott, their suits were to make only slow progress in the face of determined opposition from Mrs. Emerson and the men handling her case. Meanwhile, the climate of opinion in Missouri was changing, and judicial attitudes were bound to change with it. In the end, the Scotts as suitors for freedom would become casualties of the sectional conflict.

Owing to a crowded docket, it was June 30, 1847, when the suits came to trial and verdicts were returned. Since Harriet's case was always a repetition of Dred's, it will be sufficient to describe the proceedings in *Scott v. Emerson*, with the understanding that everything said applies also to *Harriet v. Emerson*.

The "Old Courthouse" in St. Louis, now one of the city's historical landmarks, was new and unfinished in 1847. There Judge Alexander Hamilton, a native of Philadelphia, presided over Dred Scott's first legal contest for freedom. The attorney speaking for Scott was probably Samuel M. Bay, formerly attorney general of Missouri. Mrs. Emerson was represented by George W. Goode, a Virginian of strong proslavery sentiments. It needed only to be proved that Dred had been taken to reside on free soil and that he was now claimed or held as a slave by Mrs. Emerson. Witnesses who had known him at Forts Armstrong and

Snelling established the first point beyond dispute. For the rest, his counsel relied primarily on the testimony of Samuel Russell, who declared that he had hired the Scotts from Mrs. Emerson, paying the money to her father, Alexander Sanford. On cross-examination, however, Russell acknowledged that his wife had made all the arrangements. He himself knew nothing about it, other than what his wife had told him, and he had done nothing except pay the hiring money to Sanford. None of the testimony proved that Mrs. Emerson now owned Dred Scott. With this defect in mind, the jury returned a verdict for the defendant.

Clearly, justice had been thwarted by a technical weakness in the presentation of Scott's case. His attorney moved for a new trial, and, after some delay, the motion was granted. But then Mrs. Emerson's counsel filed a bill of exceptions to the order for a new trial. Thus Dred's case—and Harriet's too—was suddenly transferred on writ of error to the supreme court of Missouri. The court considered Mrs. Emerson's appeal in April 1848 and handed down a decision against her two months later. Since a new trial had already been ordered, said Judge William Scott, there was no final judgment upon which a writ of error could lie. Dred and Harriet had won the right to make a new beginning. But it had become clear that their determination to be free was matched by that of Mrs. Emerson to retain possession of them. The legal maneuvers of defense counsel revealed an intent to win by any means available and had thus far blocked a court decision on the merits of the case.

In 1847, if not earlier, a second daughter was born to the Scotts and given the name Lizzie. During the first two years of litigation, Dred and Harriet had continued to work for the Russells on hire from Mrs. Emerson. Then, on March 14, 1848, George Goode appeared before Judge Hamilton to present his client's motion that the Scotts be taken in charge by the sheriff and hired out. The cynical nature of the Emerson defense becomes especially evident here; for according to Goode's argument before the state supreme court just a few weeks later, Scott's counsel had failed to prove that Mrs. Emerson was "in any manner connected with his being held in slavery." Judge

Hamilton granted the motion, since Missouri law provided for just such action in freedom cases. But to whom the Scotts were then hired by the sheriff is not indicated in the record.

Mrs. Emerson was thus relieved of responsibility for the Scotts during the pending litigation, but without compromising her claim to them. The arrangement may have been made to suit the young widow's new plans. Her father, Alexander Sanford, died in 1848. Either that same year or the next, Irene Emerson left St. Louis to live with one of her sisters in Springfield, Massachusetts. At this point, John Sanford apparently took over the supervision of his sister's affairs in St. Louis and hired new counsel for the second trial. George Goode gave way to Hugh A. Garland and his law partner, Lyman D. Norris. Garland was a highly respected attorney who had been a professor of Greek, a member of the Virginia legislature, and clerk of the national House of Representatives. By this time also, the firm of Alexander P. Field and David N. Hall was representing the Scotts. Field, long a prominent figure in Illinois and Wisconsin politics, was an expert trial lawyer with a special flair for damage suits.

After the Missouri supreme court dismissed Mrs. Emerson's writ of error in June 1848, another long delay ensued. Not until January 12, 1850, did the case finally come to retrial, with Judge Hamilton again presiding. Testimony of Mrs. Russell clearly established that the Scotts had indeed been hired from Mrs. Emerson. The defense accordingly changed its strategy, arguing that at Forts Armstrong and Snelling, Emerson had been under military jurisdiction and therefore not subject to laws of the civil government prohibiting slavery. This argument ignored the precedent of *Rachel v. Walker*. Besides, as Scott's counsel pointed out, it did not cover the fact that Emerson had left his slaves at Fort Snelling in the service of other persons after he was ordered to a different post. The decisive moment in the trial came when Judge Hamilton complied with a request that he instruct the jury in terms highly favorable to the plaintiff. The verdict that followed as a matter of course made Dred Scott nominally a free man.

But the Emerson forces were by no means ready to give up the struggle. After a vain effort to secure still another trial, they

took the appropriate legal steps for carrying an appeal to the
state supreme court. At this time, the opposing attorneys signed
a stipulation that the decision of the high court in Dred's case
would apply also to Harriet, since the law in both suits was
"identical." Briefs were filed in March 1850, but the supreme
court put off consideration of the case to the October term. Further postponements then followed, and a decision that might
have been reached as early as 1848 was in fact not handed down
until 1852. This long delay, stemming from the technical flaw in
Samuel Russell's testimony at the first trial, proved to be crucial
because of new influences that came to bear on the judiciary
during the interval.

The long struggle over expansion and slavery, culminating in
the Compromise of 1850, had left a bitter aftertaste throughout
the country. Southern attitudes had hardened into a grim de-
fensiveness, and the public mood of the slaveholding states was
no longer congenial to suits for freedom. Missourians were especially sensitive to the rising temperature of the sectional conflict.
Their state was in an exposed position, bordered on three sides
by free territory, and, unlike most other slaveholding states, it
had an articulate antislavery minority, whose presence and ut-
terances heightened the feeling of insecurity among slave-owners.

The slavery issue caused discord within both political parties
there, but the sharper cleavage appeared in the ranks of the Missouri Democrats. Senator Thomas Hart Benton had alienated
many members of the party by his hostility to John C. Calhoun,
his opposition to the annexation of Texas, and his moderate
views on the slavery question. Benton's enemies in the state legislature seized the opportunity to embarrass him. Early in 1849
they secured passage of the "Jackson Resolutions," which embraced Calhoun's extreme proslavery doctrines and instructed
Missouri's two senators to "act in conformity" with them. Benton, with re-election in mind, came roaring home to vindicate
himself, but the old warrior's political future was obviously uncertain. At the polls in August 1850, pro-Benton Democrats captured only about one-third of the seats in the state legislature.
The Whigs gained a plurality, while the anti-Benton Democrats
emerged holding the balance of power. With election of a sena-

tor thus depending on negotiations between any two of these three groups, the situation was ripe for political intrigue.

There is reason to believe that the author of the Jackson Resolutions was Judge William B. Napton of the state supreme court. Another member of the court, James H. Birch, had become involved in a venomous feud with Benton. Both Napton and Birch were more than willing to use their judicial power in the anti-Benton and proslavery interest. The Dred Scott case offered an opportunity to do so. According to the third supreme court judge, a pro-Benton man named John F. Ryland, his two colleagues were preparing to overrule the previous court decisions and reject Scott's claim to freedom. He, Ryland, intended to write a dissenting opinion. To the Whig leader Edward Bates, in whom Ryland confided, it appeared that there might be a plot developing to fuse the Whigs and anti-Benton Democrats, with the Whigs receiving the senatorship in exchange for swallowing the proslavery doctrine of the Jackson Resolutions. Much speculation centered on Henry S. Geyer, a well-known lawyer and Whig elder statesman whose pronounced southern sympathies made him acceptable to some of the anti-Benton men.

In this charged political atmosphere, the supreme court judges discussed the drafting of their Dred Scott decision. Birch, an aggressive partisan, wanted to declare the Missouri Compromise unconstitutional, but Napton thought it unnecessary to go that far. Meanwhile, under pressure from his colleagues, Ryland's opposition dissolved, and he agreed to concur in a ruling that under Missouri law Dred remained a slave. Napton was chosen to write the opinion of the court, but for months he put off doing so. During that period of delay, the new state legislature elected Geyer to the Senate seat that Benton had occupied for thirty years. The downfall of "Old Bullion" was viewed with regret by many Missourians and may have influenced another election held later in the same year. A recent amendment to the state constitution had changed the supreme court from an appointive to an elective body. All three of the incumbents became candidates to succeed themselves, but only Ryland, still labeled a Benton Democrat, survived the contest at the polls in September. Birch and Napton were swept from office, the latter without having delivered his Dred Scott opinion. The case would have to be considered again by a reorganized court.

Another event affecting Dred Scott's future took place in January 1851, when the Supreme Court of the United States handed down its decision in *Strader v. Graham*. This Kentucky case involved some slave musicians who were taken briefly into Ohio for performances and later fled from Kentucky to Canada. It was a suit, not for freedom by the slaves themselves, but for damages by their owner against several men who had allegedly aided the escape. Defense counsel argued that the Negroes had been liberated by virtue of the Northwest Ordinance as soon as they set foot on Ohio soil, and that their subsequent flight was therefore one of free men rather than slaves. The Kentucky Court of Appeals rejected this argument in rendering a decision for the slave-owner, whereupon the case was carried to the United States Supreme Court. Chief Justice Taney, speaking for a unanimous Court, dismissed the case for lack of jurisdiction. The Northwest Ordinance, he declared, no longer had any force in Ohio, having been superseded by the constitution and laws of that state. Consequently, the case did not present a federal question under the Judiciary Act of 1789 and so could not be reviewed by the Supreme Court. The decision of the highest Kentucky court was conclusive.

The *decision* in the *Strader* case, being simply a refusal to accept jurisdiction, did not impinge significantly upon Dred Scott's cause before the high court of Missouri. Indeed, it was irrelevant unless the Missouri judges decided against him and he attempted an appeal to the United States Supreme Court. Even then, the two cases would be far from parallel. For Scott's claim to freedom rested upon several years of residence on free soil, rather than a brief visit, and residence not only in a free state but in federal territory covered by the Missouri Compromise restriction. So the *Scott* case, unlike the *Strader* case, clearly involved a right claimed under the federal Constitution, and the Supreme Court could scarcely refuse to hear it on jurisdictional grounds.

Taney's *opinion* in the *Strader* case was a different matter. In it, he managed to cover much of the substantive ground that presumably lay beyond the Court's jurisdiction. Taney, in fact, endorsed the main line of reasoning by which the Kentucky court had arrived at its decision. Namely, whatever effect the laws of Ohio might have had upon the status of the slaves while they were in Ohio, their condition after returning in bondage to Kentucky "depended altogether upon the laws of that State and could not be influenced by the laws of Ohio." This placed a federal stamp of approval on the doctrine of reversion. But what of Dred Scott's claim to freedom under the Missouri Compromise, based on his residence at Fort Snelling? Did the doctrine of reversion likewise govern the relationship between federal territorial law and state law? To this problem Taney also addressed himself in a passage that was patently *obiter dictum*. Before concluding that the Northwest Ordinance had been superseded in Ohio, he considered the hypothetical effect of a contrary conclusion. "The ordinance in question, if still in force," he declared, "could have no more operation than the laws of Ohio in the State of Kentucky."

Taney's *Strader* opinion, if accepted as precedent despite its extraneousness, would have a controlling effect on the future disposition of any similar cases in the United States Supreme Court. Its effect on a case being heard *in a state court,* however, was permissive rather than controlling. It confirmed the principle of reversion, but left the state to decide whether it would apply the principle of reattachment. Taney's remarks, even if they should become relevant to Dred Scott's case, indicated neither that Scott was free nor that he was still a slave, but only that his condition depended solely on Missouri law. And the law expounded by the Missouri supreme court had been consistently favorable to suits for freedom like his, involving long-term residence on free soil. Legally, therefore, the *Strader* opinion ought not to have prejudiced Scott's cause, but its timing and psychological effect worked to the advantage of the other side.

The Missouri precedents for the Dred Scott case had been set by liberal-minded judges who were predisposed to favor freedom, but the times had changed and the judges were, for the most part, a different breed of men. With slavery now under fierce attack, its defenders regarded the old liberalism as a display of weakness. Coming in this new context, the *Strader* opinion assured Missourians that they were under no legal compulsion to enforce the laws of another jurisdiction hostile to slavery, and that they were entirely free to consult their own self-interest in disposing of suits for freedom relying on such laws. Thus Taney's pronouncement gave a green light to judicial reaction in Missouri.

The two new state supreme court judges elected along with Ryland in September 1851 were William Scott and Hamilton R. Gamble. As an ardent proslavery Democrat, Scott was prepared to take up where Napton had left off and overrule the Missouri precedents favorable to Dred Scott's cause. Gamble, on the other hand, was a Whig and a member of the faction that opposed collaboration with the proslavery Democrats. His presence on the court, together with the pro-Benton label still worn by Ryland, probably made Dred Scott's prospects seem brighter than they really were.

On March 22, 1852, Judge Scott finally announced the decision of the court. With Ryland concurring, he found that Dred Scott was still a slave and ordered the judgment of the lower court reversed. As a legal document, his opinion dealt essentially with the problem of comity or conflict of laws:

> Every State has the right of determining how far, in a spirit of comity, it will respect the laws of other States. Those laws have no intrinsic right to be enforced beyond the limits of the State for which they were enacted. The respect allowed them will depend altogether on their conformity to the policy of our institutions. No State is bound to carry into effect enactments conceived in a spirit hostile to that which pervades her own laws.

Comity, Scott declared, was therefore a matter of judicial discretion, to be "controlled by circumstances." But at this point the necessity of demonstrating that changed circumstances dictated the overthrow of Missouri precedent converted a legal explication into a political tract:

Times are not now as they were when the former decisions on
this subject were made. Since then not only individuals but
States have been possessed with a dark and fell spirit in relation to slavery, whose gratification is sought in the pursuit of
measures, whose inevitable consequences must be the overthrow and destruction of our government. Under such circumstances it does not behoove the State of Missouri to show the
least countenance to any measure which might gratify this
spirit.

There followed a homily on slavery as a civilizing force that had
raised the American Negro far above the "miserable" African.
"We are almost persuaded," Scott concluded, "that the introduction of slavery amongst us was, in the providence of God, who
makes the evil passions of men subservient to His own glory, a
means of placing that unhappy race within the pale of civilized
nations."

On that pious note ended the six-year effort to establish Dred
Scott's right to freedom under the laws and in the courts of Missouri. The decision was reached by a two-to-one vote; for Judge
Gamble entered a dissenting opinion. His argument was almost
entirely an appeal to the principle of *stare decisis*. Without con-
testing Judge Scott's conclusion that the extending of comity
was optional, he maintained, in effect, that Missouri had already
exercised her option by choosing to enforce the laws of other
jurisdictions against slaveholding. "I regard the question," he
said, "as conclusively settled by repeated adjudications of this
court." Furthermore, those earlier cases had been decided "when
the public mind was tranquil," and they embodied principles
that had not changed with the changing times.

As Gamble plainly implied, his colleagues had subordinated
the rights of the parties in the case to the public issues associated with it. Their decision, rendered nominally against Dred
Scott, was primarily an expression of mounting southern anger
and an act of retaliation against antislavery words and deeds.
Judge Scott's convincing legal analysis of the nature of comity
carried him only to a reassertion of state sovereignty. Beyond
that, he deserted the judicial path, lined as it was with disagreeable precedents, and followed a political route to the proslavery

position from which he delivered his opinion.* For the first time, but not the last, a court had used the Dred Scott case as a means of determining public policy.

3

Proceedings in *Dred Scott v. Emerson* did not end with the decision of the Missouri supreme court announced on March 22, 1852. The case was then remanded to the trial court for final action in the form of a judgment implementing the decision. But Judge Alexander Hamilton put off complying with the order. Instead, according to an entry in the circuit court record for January 25, 1854, the case was "continued by consent, awaiting decision of Supreme Court of the United States." The only satisfactory explanation of Judge Hamilton's curious action is that he was privately informed in 1852 of an intention to carry Dred Scott's cause to the federal Supreme Court. This does not necessarily mean, however, that the precise strategy for further litigation had been worked out at that time. From the fact that more than a year passed before new court action was initiated, one might well infer that the Scott forces were at first perplexed about how to proceed. But the delay may also have resulted from the need to find new counsel in place of Alexander Field and David Hall. Hall had died in the spring of 1851, and not long afterward, Field moved to Louisiana, where he remained for the rest of his life.

By all logic, the next move in behalf of Dred Scott should have been an appeal directly to the United States Supreme Court, as provided for in Section 25 of the Judiciary Act of 1789. Perhaps the change of counsel made the difference. If Field and Hall had continued in charge of the case, they might possibly have elected to proceed with an appeal. But the paramount *rea-*

---

* Judge Scott did not make it clear whether he regarded Dred's years in Illinois and at Fort Snelling as constituting residence or mere sojourning, but the language of his opinion was broad enough to cover both and make it out of line with all other previous southern decisions on the subject.

son for not appealing may have been the expectation that the Supreme Court, with *Strader v. Graham* in mind, would refuse to accept jurisdiction. If so, Taney's freewheeling *Strader* opinion takes on added historical significance. Not that Dred himself would have fared any better by undertaking an appeal; for the Court, if it had accepted jurisdiction, would in all probability have upheld the Missouri court decision. But whatever the outcome, it would have marked the end of Dred's legal fight for freedom. In other words, if *Dred Scott v. Emerson* had been reviewed by the United States Supreme Court, there would have been no *Dred Scott v. Sandford,* which was simply the alternative way of getting the case before that same Supreme Court. The crucial difference was that the two major issues in the *Sandford* case—Negro citizenship and the constitutionality of the Missouri Compromise restriction—did not appear on the face of the record in the *Emerson* case and would have been beyond the scope of federal court review. Thus a Supreme Court decision in *Dred Scott v. Emerson* would have been narrowly based and without the great impact attributed to *Dred Scott v. Sandford.*

By the end of 1853, Dred Scott had acquired new legal counsel, had allegedly become the property of a new owner, and had begun a new suit for freedom in the federal circuit court. Since 1851, Charles Edmund LaBeaume, brother-in-law of Henry T. Blow, had been hiring Dred and Harriet Scott from the sheriff. LaBeaume, himself a lawyer, consulted another local attorney, Roswell M. Field about the Scott case. He apparently told Field that Irene Emerson, now the wife of Calvin C. Chaffee of Springfield, Massachusetts, had recently sold the Scotts to her brother, John F. A. Sanford, now a resident of New York City, although his business affairs still brought him frequently to St. Louis. Field thereupon recommended a suit in federal court under the diverse-citizenship clause and agreed to serve as counsel. For this version of how the new case got started, the principal authority is Field himself, in a letter written just a year later.

If Field's explanation seemed entirely satisfactory, there would be little mystery about the origins of *Dred Scott v. Sandford.* Even before the case reached its conclusion in 1857, however, there were rumors that Sanford's ownership of the

Scotts had been contrived for the sole purpose of making a federal suit possible. Attorneys for both sides publicly denied that the case was fabricated, but the suspicion has persisted. In many historical accounts, the transfer of the Scotts to Sanford is labeled a "fictitious sale"—meaning, apparently, that it was nominal. More recently, historians have been disposed to believe that there was no transfer of any kind, that Sanford never owned the Scotts but instead exercised control over them in some capacity, perhaps as his sister's agent or as an executor of John Emerson's will. But if this is true, then Sanford's behavior becomes all the more curious. Why, if he was not the owner, did he allow himself to be sued as the owner without making any effort to disclaim ownership? At the same time, there is also something puzzling about the strategy of the Dred Scott forces. The earlier suit against Mrs. Emerson had been undertaken with bright prospects of success, but the action against Sanford was a different matter because of the discouraging precedent of *Strader v. Graham* and the proslavery record of the Supreme Court. Why, then, was such an unpromising battle ever begun?

Contemporary suspicion about the origins of the case was voiced by both sides in the sectional controversy. One version made Sanford a tool of abolitionist intrigue; the other pictured him as the key figure in a carefully planned judicial assault on the constitutionality of the Missouri Compromise. The task confronting the historian, then, is one of trying to determine the motives of the persons involved in the suit and the extent to which any cooperation between the opposing parties was collusive. Previous efforts have been obfuscated by the question of ownership, which is almost a red herring and yet has received so much attention that it can scarcely be ignored.

The chief reason for believing that Sanford actually did own the Scotts in 1853 is the repeated acknowledgment of such ownership by his counsel during the course of the trial. In fact, as part of his formal plea of not guilty to the nominal complaint of assault and false imprisonment, Sanford declared that the slaves were his "lawful property." On the other hand, those historians who deny that Sanford was the owner rely primarily on the circumstances of Scott's eventual emancipation. Sanford died on

May 5, 1857, two months after the Supreme Court decision in his favor, and his probate papers contain no mention of the Scotts. Moreover, just three weeks later, Dred and his family were manumitted by Taylor Blow, who had recently acquired them from *Calvin and Irene Chaffee*. Thus, if Sanford owned the Scotts in 1853, having received them from his sister, he must have returned them to her at some time before his death in 1857—all of which seems highly unlikely. The facts, in short, discourage certitude. Sanford may have owned the Scotts as he said, but there is reason to suspect that he did not. Perhaps the most credible explanation is that Sanford, continuing to act as his sister's agent, chose to shield her by permitting himself to be sued in her place.

As far as the legality of Dred Scott's suit is concerned, it makes little difference whether Sanford was acting as owner, agent, or executor when he accepted the role of defendant. In a suit for freedom, the matter at issue was not primarily the owner's title to his slave property but rather the right of *anyone* to treat the plaintiff as a slave. Thus the owner or any other person holding the Scotts as slaves was an appropriate target for legal action in the form of a damage suit. Moreover, solving the problem of ownership would not in itself solve the problem of Sanford's motives; for we would still need to know why he acquired the Scotts, or why he misrepresented himself as their owner. In neither case would an ulterior purpose be any more assumable than personal convenience, consideration for his sister, or some other private reason.

Therefore, the fact that Sanford's convenient acknowledgment of ownership made a federal suit possible may or may not be evidence of collusion. The filing of an "agreed statement of facts," signed by opposing counsel, also contributes to the appearance of coziness, but this may have been simply an effort to limit the time and costs of the trial. What aroused the most contemporary suspicion about Sanford's conduct was the revelation in 1857 of his family tie with Mrs. Chaffee and her earlier role in the case; for Calvin Chaffee by that time had taken a seat in Congress as an emphatic opponent of slavery. Many historians ever since have jumbled the chronology and portrayed Sanford as the tool of his "abolitionist" brother-in-law. But Chaffee in 1853 was still a physician in private practice and had not yet entered politics. (He served two terms in Congress from 1855 to 1859.) There is no evidence to connect him or his wife with the litigation getting under way in Missouri. Indeed, it is doubtful that Chaffee even knew of the Scotts' existence in 1853. Neither does it seem credible that Sanford, himself a slaveholder and the real manager of his sister's defense in the Missouri courts, had undergone such a complete change of heart by 1853. He retained the same proslavery attorney, Hugh Garland, who had won the earlier case and no doubt expected to win again. Nothing in Garland's strategy suggests mere token resistance to the new Scott suit. The idea that Sanford was a cardboard defendant, secretly in league with the other side, does not have enough substance to be taken seriously.

On the other hand, both before and after the Supreme Court decision in 1857, there were charges in the antislavery press that the case had been fabricated by proslavery interests. But this implied that the Scott forces, by initiating the suit, wittingly played into the hands of the enemy, which was absurd. The men behind Dred Scott's federal suit were generally the same ones who had supported him in the Missouri courts, with the exception of his new counsel. Roswell M. Field (not related to Scott's previous attorney, Alexander P. Field) was a native of Vermont and probably stronger in his antislavery convictions than any of the other lawyers who represented the Scotts. In view of the odds against success, one may question the wisdom of undertaking the suit, but not the honesty of its purpose. Field appears to have been determined that Dred Scott should obtain a hearing before the nation's highest tribunal.

What remains is the possibility that the suit, while genuine enough on the Scott side, was connived at and exploited for proslavery purposes by the defense. One New York Republican newspaper asserted that Sanford, a Democrat, had "consented to place himself in the attitude of a defendant after enduring an amount of importunity, badgering, and worrying, from persons having no other than a political interest in the case." Supportive evidence for this assertion has never turned up, however, and the explanation breaks down when one examines the manner in which Sanford's defense was conducted. Conspiratorial collusion on Sanford's part would make sense, after all, only if it was directed at securing a judicial ruling on the constitutionality of the Missouri Compromise. But the strategy of defense counsel in the courtroom, as we shall see, was plainly not aimed at that purpose or at any other purpose except winning a favorable verdict.

The United States circuit court for the district of Missouri had no permanent home in St. Louis. It moved from one rented hall to another, and by 1854 had been pushed into "a small back room over a Main Street store." There *Dred Scott v. Sandford* was tried before Judge Robert W. Wells, a Virginian with a shrill voice and awkward manner who had previously been attorney general of Missouri. The case was a suit for freedom in the customary form of an action of trespass. The declaration filed for Scott on November 2, 1853, asserted that he was a citizen of Missouri. It complained that on the preceding January 1, Sanford had assaulted and wrongfully imprisoned Scott himself, his wife Harriet, and their two children, Eliza and Lizzie. The damages claimed on these three counts totaled $9000.

At the next term, in April 1854, Sanford filed a plea in abatement challenging the court's jurisdiction on the grounds that Scott, as a Negro descended from slaves of "pure African blood," was not in fact a citizen of Missouri. This move, if successful (and it might well have been), would have foreclosed any testing of the Missouri Compromise. It therefore seems utterly incompatible with the notion of a proslavery plot. However, Judge Wells upheld Scott's demurrer to the plea, ruling that for the purpose of bringing suit in a federal court, citizenship implied nothing more than residence in the designated state and the legal capacity to own property. In his ruling, it should be noted, Wells limited himself to interpreting just the diverse-citizenship clause in Article Three, Section Two, of the Constitution. The question of whether free blacks qualified as citizens under this clause had not been settled by a federal court, the only jurisdiction in which it could arise. In a number of state court cases, the general subject of Negro citizenship had been raised under Article Four, Section Two, which declares that "the citizens of each state shall be entitled to all privileges and immunities of citizens in the several states." The decisions in those cases were generally against Negro citizenship. Wells made it clear, however, that his ruling did not extend to the privileges-and-immunities clause or define citizenship in all its aspects. By implication, he adopted the view that the meaning of the word "citizen" might vary with its context. A free Negro, he held, was *enough of a citizen* to be covered by the diverse-citizenship clause, whatever his status otherwise.

As constitutional interpretation the ruling was probably sound, and as a practical matter, it was eminently sensible. There is little reason to believe that the framers of the Constitution intended to bar native-born free Negroes from access to federal courts, a privilege extended even to aliens of every race. Such exclusion, aside from its patent injustice, would have been legally troublesome in a number of ways. For one thing, the definition of "Negro" varied from state to state but ordinarily embraced most persons of mixed ancestry from predominantly black to predominantly white. So, in a given case, the jurisdiction of a federal court might depend upon verification of the race of a great-grandmother of one of the parties. Moreover, such exclusion would not only deny a privilege but confer a special immunity; for if a Negro could not sue, neither could he be sued, under the diverse-citizenship clause.

Having failed to obtain dismissal of the suit on jurisdictional grounds, Sanford entered a plea of not guilty to the charges in Scott's declaration. Did he, by pleading over, acknowledge the court's jurisdiction and thus waive the right to reopen the subject later? This question would produce controversy bordering on confusion when the case came before the Supreme Court. The issue was especially important because of its possible bearing on the Fugitive Slave Law. The Wells ruling on the plea in abatement, as Field soon realized, would mean that an alleged fugitive might claim citizenship in the state where he was apprehended and secure a federal trial before a friendly jury. His right to do so, being derived straight from the Constitution, would presumably override the act of 1850 with its provisions for summary hearing and *ex parte* testimony. On a matter of such obvious consequence, a mere district judge like Wells was unlikely to have the final word.

It was at this point in the proceedings that opposing counsel filed their "Agreed Statement of Facts," an inaccurate summary of the Scott family's life and travels with Dr. Emerson. The document has misled many unwary historians, but for the immediate legal purpose it was adequate and fair.

The case came to trial on May 15, 1854. Arguments of counsel were based entirely on the Agreed Statement. By this time the struggle over the Kansas-Nebraska bill, which repealed the slavery restriction of the Missouri Compromise, was approaching its climax in Congress. Yet, significantly, Sanford's attorney did not seize the opportunity to challenge the constitutionality of the restriction. Instead, he relied on the line of reasoning that had been successful before the Missouri supreme court. Judge Wells instructed the jury that the law was with the defendant, and the jury accordingly returned a verdict in Sanford's favor. Later, Wells expressed a personal wish that it could have been otherwise. If Scott, he added, had been declared free under Illinois law *while he was still in Illinois,* the decision would have had full effect in Missouri. But Missouri possessed the same power to declare him a slave in Missouri under *its* laws. So Wells plainly made comity the controlling consideration, taking his cue from *Strader v. Graham* and the decision of the supreme court of Missouri in *Scott v. Emerson.*

The verdict posed an odd technical problem that went unnoticed at the time. According to the decision of the court, Dred Scott was a slave and had always been a slave. This meant that he was never a citizen of Missouri and therefore had no right to bring suit in the first place. Having sent the case to a jury and received a verdict, Judge Wells apparently did not consider a last-minute dismissal of the suit for want of jurisdiction. Yet this is precisely what he should have done, in the official view of the Supreme Court as subsequently expressed by Chief Justice Taney.

After an unsuccessful motion for a new trial, Field filed a bill of exceptions, the first step in taking the case to the Supreme Court on a writ of error. The Scott forces now faced the urgent task of recruiting a suitable attorney to argue their case before the Supreme Court, and they must either raise the money for his fee or else find someone willing to donate his services. Their first effort was to publish a twelve-page pamphlet containing a record of the recent trial. The preface, dated the Fourth of July for symbolic effect, was attributed to Dred Scott himself. It summarized the background of the case, varying in some details from the Agreed Statement of Facts, and then closed with an appeal for help:

> I have no money to pay anybody at Washington to speak for me. My fellow-men, can any of you help me in my day of trial? Will nobody speak for me at Washington, even without hope of other reward than the blessings of a poor black man and his family? I do not know. I can only pray that some good heart will be moved by pity to do that for me which I cannot do for myself; and that if the right is on my side it may be so declared by the high court to which I have appealed.

The months went by, however, and no champion for Dred Scott came forward. Finally, on Christmas Eve 1854, Field wrote to Montgomery Blair suggesting that he or some other lawyer in Washington might serve "the cause of humanity" by taking up the case. Blair, after consulting his family and certain friends, agreed to act as Scott's attorney without fee. He also enlisted the aid of Gamaliel Bailey, abolitionist editor of the *National Era*, who promised to raise the money for court costs and incidental expenses.

Montgomery Blair was the oldest son of Francis Preston Blair, who had come out of Kentucky in 1830 to edit the Washington *Globe* and become a prominent member of Andrew Jackson's "kitchen cabinet." By adhering to the Van Buren-Benton wing of Jacksonian Democracy during the 1840s, the elder Blair had incurred the enmity of many southern Democrats and made himself unacceptable to James K. Polk, who forced his retirement from party journalism. Blair and his sons had supported the Free Soil ticket in 1848, and their opposition to the Kansas-Nebraska Act in 1854 was drawing them into the new political coalition that would soon adopt the name Republican.

For many years, Montgomery Blair had practiced law in St.

Louis and served as a political lieutenant of his father's old friend, Thomas Hart Benton. He now lived in Blair House on Pennsylvania Avenue, having moved to Washington in 1853 and begun practice before the Supreme Court. At the age of forty-one, he was a man of considerable standing in the national capital, but he still regarded himself as a citizen of Missouri and gave that as one reason for accepting the Dred Scott case. His knowledge of Missouri law made him especially qualified to handle the appeal. Blair was tall and lean, with a military bearing acquired as a cadet at West Point. He had an awkward manner, a high-pitched voice, and an aversion to windy oratory. There was no streak of playfulness in his nature, no disposition to court an audience by amusing it. His legal arguments, always compact and precise, were presented with an almost religious earnestness. A onetime slaveholder and no admirer of abolitionism, Blair was nevertheless dedicated to the free-soil cause. In the Dred Scott case he may have seen an opportunity to enhance his own reputation and strike a blow against Benton's enemies in Missouri, but his decision to participate was also prompted by conviction.

Yet Blair, for all of his merits, appeared to be overmatched against the opposing counsel. The quality of the two attorneys retained by Sanford indicates that the potential importance of the Dred Scott case had at last been recognized in certain political circles. One of them was Henry S. Geyer, the man who had unseated Benton. Geyer's career in the Senate was proving to be undistinguished, but he had few peers at the Missouri bar and was earning a high reputation in Washington's legal community. With Geyer pitted against Blair, the case continued to echo the din of Missouri politics. The other counsel for Sanford stood even higher in national repute. Reverdy Johnson of Maryland, former senator and attorney general under Taylor, was probably the most respected constitutional lawyer in the country. An old friend of the Chief Justice and veteran of many famous court battles, Johnson added luster to any legal cause that he undertook. Facing such a formidable team, Blair tried several times to enlist the services of another lawyer, but without success. He therefore prepared to argue the case alone.

THE TANEY COURT IN 1857

JUSTICE	BORN	TERM OF SERVICE	STATE	PARTY	PREVIOUS JUDICIAL EXPERIENCE	PREVIOUS POLITICAL CAREER
John McLean	1785	1829-61	Ohio	Rep.	Ohio supreme court	Congressman U.S. Postmaster General
James M. Wayne	1790	1835-67	Ga.	Dem.	State judge	State legislator Mayor of Savannah Congressman
Roger B. Taney	1777	1836-64	Md.	Dem.		State legislator Md. Attorney General U.S. Attorney General Secretary of Treasury
John Catron	1786	1837-65	Tenn.	Dem.	Tenn. supreme court, CJ	
Peter V. Daniel	1784	1841-60	Va.	Dem.	U.S. district judge	State legislator Privy Councillor Lieutenant Governor
Samuel Nelson	1792	1845-73	N.Y.	Dem.	State judge N.Y. supreme court, CJ	Postmaster
Robert C. Grier	1794	1846-70	Penn.	Dem.	State judge	
Benjamin R. Curtis	1809	1851-57	Mass.	Whig		State legislator
John A. Campbell	1811	1853-61	Ala.	Dem.		State legislator

Meanwhile, the record of *Dred Scott v. Sandford* had been officially received by the Supreme Court on December 30, 1854. This late arrival placed the case far down on the docket, and to no one's surprise, it was continued to the next term. The delay meant that the case would probably be heard during the early stages of a presidential campaign.

⊰ 6 ⊱

Before the Supreme Court

For more than a year after it was docketed, the Dred Scott case awaited the attention of the Supreme Court. During that time the revolutionary effects of the Kansas-Nebraska Act became increasingly evident. Kansas itself appeared to be on the verge of civil war. Open hostilities between proslavery and free-state forces in the territory were narrowly averted in December 1855, just as the Court was beginning its new term. Meanwhile, the anti-Nebraska movement, already triumphant in many northern states, was approaching the final phase of transformation into a permanent political party. At a meeting scheduled for February 22 in Pittsburgh, Republican leaders planned to lay the foundation of a national organization. Kansas would obviously be the principal issue in the coming presidential election. The new thirty-fourth Congress, bogged down for two months in a struggle over the speakership of the House, would likewise soon find itself preoccupied with the Kansas problem. The newspapers of the nation were already rehearsing every argument on the subject. And the Kansas controversy inevitably produced another round of angry debate on the constitutional power of Congress over slavery in the territories. Thus the historical context of the Dred Scott decision was being prepared.

Yet the public was still unaware of the case. It received no advance publicity in the press. Even the Washington correspon-

dent of the *Missouri Republican* (St. Louis), though he mentioned other matters pending before the Supreme Court, said
nothing about *Dred Scott v. Sandford*. This lack of interest seems
peculiar in retrospect, but is easily explained. In almost ten
years of litigation, Dred Scott's legal struggle for freedom had
never yet elicited any extended argument or judicial pronouncement on the constitutionality of the Missouri Compromise restriction. The explosive political implications of the case remained hidden from public view.

On February 7, 1856, with the Supreme Court nearly ready
to hear the case, Montgomery Blair filed his brief. Curiously, he
devoted only four of its ten pages to the task of arguing for *reversal* of the circuit court's decision against Scott's right to freedom. The remainder of the brief was a *defense* of the circuit
court's ruling (on the plea in abatement) that free Negroes
were citizens to the extent of being qualified to bring suit in
a federal court. That is, Blair gave more attention to defending ground already won than to mounting the attack necessary for victory. It is possible that Blair, in adopting this odd
strategy, was influenced by a letter he had received from
Roswell Field. If the ruling of Judge Wells on the plea in abatement were allowed to stand, Field wrote, the resulting constitutional right of black persons to sue in federal courts would probably make the Fugitive Slave Act "of little value" to southern
masters. Field thought it "very desirable" to obtain the Supreme
Court's opinion on the subject. Blair was apparently willing to
invite such opinion in his brief, even though the strategy was
unlikely to benefit his client. Dred Scott, out of sight back in
St. Louis, was becoming more clearly a pawn in the political
game.

As for Blair's limited argument on the merits, perhaps the
most striking feature is that it claimed freedom for Dred Scott
solely on the ground that he had been "emancipated by his master's having taken him to reside in the State of Illinois." Blair
made no mention of Scott's residence at Fort Snelling. Thus he
avoided the territorial issue entirely, perhaps seeing no advantage to his client or to the Republican cause in having it tested.

In this part of his brief, Blair drew heavily on Judge Gamble's dissenting opinion in *Scott v. Emerson,* whereas the verdict of the lower federal court had followed the majority opinion of Judge Scott in that case. Gamble had demonstrated that precedents in Missouri were generally on Dred's side. Judge Scott had cited Taney's opinion in *Strader v. Graham* as authority for reversing the earlier Missouri decisions. Blair discreetly omitted reference to the Strader precedent but made it all the more relevant with his strategy of concentrating on Dred's residence in Illinois.

If Henry S. Geyer or Reverdy Johnson filed a brief, it has apparently not been preserved. Our knowledge of the case presented for the defense is therefore limited to fragmentary newspaper reports. Argument before the Court began on February 11, 1856, and extended over four days. Blair spoke first, followed by Geyer and Johnson, with Blair then closing for the plaintiff. Defense counsel reiterated the arguments previously used in Sanford's behalf, including the plea to jurisdiction that a Negro was not a citizen. In addition, both Geyer and Johnson advanced to new ground by attacking the constitutionality of the Missouri Compromise restriction. Thus, in February 1856, the Dred Scott case and the major political issue of the day had finally converged. From this point on, Sanford became merely the nominal defendant. Stricken with mental illness, he would be in an asylum before the end of the year. Reverdy Johnson had taken up the case at the suggestion of a "southern gentleman," and appropriately so; for the real client that he and Geyer now represented was the slaveholding South.

During the latter part of February, the Court conferred at least twice on the case without making much progress. Then it recessed for the entire month of March so that the justices could spend some time on their circuits. Not until April 5 was the next conference held, and three more followed it within a week. The justices seemed disposed to be prudent. In a letter to his uncle on April 8, Justice Benjamin R. Curtis confided: "The Court will not decide the question of the Missouri Compromise line,—a majority of the judges being of opinion that it is not necessary to do so." This probably meant either that jurisdiction would be denied or that the decision of the circuit court would be upheld, but Curtis did not say which choice was likely.

From other evidence it appears that the Court was divided on the question of jurisdiction, and more particularly on the technical problem of whether the plea in abatement was subject to review. Four justices were aligned on each side of this issue, with Samuel Nelson leaning toward the affirmative but uncertain about it and reluctant to cast a deciding vote. On May 12, the Court ordered that the case be reargued in the next term with special attention to two questions: 1) Was the plea in abatement properly before the Supreme Court? 2) If so, had the circuit court ruled correctly on the plea—that is, did a Negro have a right as a citizen to bring suit in a federal court?

Many observers were convinced, however, that the postponement was dictated by political considerations and especially by the fear that Justice McLean would use the case to improve his chances of winning the Republican presidential nomination. Yet McLean himself apparently offered no objection to the order for reargument. Abraham Lincoln, on the other hand, later accused the Court of delaying its decision in order to conceal the pro-slavery intentions of the Democratic party until after the presidential election. This was part of his famous conspiracy charge in the House-Divided speech, but there is no evidence to support his reading of judicial motives. What does seem likely, however, is that some justices, at least, were reluctant to render such a controversial decision on the eve of a major political campaign.

Democrats assembled in Cincinnati on June 2 for their national convention and nominated James Buchanan on a platform endorsing popular sovereignty in vaguely southern terms while by-passing the constitutional issue of congressional power over slavery in the territories. The Republicans, meeting two weeks later in Philadelphia, expressly affirmed the existence of such power, and of course many southern spokesmen categorically denied it. Yet the issue was not clearly drawn between the parties in the campaign. The election did not become a referendum on the question laid before the Supreme Court in the Dred Scott case.

McLean had strong support at the Republican convention, but the new party preferred younger, more colorful leadership, and its presidential nomination went to the western adventurer, John C. Frémont. With Millard Fillmore already nominated by the American party, there were three contestants in the field. Kansas was the principal issue of the campaign, and from the South came threats of secession in the event of a Republican victory. Buchanan's election by a narrow margin in November postponed the day of reckoning for another four years. When the Supreme Court convened for its new term in December, the atmosphere was one of a storm weathered and of tensions relaxed.

But sectional and partisan animosities were quickly revived by the retiring President, Franklin Pierce, in his final annual message. Half of this extraordinary document was a savage denunciation of the Republican party. Pierce, having suffered the humiliation of being denied renomination, now hailed the outcome of the election as a personal vindication and as an emphatic condemnation of the antislavery movement. The American people, he said, had refused to be led down "this path of evil"; the Republicans had failed in their efforts to "usurp the control of the Government of the United States." As for the Missouri Compromise restriction, it was already "a mere nullity . . . a monument of error . . . a dead letter in law" at the time of its repeal.

There was an immediate flurry of angry replies from Republicans in Congress, and the resulting debate had been going strong for two weeks when reargument of the Dred Scott case got under way on December 15. Obviously, postponement of the case had not defused it. Many more people were now aware of what might be at stake in one Negro's suit for freedom. The reargument accordingly drew a large audience that included "many distinguished jurists and members of Congress."

At first it appeared that Montgomery Blair would again be Scott's only counsel, but at the last moment he acquired the limited assistance of George T. Curtis, a conservative Massachusetts Whig. Curtis, the brother of Justice Benjamin R. Curtis, agreed to present a defense of congressional power in the territories. Now that the political implications of the case were widely recognized, it became more noticeable that Dred Scott had no prominent antislavery champion in his corner. This state of affairs inspired comment at the time, and the failure of antislavery radicals to take an earlier interest in the case remains something of a puzzle. Yet Scott himself was better off with relatively conservative counsel; for his hope of freedom depended upon the Court's rising above political and sectional considerations.

Again the Court heard some twelve hours of argument extending over four days. Blair led off alone, with Geyer and Johnson following, and Blair then used up another two hours on the final day, leaving just one hour for Curtis. The technical question of whether the plea in abatement was before the Court, supposedly the moot issue that had prompted the order for reargument, received only brief attention. Blair predictably maintained that Sanford, by pleading over to the merits, had waived any further right to raise the question of jurisdiction. Among the precedents that he cited were several rulings by the Taney Court itself. Geyer, in turn, emphasized the limited nature of federal jurisdiction in civil suits brought under the Judiciary Act of 1789. Scott's averment, he argued, must be without defect or there could be no jurisdiction. If the circuit court's ruling on the plea in abatement was erroneous, then "it was error to proceed further, and the defendant's pleading over could not give jurisdiction."

On the question of Negro citizenship, Blair spoke for more than an hour, going over much the same ground that he had covered in February. He demonstrated that the word "citizen" had been used frequently in both state and federal law to mean "free inhabitant." He pointed to the mingling of those terms in the privileges-and-immunities clause of the Articles of Confederation. The Constitution, to be sure, spoke only of "citizens" in its version of the clause. But this verbal change, Blair insisted, implied no change in substance, no intention to exclude free Negroes; for it had been made without the objections and debate that would surely have greeted any effort at such exclusion. Blair also distinguished between "civil rights" and "political functions," such as voting and jury service—functions from which various classes of citizens were excluded. Political disabilities, in short, did not deprive free blacks of citizenship. At the very least, Blair argued, they were "*quasi* citizens," possessing the right to own property, carry on business, and seek redress in the courts. Thus Blair's last line of defense was the concept of limited citizenship that Judge Wells had adopted in ruling against Sanford's plea in abatement.

Geyer's treatment of the citizenship question was briefer and less coherent than Blair's, but it contained the elements of a clever argument. He began by asserting that parties in a federal suit must be able to prove their national as well as their state citizenship. Citizens of the United States, he continued, were either born to that status or they had acquired it by naturalization. But Dred Scott, admittedly, was by birth a slave rather than a citizen, and he had never been naturalized. Therefore, even if his travels with Emerson had made him a free man, they had not made him a citizen of the United States. What seemed to be emerging here was a distinction between free-born free Negroes and slave-born free Negroes, with the latter more obviously excluded from United States citizenship. Geyer failed to clinch his argument, however. Instead, he obscured it by mixing in statements and citations to the effect that *all* free blacks were excluded from citizenship. Nevertheless, in shifting the focus from state to federal citizenship, he anticipated the line of reasoning that Taney would follow.

It was likewise Blair and Geyer, primarily, who dealt with the question of whether Dred Scott's two-year stay in Illinois had worked his emancipation. Geyer, for the negative, merely reiterated two familiar arguments: 1) Emerson, as an army officer at a military installation in Illinois, had been a sojourner rather than a resident of the state, and as such he had not forfeited ownership of his slave; 2) whether free or not under Illinois law, Scott's status after his return to Missouri was determined by Missouri law as interpreted by the highest court of that state (the doctrine of reversion).

Blair's treatment of the subject showed more originality and indicated that he had given the case much additional study since the first round of arguments. For one thing, he now came to grips with the *Strader* case and put his finger accurately on the fallacy of regarding it as a controlling precedent. To wit, the

Supreme Court had refused to accept jurisdiction on the ground that the case involved no federal question. The ruling therefore affirmed only the *finality*, and not the *legal soundness*, of the decision rendered in the supreme court of Kentucky. No such jurisdictional question arose in *Dred Scott v. Sandford*, where federal jurisdiction was original and depended upon the character of the parties rather than the nature of the law to be applied.

As for the military sojourner argument, Blair neatly inverted it by pointing to the lack of any evidence in the record "that Dr. Emerson had or claimed a residence elsewhere whilst he was living at these [military] posts." And he reminded the Taney Court that according to one of its own decisions, "where a person lives is taken *prima facie* to be his domicil."

Blair's principal task was to discredit the majority opinion of Judge Scott in *Scott v. Emerson,* which had in turn largely governed the decision of Judge Wells in the federal circuit court. First Blair minimized the legal weight of the *Emerson* opinion, declaring that it in no way limited a federal court's freedom of judgment. Then he attacked its central argument that Dred Scott, even if temporarily freed by Illinois law, had resumed the status of slavery when he went back to Missouri with his master (the doctrine of reattachment). The decision of the Missouri supreme court, he said, had been made in defiance of longstanding Missouri precedent and for admittedly political reasons. Furthermore, the Missouri court had been wrong in viewing enforcement of Illinois antislavery law as a forfeiture of property. Emancipation in cases like Scott's was not a penalty imposed upon the slaveholder, but rather a recognition of the legal effect produced by the master's voluntary act of taking his slave to reside in a free state. Thus no "penal" justice was involved, and the obligations of interstate comity were binding on Missouri. Blair acknowledged that a sovereign state might put some limits on this obligation by refusing to enforce laws of other states that it found repugnant. But Missouri, he argued, had never manifested hostility to suits for freedom. On the contrary, its code of laws made such suits "favored actions," no matter where a plaintiff had acquired his asserted right to freedom.

Fundamentally at issue here were the nature and operation

of interstate comity. The general principles were not in dispute.
They had been laid down by Joseph Story in his classic work,
Conflict of Laws, and had been endorsed by Chief Justice Taney
in *Bank of Augusta v. Earle* (1839). A state law had extraterritorial force within the boundaries of another state only with the
latter's consent. Such consent might be assumed, however. "In
the silence of any positive rule, affirming or denying, or restraining the operation of foreign laws," Taney had written in 1839,
"courts of justice will presume the tacit adoption of them by
their own government, unless they are repugnant to its policy, or
prejudicial to its interests." The critical importance of Taney's
exception is obvious. Presumably, a "positive rule" would have
to come from a state legislature, but the Chief Justice had plainly
indicated that "courts of justice" might, on their own responsibility, find a foreign law to be "repugnant" or "prejudicial." And
that was precisely what the supreme court of Missouri had done
in *Scott v. Emerson*. Thus, in spite of Blair's able argument, the
weight of judicial precedent seemed to be on Sanford's side.

As for Dred Scott's claim to freedom by virtue of his residence
at Fort Snelling, there was no compelling legal reason why it
should not have been argued on the same ground. The federal
law prohibiting slavery north of 36° 30' was municipal rather
than national in character. It could scarcely have any more extraterritorial force than the law of a sovereign state like Illinois.
Inside Missouri, the federal prohibition was as "foreign" as the
law of Illinois and therefore just as unenforceable without Missouri's consent. Such, at least, had been the reasoning of Judge
Scott in the state supreme court, and it accorded with Taney's
dictum in *Strader v. Graham*.

However, both Geyer and Johnson neglected this line of defense, which might have benefited their client but not the slaveholding South in any significant way. Instead, they relied wholly
on the argument that Dred Scott had remained a slave during
his years at Fort Snelling because the federal law forbidding
slavery in that region was unconstitutional. The constitutionality
of the Missouri Compromise restriction, it will be remembered,
had never been at issue in the earlier deliberations of three
courts that heard the case. Neither had it received any special

mention in the Supreme Court's order for re-argument. Yet this constitutional question, the only subject taken up by all four counsel, was now plainly the center of attention.

In challenging congressional power over slavery in the territories, Geyer and Johnson rested their argument largely upon a narrow interpretation of the territory clause and a broad appeal to the principle of state equality. In response, Blair and Curtis maintained that broad construction of the territory clause had been intended by the framers of the Constitution, implemented repeatedly by Congress, confirmed by the Supreme Court, and accepted virtually without question by the American people for half a century. Instead of attempting to summarize the entire debate on the subject, it may be more illuminating to abstract a few significant exchanges of argument:

Geyer-Johnson: The word "territory" as used in the Constitution means nothing more than "land." A clause intended merely to provide for disposal of soil cannot endow Congress with "supreme, universal and unlimited power" over the persons and property of territorial inhabitants. *Blair-Curtis:* The territory clause comprises two distinct powers, originating in two separate proposals by Madison at the Constitutional Convention. One is the power to dispose of public lands and other federal property. The other is the power, in Madison's words, to "institute temporary governments," rephrased to read: "make all needful rules respecting the territory." The fact that the territory clause is combined with the clause providing for admission of new states, the two constituting a separate section of Article Four, indicates that the framers were dealing with the problem of government, as well as the disposal of soil, in the western territories.

Geyer-Johnson: The power of Congress to institute temporary governments in the territories is acknowledged. But it is an implied power, rather than an expressly enumerated one, and arises out of necessity. Only legislation that is "needful" for the establishment of such government can be constitutionally justified, and a law prohibiting slavery does not fall within that category. *Blair-Curtis:* The question of whether any particular piece of legislation is "needful" cannot be settled by judicial action. It is, instead, a political question, and aggrieved persons must seek political remedies. Slavery has been a subject of legislation wherever legislative power exists and is as much so in the territories as in the states.

Blair-Curtis: Southerners like John C. Calhoun have frequently acknowledged the power of Congress to prohibit slavery in the territories. They accepted the Missouri Compromise line, for example, and later proposed extending it to the Pacific. *Geyer-Johnson:* The Missouri Compromise was a "compromise of principle necessary to the existence of the Union," and the Supreme Court has never upheld its constitutionality. The measure is therefore no final authority for a court of justice.

Geyer-Johnson: The Missouri Compromise restriction violates the spirit of the Constitution by disparaging the domestic institutions of certain states and denying their citizens equal access to western territories. *Blair-Curtis:* The law excludes no citizen from any territory, and southerners have in fact emigrated to free territories in large numbers. Instead, the law forbids the holding of a kind of property that can be legally held in certain states. To find it unconstitutional would be to make the constitutionality of federal legislation dependent on the variable property laws of the states.

Geyer-Johnson: The restriction is unconstitutional because the power to prohibit slavery is not expressly conferred on Congress by the Constitution. *Blair-Curtis:* The restriction is a valid exercise of the legislative power because it is nowhere expressly forbidden in the Constitution.

Thus the second round of arguments ended. For all its dry legal content, the debate in the crowded little courtroom was also at times intensely political, especially on the part of Geyer and Johnson. Their case argument turned frequently into general vindication of the South and slavery—an institution, said Johnson, that would last "for all time." In the background all the while, like an orchestral accompaniment to the arguments of counsel, were the echoes of acrimonious congressional debate on the same subject in the same building, heightening the sense of urgency with which many Americans watched the judicial proceedings.

In summary, the Court had a series of four questions before it, presumably to be answered in the following order:

1. *Was the plea in abatement before the Court?* On this question, the justices themselves were badly divided; for although the common-law rule of pleading seemed to support a negative answer, it was by no means clear that the rule applied within the federal court system. A negative answer, desired by Scott's counsel, would leave standing the lower court's ruling against the plea, and the Supreme Court would move directly to consideration of the merits of the case—that is, to questions 3 and 4. An affirmative answer would lead the Court to a review of the lower court ruling and to a decision on the second question.

2. *Was Dred Scott (if free) a citizen of Missouri and thus capable of bringing suit in a federal court?* Here, precedent and logic seemed to favor the answer previously returned by the lower court, but it remained to be seen whether any southern justice would be willing to accord Negroes even limited citizenship. A negative answer would presumably conclude the action in Sanford's favor with an order directing the lower court to dismiss the case for lack of jurisdiction. An affirmative answer would carry the Court on to a consideration of the case on its merits.

3. *Was Scott free as a consequence of his residence in Illinois?* Much depended here upon whether Scott's residence at Forts Armstrong and Snelling was regarded as mere sojourn or as the equivalent of domicile. Yet, even if the latter view were to prevail, the sweeping character of Judge Scott's pronouncement in *Scott v. Emerson,* together with the *Strader* "precedent" and established judicial doctrine on interstate comity, gave the advantage to Sanford. An affirmative answer would, of course, mean victory for Scott. A negative answer would necessitate consideration of question 4.

4. *Was Scott free as a consequence of his residence at Fort Snelling?* Insofar as the answer depended upon a decision regarding the constitutionality of the Missouri Compromise restriction, the weight of history appeared to be on Scott's side. However, the same principles of reversion and reattachment with

which the defense had responded to question 3 were arguably applicable here as the basis for a decision in Sanford's favor.

Given the makeup of the Court, a decision against Scott seemed likely, but the political magnitude of the case depended upon the way in which that decision was reached. One simple solution would have been to answer question 1 in the affirmative and question 2 in the negative, thereby reversing the lower court's ruling against the plea in abatement and causing the case to be dismissed for want of jurisdiction. Excluding free Negroes from citizenship would no doubt arouse anger in abolitionist circles, but not among the great majority of northerners who equated black skins with natural inferiority. The Court, however, was so evenly divided on the status of the plea in abatement that an effective decision could scarcely be reached in this manner.

Another solution, equally simple and even less controversial, was also available. The Court could merely uphold the decision of the lower court, using the *Strader* doctrine as the basis for returning negative answers to both question 3 and question 4. It was toward this strategy of self-restraint that a majority of the justices, with some reluctance, began to move.

2

Contrary to some expectations of a prompt decision, another delay of many weeks set in. The principal reason, it appears, was the prolonged absence of Justice Daniel and a general reluctance to dispose of such an important case without the full Court present. Daniel's wife suffered a horrible death on January 3 when her clothing caught fire, and he did not attend another session until the middle of February. Accordingly, it was on February 14 that the Court held its first conference of the term on the Dred Scott case.

As the conference proceeded, two things became clear. First, Nelson had come over to the side of the four justices who held that the plea in abatement was not before the Court; or at least he now believed that this jurisdictional problem need not and should not figure in the decision. Second, only the five southern justices were willing to invalidate the Missouri Compromise restriction. Curtis and McLean took the opposite view, while Nelson and Grier preferred simply to uphold the circuit court's decision. The prospect of having such a momentous pronouncement supported by just the bare majority of a court divided along sectional lines could not fail to inspire misgivings. At any rate, the relatively innocuous strategy of Nelson and Grier won approval. Nelson was appointed to write the opinion of the Court, in which six other justices would presumably concur. This would mean no decision on the citizenship issue or on the power of Congress to prohibit slavery in the territories.

Yet the very setting in which they deliberated tended to press the justices toward a broader decision. Here, it seemed, was an opportunity for judicial statesmanship. By acting boldly, the Court might be able to dispose of a dangerous public issue and perhaps save the nation from disaster. In addition, some of the southern justices may have been subjected to sectional pressures of a more definite kind; for here also was an opportunity to rescue the South officially from the discrimination and insult discernible in federal laws hostile to slavery. Alexander H. Stephens informed his brother that he was urging the Court to a prompt decision, with the full expectation that it would settle the territorial issue in the South's favor. A likely object of Stephens's influence was his fellow Georgian, Justice Wayne, and Wayne proved to be the pivotal figure in an abrupt reversal of the strategy first adopted by the Court's majority.

There was also pressure from the President-elect. James Buchanan, fussing with the problem of what to say about the territorial issue in his inaugural address, wrote to his old friend Justice Catron asking whether the Court would soon hand down a decision. Catron replied with what must have been disappointing news. The Dred Scott case, he revealed, would be decided in a conference on February 14, but not in a way to help Buchanan with his inaugural; for the Court would probably not pass judgment on the power of Congress over slavery in the territories.

The assignment of the majority opinion to Nelson soon confirmed Catron's prediction.

Nelson set to work promptly and produced a short opinion of about five thousand words. It began with an equitable summary of the opposing views on the plea in abatement. Tactfully, as the spokesman of the Court, Nelson left the issue open, saying only: "In the view we have taken of the case, it will not be necessary to pass on this question." Turning to the merits of the case, he began by assuming that Dred had been taken from Missouri into Illinois "with a view to a temporary residence." He then reasoned his way from the accepted definition of comity to the principle of reversion, with the resulting conclusion that Dred Scott's status when he brought suit depended entirely on the law of Missouri as previously determined by the highest court of that state in *Scott v. Emerson*. If Scott became free at Fort Armstrong, Nelson said, he did so because Illinois refused to recognize and enforce the slave law of Missouri. Once he returned to Missouri, the situation was reversed. "Has the law of Illinois any greater force within the jurisdiction of Missouri than the laws of the latter within the former? Certainly not. They stand upon equal footing." For the same reasons, Nelson continued, Scott did not become free by virtue of the Missouri Compromise restriction during his residence at Fort Snelling. A territorial law of Congress had no extraterritorial force superior to that of a state law. Taney had made this clear in *Strader v. Graham*, declaring that the Northwest Ordinance, if still in force, "could have no more operation than the laws of Ohio, in the State of Kentucky." Thus Missouri law likewise controlled Scott's status after his return to that state from Fort Snelling. Nelson's logic was by no means impeccable, and his conclusions rested upon more than one dubious assumption. Still, it appeared that his opinion, as the official opinion of the Court, would affect only a relatively few Negroes, and he had made effective use of the Chief Justice's own words to demonstrate that there was no need to consider the constitutionality of the Missouri Compromise restriction.

The ink was scarcely dry on Nelson's draft, however, before the Court majority reversed itself and decided to take hold of the thornier problems that he had so carefully avoided. On the motion of Wayne, it was agreed that Taney should write the opinion of the Court, covering all the questions arising in the case. This change occurred after February 14 but apparently no later than February 19; for on the latter date, Catron wrote again to Buchanan, indicating that the Court *would* render a decision on the constitutionality of the Missouri Compromise restriction. Wayne justified his crucial motion with the argument that public expectation had made it the Court's duty to decide the larger issues in the case. But Catron offered a different explanation in his letter to Buchanan. The Court majority, he asserted, had been "forced up" to its change of plan by the determination of Curtis and McLean to present extensive dissenting opinions discussing all aspects of the case. Justice Grier said about the same thing in a letter written to Buchanan four days later. This evidence has been enough to convince many historians that the willfulness of the two dissenting justices compelled the shift from Nelson's supposedly innocuous treatment of the case to Taney's broader and more inflammatory opinion. The explanation is open to question, however.

For one thing, the statements of Catron and Grier are self-serving and unsupported by any contemporary testimony from Curtis and McLean themselves, or from any of the other four southern justices who were supposedly "forced up" to changing their plans. There is reason to believe that Curtis in later years denied the accuracy of the Catron-Grier explanation and insisted that his opinion had been a response to that of the Chief Justice. And of the four southern justices besides Catron, only Campbell ever wrote out an account of the last-minute change of strategy, and he said nothing about pressure from the dissenters.

The principal mistake of some scholars has been their assumption that the five southern justices were all willing at first to let Nelson speak for them, and that only McLean and Curtis insisted on discussing the territorial question. The majority never came to such complete agreement, however, and multiple opinions, as we have seen, were common in the Taney Court. Wayne prepared a separate Dred Scott opinion that undoubtedly dealt with the Missouri Compromise, since he laid it aside as unnecessary when Taney replaced Nelson as spokesman for the Court. There is also evidence that Daniel intended to file his own opinion, and the same may have been true of Taney and Campbell. Thus what seems to have been in prospect was a debate carried on over Nelson's head between dissenting and concurring justices. The Court majority, it appears, had maneuvered themselves into an absurd situation, and their abrupt change of plan was a way of getting out.

But the best explanation may well be the most obvious one. That is, the change did spell victory for those justices who had wanted all along to issue an emphatically pro-southern decision. Here, the conspicuous figure was Wayne. He made the key motion in conference and later claimed that the initiative had been his alone. Yet one should not discard the possibility that Taney played a more important part than is visible on the surface. Behind his mask of judicial propriety, the Chief Justice had become privately a bitter sectionalist, and his ostensibly passive role in the conferences is inconsistent with the temper of the opinion that he ultimately delivered. It seems unlikely that Wayne offered his motion shifting the opinion of the Court to Taney without first sounding him out. Furthermore, Wayne specified that the Chief Justice should cover *all* the major issues raised in the case. This meant including the question of Negro citizenship, which a majority of the justices had supposedly waved aside, but which Taney was anxious to discuss, as his opinion subsequently revealed. In short, the voice was Wayne's but the hand may have been the hand of Taney.

There remained the problem that a five-man decision on the territorial issue would be of dubious effect and might damage the Court's prestige. Accordingly, pressure was brought to bear on Grier, the one likely recruit among the four northern justices. Buchanan, at the urging of Catron, wrote to Grier, who promptly conferred with Taney and Wayne and then replied:

> I am anxious that it should not appear that the line of latitude should mark the line of division in the court. I feel also that the opinion of the majority will fail of much of its effect if founded on clashing and inconsistent arguments. On conversation with the chief justice, *I have agreed to concur with him.*

. . . But I fear some rather extreme views may be thrown out by some of our southern brethren. There will therefore be six, if not *seven* (perhaps Nelson will remain neutral) who will decide the compromise law of 1820 to be of non-effect. But the opinions will not be delivered before Friday the 6th of March.

Thus Buchanan's intervention contributed significantly to the change in the substance of the Dred Scott decision.

On March 4, a bright spring day, the new President took the oath of office administered by the aged Chief Justice. The two men held a brief conversation during one pause in the ceremonies, and the exchange did not go unnoticed. For some hostile onlookers, the incident assumed a sinister meaning as they listened to a passage in the inaugural address. Fortunately, said Buchanan, Congress had determined that the principle of majority rule should prevail in the territories, where the people were left perfectly free (by the Kansas-Nebraska Act) to deal with the institution of slavery in their own way, subject only to the Constitution. There was, to be sure, a minor problem still awaiting solution:

> A difference of opinion has arisen in regard to the point of time when the people of a Territory shall decide this question for themselves.
> This is, happily, a matter of but little practical importance. Besides, it is a judicial question, which legitimately belongs to the Supreme Court of the United States, before whom it is now pending, and will, it is understood, be speedily and finally settled. To their decision, in common with all good citizens, I shall cheerfully submit, whatever this may be.

These disingenuous words were made to seem all too pat by the issuance of the Dred Scott decision just two days later. In antislavery circles, remembrance of the little chat preceding the inaugural soon blossomed into a tale of high-level intrigue. Taney, it was said, had revealed the substance of the forthcoming decision to Buchanan, who had then altered his text to make use of the information. Many years afterward the ironic truth would come to light—that no such revelation was necessary because the

President already knew, and the Chief Justice knew that he knew, what the Court would decide.

But there is something more to puzzle over—a remarkable discrepancy that has somehow escaped the attention of historians. Both Catron and Grier had informed Buchanan that the Court would rule on the constitutionality of the Missouri Compromise restriction—that is, on the power of *Congress* to prohibit slavery in the territories. In his inaugural, however, Buchanan addressed himself to a different problem entirely. He predicted a ruling on popular sovereignty—that is, on the power of a *territorial legislature* to prohibit slavery. This was an issue primarily between northern and southern Democrats. Now, since Dred Scott had laid no claim to freedom by virtue of a territorial law, the issue was not present in his suit and had never been argued by counsel. What, then, had led Buchanan to think that the Court would settle the question?

Only one justice actually answered the question Buchanan had so ostentatiously turned over to the Court. That was Taney, who slipped into his opinion a few lines on the power of a territorial legislature over slavery. Although there is no evidence of any secret communication between the two men, one must at least consider the possibility that Buchanan, before Inauguration Day, saw a draft of the Taney opinion or received information in detail about its content. The alternative explanation, difficult to believe, is that Buchanan not only misunderstood the nature of the Dred Scott case but somehow misread the explicit statements of Catron and Grier.

On March 6, Taney led off the reading of opinions in a crowded courtroom. He spoke in a low voice that became almost inaudible before the end of his two hours. Nelson and Catron followed the Chief Justice with their relatively brief opinions. McLean and Curtis, the two dissenters, were heard the next day, taking up about five hours. The remaining justices filed their opinions without reading them from the bench. In the explosion of editorial comment that ensued, Taney's "opinion of the Court" naturally received the most attention. It was lavishly praised by Democrats and furiously denounced by Republicans, although its contents were but imperfectly known. Whereas Mc-

Lean and Curtis promptly released the full texts of their opinions for newspaper publication, the Chief Justice withheld his manuscript for revision. The public had access only to a summary of the opinion, taken down in court by an Associated Press reporter and printed in major newspapers throughout the country. This gave Republicans a definite advantage in the war of words. Taney found the situation embarrassing, and he nursed his resentment of the action taken by the two dissenters, which seemed not only improper and disrespectful but deliberately intended to encourage the violent outcry against the decision.

As weeks passed and Taney's full opinion did not appear in print, the word spread that he was undertaking extensive revisions. The rumor worried Justice Curtis especially, for his dissent had been keyed to Taney's opinion. On April 2, he wrote to William T. Carroll, Clerk of the Supreme Court, asking for a copy of the opinion whenever it should be available in printed form. Carroll replied four days later that he had been directed not to give anyone a copy of the opinion before it was published officially in Howard's *Reports.* The directive had been issued by the Chief Justice with the concurrence of Daniel and Wayne, the only other justices remaining in Washington after the close of the term. It was obviously aimed at Curtis, for Taney's written confirmation of the order bore the same date as Carroll's reply to Curtis (April 6).

After another exchange of letters with Carroll, Curtis wrote to Taney for an explanation, saying that he did not suppose the Chief Justice intended to deny a colleague access to the opinion of the Court. Taney responded with a hostile letter declaring that Curtis had no right to a copy of the opinion because he wanted it for use by partisan critics of the Court. Stung by the accusation, Curtis unwisely elected to continue the quarrel. In a letter dated May 13, he protested the impugnment of his motives, questioned the authority of three justices to impose such a restriction, and suggested that it was a violation of the rules of the Court to withhold an opinion for so long a time.* He reas-

* The Supreme Court's *Rules of Practice,* rule 25 (in force since 1834) declared: "All opinions delivered by the court shall, immediately upon the delivery thereof, be delivered over to the clerk to be recorded."

serted his own official right to examine an opinion of the Court that, according to reports, had been "materially altered" since its oral delivery.

The Chief Justice fumed for nearly a month before firing off an eleven-page answer. (Meanwhile, the whole argument became academic with the official publication of the Dred Scott decision late in May.) He had no desire, Taney wrote on June 11, to continue the "unpleasant correspondence" that Curtis had seen fit to commence, but certain statements could not be passed by without notice. Having published his own opinion without consulting the Court, Curtis had no right to share in the disposition of the opinion of the Court, especially when his avowed object was to "impair its authority and discredit it as a judicial decision." As for the report that he, Taney, had substantially altered his opinion, it was utterly untrue.

> There is not one historical fact, nor one principle of constitutional law, or common law, or chancery law, or statute law in the printed opinion which was not distinctly announced and maintained from the Bench; nor is there any one historical fact, or principle, or point of law, which was affirmed in the opinion from the Bench, omitted or modified, or in any degree altered, in the printed opinion.

What had been added, Taney continued, were certain proofs and authorities to support historical facts and legal principles asserted in his oral opinion but denied in the dissenting opinions. "And until the Court heard them denied, it had not thought it necessary to refer to proofs and authorities to support them— regarding the historical facts and the principles of law which were stated in the opinion as too well established to be open to dispute." Here, covered over with some self-righteous indignation, was the plain acknowledgment that the Taney revisions were indeed rebuttal to certain parts of the dissenting opinions.

A few days later, Taney confided to a close friend: "When I saw you I thought Mr. Justice Curtis would not answer my [first] letter. You thought otherwise, and that his letter would be in the tone of a demagogue. You were right and I have received from him just such a letter as you predicted. . . . It was of a

character that made it proper to reply to it." Taney added that
he expected Curtis to answer again. "But every attempt to justify
what cannot be justified, can only plunge one in further difficul-
ties. Yet he cannot feel comfortable in his present position." Curtis did write still another letter, to which Taney responded with
a short acknowledgment that brought the exchange to a close.
And Curtis did feel uncomfortable about the dispute—so uncomfortable that by September he had submitted his resignation
from the Court. His had been the initial blunder that provoked
the quarrel, but thereafter Taney was the aggressor, venting his
resentment of the personal abuse to which he had been subjected
since the announcement of the Dred Scott decision.

When he finally acquired a copy of Taney's published opinion, Curtis compared it with his recollection of the oral version,
which he had heard twice—first in conference and then again on
March 6. He concluded that "upwards of eighteen pages" had
been added. "No one can read them," he declared, "without per-
ceiving that they are *in reply* to my opinion." Thus Curtis maintained that about one-third of the published opinion was new
material introduced as rebuttal, whereas Taney insisted that he
had made no significant changes or additions. Which man's reckoning is more trustworthy? How much did Taney change his
opinion after delivering it from the bench?

Unfortunately, the opinion that Taney read from the bench
was not preserved, and the newspaper summary is inadequate
for systematic comparison with the published version. There are,
nevertheless, some indications of the extent to which he revised
the original document. For one thing, the Chief Justice read his
opinion on March 6 in two hours or a little more, but at his measured pace, the published version (containing about 23,000
words) would have required at least three hours for reading.
If so, the opinion was ultimately expanded about 50 per cent,
making it some eighteen pages longer, as Curtis calculated.

This conclusion is partly confirmed by more definite evidence
in the National Archives, where two different sets of page proofs
of the Taney opinion have been preserved. Handwritten additions to the proofs constitute about eight pages of the version
finally published. The three most lengthy additions are as follows:

1. Five paragraphs (19 Howard 428-430) supplementing a passage of three paragraphs in which Taney defended the right of the Court to examine the facts in the case after having upheld the plea in abatement. All eight paragraphs are plainly rebuttal to the assertion of Curtis (and McLean) that much of Taney's opinion was without authority.

2. Fifteen paragraphs (19 Howard 442-446) in which Taney attempted to reconcile his views on the territorial clause with those of John Marshall in *American Insurance Company v. Canter*. This was likewise rebuttal, but primarily to McLean rather than Curtis.

3. Three paragraphs (19 Howard 453-454) near the end of the opinion, denouncing the manner in which the case had been brought before the Supreme Court. This introduced a new question that had not been argued by counsel.

Now, if Taney added eight pages *after* the document had been set in type, it is not difficult to believe that he had expanded the original manuscript by as much as ten pages *before* he sent it to the printer. It therefore appears that Curtis was substantially correct in his critique of the published opinion. Taney's denial of having made any significant changes must be labeled inaccurate. The so-called opinion of the Court included a considerable amount of material that few if any of the other justices heard or read before its publication. And much of this new material was rebuttal to the dissenting opinions of Curtis and McLean. Another complication is thus added to an already labyrinthine case, and especially to the question that has fascinated and confused several generations of historians and legal scholars: What did the Court actually decide?

3

Only one thing was absolutely certain. Dred Scott had lost his eleven-year legal battle for freedom. Seven of the nine justices agreed that at law he was still a slave. Beyond that simple fact, the results of the contest were far from clear. In his "opinion of the Court," Taney had excluded Negroes from citizenship and denied Congress the power to prohibit slavery in the territories. But were these declarations part of the *ratio decidendi* and therefore authoritative?

The perplexities of the Dred Scott decision were partly inherent in the case as it came before the Supreme Court and partly a result of the manner in which the Court handled the case. Confusing enough in itself was the double-layered jurisdictional problem presented by the plea in abatement. But in addition there was the peculiar circularity of relationship between the jurisdictional question and the merits of the case; for the latter could be subsumed entirely under the former. And then the complications were multiplied by the number of concurring opinions and by the widespread doubt that Taney, in some of his principal conclusions, actually spoke for a majority of the Court.

From one point of view, there is nothing to puzzle over. What the Court decided was what the designated "opinion of the Court" announced as having been decided. To wit:

1. The ruling of the circuit court on the plea in abatement was subject to review by the Supreme Court.

2. Negroes were not citizens of the United States and therefore had no right to bring suit in a federal court under the diverse-citizenship clause of the Constitution.

Consequently, the circuit court had been wrong in its ruling on the plea in abatement and should not have accepted jurisdiction of the case.

3. Dred Scott, a slave, had not become a free man during his residence at Fort Snelling; for the Missouri Compromise restriction under which he claimed freedom was unconstitutional because Congress had no power to prohibit slavery in the federal territories.

4. Scott was not free as a result of his residence in Illinois; for his status, after his return to Missouri, depended entirely upon the law of that state as determined in *Scott v. Emerson*.

Consequently, Scott was still a slave, therefore not a citizen, and therefore incapable of bringing suit in a federal court under the diverse-citzenship clause.

5. For these reasons, the suit must be returned to the circuit court with instructions that it be dismissed for want of jurisdiction.

For the most part, however, historians have been unwilling to accept Taney's opinion as a definitive statement of what the Court decided. Instead, they have examined all of the opinions and endeavored, in effect, to count the "votes" of the justices on each of the major issues. This calculation of box scores has produced various results, but here is the most common summing-up:

BOX SCORE

1. Four justices held that the plea in abatement was properly before the Court (Taney, Wayne, Daniel, and Curtis).

2. Three justices held that a Negro could not be a citizen of the United States (Taney, Wayne, and Daniel).

3. Six justices held that the Missouri Compromise restriction was invalid (Taney, Wayne, Grier, Daniel, Campbell, and Catron).

4. Seven justices held that the laws of Missouri determined Scott's status as a slave after his return to that state from Illinois (Taney, Wayne, Nelson, Grier, Daniel, Campbell, and Catron).

5. Seven justices held that Scott was still a slave, but there were differences on what the final judgment of the Court should be (same as in number 4).

From these tabulations it has been easy enough to infer that "there was no judicial decision on the question of Negro citizenship." Taney's pronouncement on this issue appears to have been extrajudicial (because only a minority of justices thought that it was before the Court), and in any case, only two other justices endorsed his ruling. From the tabulations it has also been possible to argue that there was no effective decision on the constitutionality of the Missouri Compromise restriction. The reasoning is that three of the six justices making up the majority on this question (Taney, Wayne, and Daniel) had no right to consider the merits of the case after having found that the circuit court lacked jurisdiction from the beginning. By such logic, the deci-

sion of the Court has sometimes been reduced to nothing more
than what was contained in Nelson's opinion—namely, that Dred
Scott remained a slave because his status was governed by the
laws of Missouri. James Bradley Thayer, in preparing his *Cases
on Constitutional Law* (1895), included Nelson's opinion rather
than Taney's because it alone was limited, he said, "to grounds
agreed upon by a majority of the court."

The whole argument is self-destructive, however, and it leads
to an absurdity. If, because of their stand on the jurisdictional
question of Negro citizenship, three of the six justices invalidating the Missouri Compromise restriction actually had no right
to consider the issue, then the same three obviously had no right
to consider the other major substantive issue—that is the effect of
Missouri law upon Scott's status after his return from Illinois. To
put it another way, if the three justices listed in item 2 of the
box score must be subtracted from the total of six in item 3, then
they must also be subtracted from the total of seven in item 4.
Nelson's opinion is therefore not a bit more valid than Taney's.
This would leave us with *nothing* decided by the Court except
the judgment itself—that Scott, for some reason or other, was still
a slave.

The absurdity results from confusing the logic of individual
justices with the decision-making of the Court. And the confusion begins with the assumption that any justice who favors dismissal on jurisdictional grounds is automatically disqualified from
considering the merits of the case. But jurisdiction is decided on
by the Court, not by individual justices, and if the Court accepts
jurisdiction, then all members, whatever their views on the jurisdictional question, have a right to join in reviewing the case on
its merits. As a matter of personal consistency, a justice may decline to participate in consideration of the merits after having
opposed acceptance of jurisdiction. But there was no rule of the
Court, then or later, *compelling* such an abstention. Thus, whatever personal inconsistency may be attributed to Taney, there is
no basis for arguing that he had no right to go to the merits, unless one accepts that his ruling on Negro citizenship (in spite of
the box score) was authoritative. In short, critics of the Dred
Scott decision cannot have it both ways. Either the Court did

rule authoritatively against Negro citizenship, or else it did legitimately consider and settle the substantive issues in the case. It cannot have done *neither;* presumably it must have done *one or the other;* but what greatly complicates matters is the possibility that it may have managed to do *both.*

The box scores are in fact open to question because they rest upon the dubious assumption that only those justices *expressly agreeing* with Taney are to be counted on his side. This means that justices not committing themselves on a certain issue are counted with the opposition. Yet, since Taney's opinion was the authorized opinion of the Court, it seems more reasonable to regard only those justices *expressly disagreeing* with him as constituting the opposition. Such was the view of Judge Woodbury Davis of the Maine supreme court. Speaking of Taney's opinion, Davis said: "I do not perceive why the other members of the court should not be regarded as concurring in it, except upon those points which they have expressly disclaimed." Counting the votes in this way, one finds that only two justices (Catron and McLean) denied that the plea in abatement was properly before the Court; and that only two justices (McLean and Curtis) held that Negroes were eligible for United States citizenship, upheld the validity of the Missouri Compromise restriction, and held that Scott, having become free in Illinois, remained so after his return to Missouri. From these facts one can readily draw the conclusion that Taney's opinion, being the official opinion of the Court and never encountering explicit dissent from more than two justices, was authoritative on all the major questions presented by the case. So much for the conclusiveness of box scores. Their meaning is derived less from the raw data than from the manipulation of the data by the respective scorekeepers.

The question of what the Court decided actually presents two distinct problems, with the second contingent on the first: 1) When Taney reviewed and reversed the ruling of the circuit court on the plea in abatement, thereby denying citizenship to Negroes, did he speak for a majority of the Supreme Court? If he did, and *only* if he did, the second problem arises. 2) Was it then legally possible for him and the Court to review the facts of the case and render judgment on whether Dred Scott had become a free man either by virtue of Illinois law or by virtue of the Missouri Compromise restriction?

The belief that Taney did not have a majority with him in his determination to review the plea in abatement stems not only from the box-score method but also from knowledge of what went on in conferences preceding the decision. At first, it will be remembered, the Court had been evenly divided on this technical question, with Nelson undecided but leaning toward Taney's side. Then, after the reargument, Nelson ostensibly shifted toward the other side, thus producing an anti-Taney majority, and as a consequence he was momentarily designated to write the opinion of the Court. But from his published opinion it is plain that Nelson remained undecided about the plea in abatement, having concluded only that it would be good strategy for the Court to by-pass an issue on which it was so badly divided. Furthermore, the decisions reached at this time lasted no more than a few days. Taney replaced Nelson as official spokesman for the Court majority, which, by approving Wayne's motion, instructed the Chief Justice to write an opinion covering *all* the questions arising in the case. Now, since Taney could not review the citizenship question if it were not before the Court, the majority's approval of the Wayne motion amounted to a reversal of its earlier stand and a vote for consideration of the plea in abatement.

But of course the only legitimate basis for a determination of what the Court decided is the official record of the Court, rather than the unofficial reports and recollections of what occurred in conference. According to that record, four justices (Taney, Wayne, Daniel, and Curtis) expressly maintained that the plea in abatement was properly before the Court, while two justices (Catron and McLean) expressly argued that it was not. What of the other three?

Nelson summarized the opposing arguments and then left the question moot, but his phrasing suggests that he was still leaning to Taney's side. Grier concurred with Nelson "on the questions discussed by him," but he also concurred with Taney on several points, including the judgment that "the record shows a *prima facie* case of jurisdiction, requiring the court to decide all questions properly arising in it." This seems to place Grier on Taney's side; certainly he cannot be counted as an opponent of Taney on the jurisdictional question. Campbell's treatment of the issue is the most puzzling of all. We have his own later statements counting himself among the anti-Taney group and insisting that the group constituted a five-man majority (including Nelson and Grier) that determined the question by declining jurisdiction. In his concurring opinion, Campbell originally wrote: "My opinion in this case is not affected by the plea to jurisdiction (for reasons stated in the opinion of Justice Catron)." By associating himself with Catron, he plainly embraced the view that the plea in abatement was not properly before the Court. But then, when the opinion was in page proof, he struck out the words enclosed in parentheses, leaving a statement of considerable ambiguity. With this revision, Campbell accommodated his opinion in some degree to that of the Chief Justice. That is, he avoided an open dissent from Taney's holding on the plea in abatement. So a survey of the individual opinions does not indicate that Taney was speaking only for a minority of the Court when he declared, "The plea in abatement is necessarily under consideration." Indeed, the contrary seems true, particularly when we consider the words of Grier.

But for the confusion caused by the plea in abatement, Taney probably would have had little trouble getting the support of a clear-cut majority for his ruling against Negro citizenship. As it was, only two justices (Wayne and Daniel) expressly endorsed the ruling, and two others (McLean and Curtis) expressly dissented from it. The four remaining justices offered no opinions on the issue and can be counted either way, as we have seen. But instead of asking how many justices are recorded as agreeing with Taney's ruling against Negro citizenship, let us ask how many are recorded as *believing* that the Court had ruled against Negro citizenship. The answer is "five." This number includes the two dissenters, McLean and Curtis, both of whom realized, as so many historians have not, that only if the Court did so rule was there any basis for asserting that the decision on the Missouri Compromise was extrajudicial. More than one scholar has noted with some puzzlement that this evidence contradicts the standard box score. "How is it," one of them asks, "if only three of the judges held that no Negro could be a citizen, that five of the judges could, in their opinions, speak of this question as having been 'decided' by the Court?" The simplest explanation of the discrepancy would seem to be that on this point, at least, the standard box score is unreliable.

In summary, the opinion of the Court declared that Negroes were not citizens; this ruling was neither expressly endorsed nor expressly challenged by a majority of justices; but a majority did apparently regard the ruling as authoritative. Thus the evidence seems to support the unorthodox view that Taney's ruling was indeed the Court's decision on the subject of Negro citizenship.

If the court did authoritatively decide that Negroes were not citizens, then we must seriously consider the possibility that it had no right to proceed further and examine the facts of the case. Instead, it has often been asserted, the case at that point should have been returned to the circuit court with the order that it be dismissed for lack of jurisdiction.

The Republican cry of *obiter dictum*, raised in 1857 and inspired by the two dissenting justices, has echoed persistently down through the years. But the words themselves are somewhat misleading, and the charge no longer carries much conviction in the face of scholarly judgment to the contrary. The phrase *obiter dictum* is ordinarily used to describe an opinion offered more or less in passing on some point of law that is not at issue in the case before the court. Very often, the point is one that has not been argued by counsel or discussed in conference. These criteria obviously do not fit the Court's ruling on the Missouri Compromise restriction. McLean, Curtis, and others like them were in fact accusing the Court of indulging in another kind of improper behavior—that of reviewing the Dred Scott case on its merits after having decided that the federal courts had no jurisdiction.*

---

* In the view of many legal experts, *"dictum"* may be appropriate to describe this kind of extrajudicial behavior. It is worth noting, however, that neither McLean nor Curtis used the term. McLean declared that the Court's rulings on the merits were "of no authority." Curtis said that they were "not binding."

What the accusation ignores or rejects is Taney's contention that throughout the whole of his opinion he was canvassing the question of jurisdiction. His line of reasoning took advantage of the peculiar circularity of the case. That is, in order to bring suit, Dred Scott had to affirm that he was a citizen of Missouri, which meant assuming that he was a free man. But if it should be determined from the facts that he remained a slave, this would mean that he was never a citizen and had no right to bring suit in the first place. Thus Taney, after having held that Scott could not be a citizen because he was a Negro, proposed to demonstrate also that Scott could not be a citizen because he was still a slave. He therefore proceeded to examine the facts of the case. In doing so, he was not, technically, turning to the case on its merits, but rather still pursuing the question of jurisdiction and "fortifying" his decision on it. Such reinforcement was especially appropriate in the Dred Scott case because of the confusion surrounding the plea in abatement. At any rate, the question now under consideration is what the Court decided, not whether its decision was sound. In this instance, a conclusive answer seems to emerge from the record. The mandate to the circuit court, it must be remembered, ordered dismissal of the suit *for want of jurisdiction.* One must assume that this mandate had the support of a majority of the Supreme Court. But how was that majority formed? Four justices held that the circuit court had lacked jurisdiction, but their reasons varied—because Scott was a Negro (Daniel), because Scott was a slave (Campbell), and for both reasons (Taney and Wayne). Three justices favored a decision on the merits (Nelson for affirming the lower court's decision; McLean and Curtis for reversing it). Grier indicated a willingness either to deny jurisdiction or to affirm the previous judgment, thus supporting both Taney and Nelson. Catron said nothing explicitly on the subject, but his final sentence permits placing him with Campbell: "I concur with my brother judges that the plaintiff, Scott, is a slave, and was so when this suit was brought." Thus the majority supporting disposal of the case on jurisdictional grounds reached agreement along the two different routes marked out by Taney. In order to speak for the majority, it was necessary for him to demonstrate that Scott was doubly not a citizen—*both* because he was a Negro and because he was a slave.

It therefore appears that none of the major rulings in Taney's opinion can be pushed aside as unauthoritative. The charge that one of them was extrajudicial does not stand up under close scrutiny, and the evidence indicates that in each of the rulings he did present the opinion of the Court. On this latter point, something further must be said, however. The whole argument over "what the Court really decided" has been in one important respect merely an academic exercise. For there can be no doubt that Taney's opinion was accepted as the opinion of the Court by its critics as well as its defenders. In all branches of government and in popular thought, the "Dred Scott decision" came to mean the opinion of the Chief Justice. As a matter of historical reality, the Court decided what Taney declared that it decided. This places only the stamp of legitimacy on his opinion, however. Whether it was based on sound law, accurate history, and valid logic is another question, still to be considered.

≈ 7 ≈

The Opinion of the Court

Historians have been preoccupied with counting noses to determine "what the Court really decided" in the Dred Scott case, and with evaluating the charge of *"obiter dictum"* leveled against the Court's most important pronouncement. Scholarly interest, in short, has centered on the question of how much of Taney's opinion was authoritative. Systematic analysis of the content of the opinion is remarkably scarce and largely limited to contemporary critiques published in 1857 or soon thereafter. Yet the Taney opinion is, for all practical purposes, the Dred Scott decision and therefore a historical document of prime importance. Consequences attributed to the decision are actually consequences of the opinion. And it was because of Taney's opinion that the Dred Scott decision constituted a landmark in the history of judicial review and cast the Supreme Court in a new role as the arbiter of current political controversy. Furthermore, the opinion can be read as a sectional credo no less revealing than Lincoln's House-Divided speech or a series of Greeley editorials. It is not only a statement of southern assumptions and arguments but also an expression of the southern mood—fearful, angry, and defiant—in the late stages of national crisis.

The fifty-five pages of Taney's opinion, as printed in Howard's *Reports,* were apportioned approximately as follows:

Introductory summary of the litigation	1 page
Plea in abatement	3 pages
Negro citizenship	24 pages
Propriety of reviewing facts of the case	4 pages
Territorial question	21 pages
Comity question (Scott in Illinois)	1 page
Criticism of suit as improper	1 page

The amount of attention given to the territorial issue was to be expected. More surprising are the number of pages devoted to proving that Negroes were not citizens and, in contrast, the brevity of the argument on the comity question. But to Taney, a Marylander, the status of free blacks was a matter of critical importance, and on the comity issue he was apparently allowing for the more elaborate treatment by Nelson.

Taney, in deciding that the plea in abatement was before the Court, based his ruling on the limited nature of federal court jurisdiction and on the inclusiveness of appellate review by writ of error. The principal argument of Montgomery Blair, echoed by Justices Catron and McLean, had been that Sanford, by pleading over to the merits after failing in his plea to jurisdiction, waived his right to raise the jurisdictional issue again. Taney insisted, however, that the principle of waiver had been drawn from the common law of England and the various states, which did not govern pleadings in the courts of the United States. The record, when it came before the appellate court, "must show, affirmatively, that the inferior court had authority, under the Constitution, to hear and determine the case." If the averment of citizenship was challenged by a plea in abatement, that challenge likewise became a part of the record. And a writ of error "always brings up to the superior court the whole record of the proceedings in the court below."

On this technical question, Taney had the support not only of Wayne and Daniel but also of Curtis, who demonstrated that under the law of Congress regulating appellate procedure, lower federal courts were not intended to be "the final judges of their own jurisdiction in civil cases." Furthermore, as Curtis insisted, it is doubtful that Sanford's pleading over to the merits actually constituted a waiver of the jurisdictional issue; for waiver implies consent, and Sanford had no choice but to plead over.

Taney's argument, reinforced by that of Curtis, seems convincing, and the Court in subsequent years reaffirmed its duty to examine the jurisdiction of the lower court whenever such jurisdiction was not plain and unchallenged on the face of the record. But the issue involves something more than the technicalities of pleading. It also raises a question about the role of the Supreme Court in the American judicial system. The Court's primary function is not to see that justice is done to individuals such as Dred Scott and John Sanford, but rather, in the process of deciding a limited number of cases, to lay down the general lines of interpretation for the instruction of other federal courts and, to some degree, of state courts as well. Thus the rulings of the Supreme Court affect the disposition of countless cases that it never hears, and the Constitution, laws, and treaties of the United States are interpreted and applied with some consistency throughout the nation. Now, the question of whether a Negro could be a citizen was clearly the kind of legal question that deserved the Court's attention. It was not a matter that could be left permanently to the decision of a lower federal court. Taney's determination to review the plea in abatement therefore appears to have been not only technically sound but in accordance with the broader functional responsibilities of his Court. At the same time, in insisting upon consideration of the citizenship question, he produced a large amount of technical confusion that seriously weakened the force of his ruling on the Missouri Compromise.

2

To the Negro citizenship issue, then, Taney devoted some 44 per cent of his entire opinion. In his argument he returned to what he had written twenty-five years earlier about the status of blacks in American society. As Jackson's attorney general, it will be remembered, he had prepared an opinion declaring that the African race was a "degraded class" not intended to be embraced in any provisions of the Constitution except those dealing with slavery. Now he found that he could use the Dred Scott case to vindicate his extreme views at length and graft them authoritatively onto American constitutional law.

But there was more involved than personal conviction. Free Negroes, as a category, had not been objects of great concern during the first years of the American republic. Laws excluding them from the suffrage and from other privileges, like laws discriminating against women, reflected the dominant view of the order of creation and were not drafted as solutions to pressing social problems. Long before 1857, however, free Negroes had become a serious social problem in the South, where they were regarded as a disturbing element among the slave population, and southerners had grown increasingly sensitive about any suggestion of federal interference with their slave system or their racial arrangements. Taney was determined to protect the South by separating the Negro race absolutely from the federal Constitution and from all the rights that it bestowed, thus leaving the states in complete control of black men, whether free or slave.

The question before the Court, it should be borne in mind, was whether Dred Scott, if he were a free Negro, could be regarded as a citizen of Missouri, at least to the extent of being eligible to bring suit in a federal court under the diverse-citizenship clause. Judge Wells, in the circuit court, had held simply that any resident capable of owning property was a citizen in that respect. For Taney, however, it was not enough to settle such a limited issue. He began by redefining the problem:

> The question is simply this: Can a negro, whose ancestors were imported into this country and sold as slaves, become a member of the political community formed and brought into existence by the Constitution of the United States, and as such become entitled to all the rights, and privileges, and immunities, guaranteed by that instrument to the citizen. One of which rights is the privilege of suing in a court of the United States in the cases specified in the Constitution.

Taney thus shifted the focus of inquiry from state citizenship to federal citizenship, and he made the right to bring suit in federal courts dependent upon the confirmation of *all* rights enjoyed under the federal Constitution.

To be a citizen, said the Chief Justice, was the same thing as being one of the "sovereign people" of the United States, and at the time of the Constitutional Convention, Negroes had not been regarded as "constituent members of this sovereignty."

> On the contrary, they were at that time considered as a subordinate and inferior class of beings, who had been subjugated by the dominant race, and, whether emancipated or not, yet remained subject to their authority, and had no rights or privileges but such as those who held the power and the Government might choose to grant them.

Here we are introduced to a fundamental assumption underlying Taney's argument, summed up in the words, "whether emancipated or not." All blacks, according to his view, stood on the same ground. Emancipation made no difference. The status of the free Negro was fixed forever by the fact that he or his ancestors had once been enslaved.

Before the adoption of the Constitution, Taney continued, every state had the right "to confer on whomsoever it pleased the character of a citizen." But this character "was confined to the boundaries of the State, and gave him no rights or privileges in other States beyond those secured to him by the laws of nations and the comity of States." Somehow, in writing these mistaken words, Taney had managed to overlook the fourth Article of Confederation, which declared: "The free inhabitants of each of these states (paupers, vagabonds and fugitives from justice excepted) shall be entitled to all privileges and immunities of free citizens in the several states."

The right of a state to confer citizenship on any class of person remained intact after 1789, said the Chief Justice. "Yet he would not be a citizen in the sense in which that word is used in the Constitution of the United States, nor entitled to sue as such in one of its courts, nor to the privileges and immunities of a citizen in the other States. The rights which he would acquire would be restricted to the State which gave them." Nevertheless, the Constitution did make a significant change, Taney declared:

> It gave to each citizen rights and privileges outside of his State which he did not before possess, and placed him in every other State upon a perfect equality with its own citizens as to rights of person and rights of property; it made him a citizen of the United States.

In this passage, Taney referred to the privileges-and-immunities clause of the Constitution as though it were something brand new, giving a citizen rights "which he did not before possess." Again it is clear that he had forgotten about the equivalent clause in the Articles of Confederation. There was method in his historical inaccuracy, however; for Taney was determined to associate the privileges-and-immunities clause with United States citizenship. And national citizenship, in his view, did not exist under the Articles. It was created by the Constitution. His purpose was clearly revealed when he undertook to restate the question before the Court. It was, he asserted, whether a single state, by endowing a Negro with citizenship, could thereby "make him a citizen of the United States, and endue him with the full rights of citizenship in every other State without their consent." The Court, he continued, had decided that an affirmative answer to this question could not be maintained. "And if it cannot, the plaintiff in error could not be a citizen of the State of Missouri, within the meaning of the Constitution."

The crucial phrase here, already used twice before, was "within the meaning of the Constitution." Taney had fashioned *two different kinds of state citizenship*. One, existing under the Articles and continuing under the Constitution, was entirely within the control of the states, but it qualified no one for the extraterritorial rights and privileges guaranteed by the Constitution. The second kind of state citizenship, created by the Constitution, embraced only those persons who were also citizens of the United States (that is, part of the "sovereign people"), and they alone were covered by the privileges-and-immunities clause or had the right to bring suit under the diverse-citizenship clause.

By conjuring up a special kind of state citizenship that was "within the meaning of the Constitution," Taney converted the question of whether Dred Scott was a citizen of Missouri into the question of whether he was a citizen of the United States. For, as he used the phrase, state citizenship "within the meaning of the Constitution" was virtually synonymous with federal citizenship. In addition, Taney demonstrated to his own satisfaction that no state could, by virtue of laws passed after the adoption of the Constitution, admit any new classes of persons to citizenship of the kind that enjoyed the protection of that instrument. Only Congress could do so, under its exclusive power over naturalization. So any state laws conferring citizenship on Negroes after 1789 were irrelevant. They could not and did not make such persons state citizens "within the meaning of the Constitution."

The Chief Justice did acknowledge that all persons "who were at the time of the adoption of the Constitution recognized as citizens in the several States, became also citizens of this new political body." This would seem to mean that some blacks, recognized as citizens by their states at the time of the Revolution, acquired national citizenship in 1789. Not so, however. Having earlier concluded that Negroes had never been citizens of the United States because they were not a part of the sovereign people who made the Constitution, Taney now asserted that Negroes were not state citizens at the time of the Revolution (no matter what the states themselves may have said about it) because they did not belong to the sovereign people for whom the Declaration of Independence was written. The basic reasons were the same, and so Taney's argument repeated itself. "It is difficult at this day," he wrote, "to realize the state of public opinion in relation to that unfortunate race, which prevailed in the civilized and enlightened portions of the world at the time of the Declaration of Independence, and when the Constitution of the United States was framed and adopted."

> They had for more than a century before been regarded as beings of an inferior order, and altogether unfit to associate with the white race, either in social or political relations; and

so far inferior, that they had no rights which the white man was bound to respect; and that the negro might justly and lawfully be reduced to slavery for his benefit. He was bought and sold, and treated as an ordinary article of merchandise and traffic, whenever a profit could be made by it. This opinion was at that time fixed and universal in the civilized portion of the white race.

One clause in the above paragraph inspired an outburst of anger and recrimination that in the end redounded to Taney's advantage. His statement that Negroes "had no rights which the white man was bound to respect" was part of his analysis of the state of public opinion at the time of the founding of the Republic. He did not say that such a view still prevailed in 1857, but many Republican newspapers—which were accused of taking the statement out of context—gave the impression that he did. As a consequence, he is often pictured as a victim of partisan misrepresentation. "By the brazen propagation of this lie the country was long deceived," writes one constitutional historian, "and the prejudices and passions aroused against the Court and its decision were due far more to Taney's alleged statement than to the point of law decided by him." Yet Republicans were not entirely wrong in regarding the clause as a fair representation of the whole decision. For if Negroes in 1789 had no rights that white men were bound to respect, and if, as Taney maintained, they had acquired no rights since that time "within the meaning of the Constitution," then their condition remained substantially unchanged, from the viewpoint of a federal judge. In 1857, they still had no rights under the Constitution that a white person was bound to respect.

Moreover, the furor over this one clause has diverted attention from the shortcomings of the entire paragraph in which it appears. The question under consideration at this point, as formulated by Taney himself, was whether *free* Negroes possessed *state citizenship* in the period from *1776 to 1789*. Yet the Chief Justice persisted in his refusal to regard free Negroes as a category of persons distinct from slaves. Punishment for crime aside, they could not be "justly and lawfully" hunted down and reduced to slavery in the African manner, or be "treated as an ordinary article of merchandise." Even slaves had some rights at law before 1789, and free Negroes had many more. In some respects, such as property rights, a black man's status was superior to that of a married white woman. He could marry, enter into contracts, purchase real estate, bequeath property, and, most pertinently, seek redress in the courts. The effect of Taney's statement was to place Negroes of the 1780s—even free Negroes—on the same level, legally, as domestic animals.

Just as he failed to concentrate on free Negroes as a class, although they were presumably the subject of his inquiry, so Taney also refused to confine his attention to the relevant period of time, 1776-1789, for determining whether free Negroes were state citizens before the Constitution went into effect. Except for a Connecticut law of 1774 requiring Negroes to carry passes when they traveled, and a Massachusetts law of 1786 forbidding miscegenation, his citations were to colonial legislation and to state laws passed in the nineteenth century. In the latter instances, his logic was peculiar, to say the least. Having earlier held that no state law passed after 1789 could make a Negro a citizen "within the meaning of the Constitution," he now cited state laws passed after 1789 as part of his proof that Negroes were not citizens *before* the adoption of the Constitution.

Seldom in his argument did Taney stick to the subject of state citizenship. Instead of examining state laws and constitutions of the Confederation period to see whether the word "citizen" was used in such a way as to include or exclude free Negroes, he merely cited various discriminatory acts as evidence that Negroes were regarded as "beings of an inferior order and altogether unfit to associate with the white race." More than anything else, he cited laws against interracial marriage. Such legislation did, of course, spring from the dominant assumption of black inferiority and did contribute to the social degradation of the Negro. But in legal terms, it can scarcely be regarded as having marked the limits of citizenship. For miscegenation laws placed restrictions on both white and black races, with punishments for both parties when a violation occurred. The fact that laws of this kind remained common and in force long after the ratification of the Fourteenth Amendment is perhaps the best indication that Americans did not associate them with citizenship.

In the midst of his citations of colonial and state laws discriminating against the Negro, Taney also discussed the Declaration of Independence and the Constitution. Both documents seem irrelevant to an examination of *state* citizenship before 1789, but his purpose was to show that the public attitude toward Negroes in the early years of American independence made it impossible to believe that they could have been regarded as citizens.

The language of the Declaration of Independence, said Taney, was "conclusive" on the subject. Then he proceeded to argue that the language did not really mean what it plainly said. Jefferson's self-evident truths "would seem to embrace the whole human family," but it was "too clear for dispute that the enslaved African race were not intended to be included." Otherwise, "the conduct of the distinguished men who framed the Declaration of Independence would have been utterly and flagrantly inconsistent with the principles they asserted." The Chief Justice, it should be noted, ignored the obvious fact that the opening generalizations in the Declaration were statements of aspiration for mankind, not descriptions of its condition. Yet, even if it is true that the words "all men are created equal" were written and endorsed with fingers crossed for slavery, Taney was manifestly up to his old trick of lumping free blacks with slaves. What seems "too clear for dispute" is that the language of the Declaration of Independence is utterly inconclusive as an indication of whether free Negroes were or were not state citizens prior to the adoption of the Constitution.

As for the Constitution, Taney continued, it contained two clauses that pointed "directly and specifically to the negro race as a separate class of persons" and indicated clearly that they were not regarded as "a portion of the people or citizens of the Government then formed." The clauses to which he referred were those dealing with the African slave trade and the recovery of fugitive slaves. "And these two provisions show conclusively," he declared, "that neither the description of persons therein referred to, nor their descendants, were embraced in any of the other provisions of the Constitution." Now, although the purposes of both clauses were clear, neither was in fact phrased in such a way as to refer exclusively to Negro slaves. And there was certainly nothing in them affecting the *descendants* of slaves, unless those descendants were slaves themselves. The Fugitive Slave Act, for example, had no legal bearing on the legal status of free Negroes. Except in the thinking of Roger B. Taney, who brushed aside free Negroes with the casual remark that they were few in number at the time of the Constitutional Convention and were in any case "regarded as part of the slave population rather than the free."

Thus Taney revealed again and again his determination to treat emancipation as legally meaningless and to mix free blacks with slaves in one legal category based on race. But his very words were belied by a third provision of the Constitution that he conveniently ignored. Article One, Section Two, apportioned representation and direct taxation among the states according to the number of "free persons" in each, plus three-fifths of the number of slaves. Here, then, was a clause of the Constitution that plainly separated slaves from free Negroes, and more than that, it appeared to make the latter a part of the "people" upon whom the federal government was to be founded. It is therefore not surprising that Taney preferred to overlook this clause. It was never mentioned in his whole opinion.

Taney had now demonstrated to his own satisfaction: 1) that Negroes were not state citizens before 1789; 2) that the protection of the Constitution did not extend to Negroes, whom it recognized neither as citizens of the United States nor even as state citizens within its use of the term; and 3) that no state had the power to make Negroes state citizens "within the meaning of the Constitution." Yet his argument rambled on as though he could not find his way to a conclusion, and before long he had let the sectional cat out of the bag. The slaveholding states, he asserted, would never have accepted the Constitution if free Negroes had been embraced in the word "citizens."

> For if they were . . . entitled to the privileges and immunities of citizens, it would exempt them from the operation of the special laws and from the police regulations which they considered to be necessary for their own safety. It would give to

persons of the negro race . . . the right to enter every other
State whenever they pleased, . . . to go where they pleased
at every hour of the day or night without molestation, . . .
and it would give them the full liberty of speech in public and
in private upon all subjects upon which its own citizens might
speak; to hold public meetings upon political affairs, and to
keep and carry arms wherever they went. And all of this would
be done in the face of the subject race of the same color, both
free and slaves, and inevitably producing discontent and in-
subordination among them, and endangering the peace and
safety of the State.

Obviously, Taney was reading southern apprehensions of the
1850s back into the minds of southerners in 1787, forgetting his
earlier assertion that free Negroes were then so few in number
that they "were not even in the minds of the framers of the Constitution." What the Chief Justice desperately feared was that if
the Negro were recognized as a citizen under the diverse-
citizenship clause, he would have a firm basis for claiming the
rights of a citizen under the privileges-and-immunities clause,
and there lay a more serious threat to southern security.

Taney, it should be noted, repeatedly shifted the focus from
the diverse-citizenship clause, where it belonged, to the privileges-and-immunities clause, which was irrelevant to the case.
He ignored Judge Wells's simple formula for determining citizenship under the former clause (residence and the capacity to
own property) and instead persisted in treating the word "citizen" as one of fixed and precise meaning, regardless of context.
This was directly contrary to the Taney Court's interpretation
when the citizenship of corporations, rather than the citizenship
of Negroes, had been the issue. As pointed out on an earlier
page, Taney in 1839 had ruled that corporations were not entitled to the rights and protections of citizenship under the
privileges-and-immunities clause. Five years later, however, the
Court had declared a corporation to be "within the meaning of
the law, a citizen of the state which created it, and where its
business is done, for all the purposes of suing and being sued."
Citizenship at least to the extent of having access to federal
courts for interstate suits—this was exactly the status that Judge

Wells had accorded to Dred Scott, but Taney would have none of it.

Further along in his meandering argument, Taney's attention was at last drawn to the clause in the Articles of Confederation that he had previously overlooked and contradicted. Earlier, he had asserted that the privileges-and-immunities clause of the Constitution gave each citizen rights "outside of his State which he did not before possess." Now, without going back to correct his error, he noted that the Articles contained a "similar" clause, using, however, the words "free inhabitants" instead of "citizens" at one point. This terminology would, he conceded, "in the generality of its terms . . . certainly include one of the African race who had been manumitted."

> But no example, we think, can be found of his admission to all the privileges of citizenship in any State of the Union after these Articles were formed. . . . And, notwithstanding the generality of the words "free inhabitants," it is very clear that, according to their accepted meaning in that day, they did not include the African race, whether free or not.

So black inhabitants, even if free, were not free inhabitants, and the fact that some rights had been denied them meant that they had no rights at all!

Another statement in this passage illustrates Taney's chronic inability to get the facts straight. Speaking of the privileges-and-immunities clause of the Constitution, he said that by the intention of the framers, "this privilege was about to be placed under the protection of the general government, and the words expounded by its tribunals, and all power in relation to it taken from the State and its courts." In fact, there is no evidence whatever that federal courts were intended to be the sole interpreters and enforcers of the privileges-and-immunities clause. The clause did provide the basis for the appeal of decisions from state courts to the Supreme Court. But it did not prevent state courts from interpreting the clause in decisions that might be intermediate or might be final if there were no appeal to the Supreme Court. Furthermore, state courts *had* actually set forth interpretations of the clause in a number of significant decisions before 1857, and Taney *had cited* one of them just a few pages earlier in his opinion.

Still not ready to leave the subject, Taney next turned to federal legislation for evidence that Negroes were never intended to be citizens. He cited three laws, ignoring others that did not suit his purpose. First there was the act of 1790 regulating naturalization and confining that privilege to aliens of the white race. No doubt the statute reflected the racial attitudes of the time, but it in no way clarified or impinged upon the status of free American Negroes. In fact, it could be regarded as expressing a determination to have *no more* Negro citizens besides those already present in the United States.

Taney also cited the act passed in 1792 requiring enrollment in the militia of every "free able-bodied white male citizen." But this phrasing tended to contradict his whole argument, as Taney himself inadvertently made clear. "The word 'white'," he wrote, "is evidently used to exclude the African race, and the word 'citizen' to exclude unnaturalized foreigners." Exactly! If free Negroes were nowhere at that time considered to be citizens, as Taney insisted, the word "white" would have been unnecessary. The word "citizen" should have been enough to exclude both aliens *and* Negroes.

The third law cited by Taney restricted employment on American ships to "citizens of the United States" and "persons of color, natives of the United States." Here, the phraseology did indeed plainly imply that Negroes were not part of the national citizenry. But this statute was enacted in 1813, and Taney had already undercut its value by stressing the fact that the other two laws were passed soon after the drafting of the Constitution when many of the framers were sitting in Congress. Elsewhere, Taney insisted that the Constitution "must be construed now as it was understood at the time of its adoption." A law passed in 1813 was scarcely best evidence of what the word "citizen" meant in 1789.

Taney then turned to the policies of the federal executive branch. In 1821, he said, Attorney General William Wirt had ruled that "free persons of color were not citizens." Quite recently, he added, that ruling had been confirmed by Attorney General Caleb Cushing, with the result that Negroes could not obtain passports as citizens of the United States. For whatever it might be worth, the general tendency of federal executive rulings had indeed been unfavorable to Negro citizenship. Yet Taney overstated his case. He misrepresented Wirt's opinion, which, by implication, actually left room for Negroes to become United States citizens through equality of treatment by their own states. As for passports, they had sometimes been issued and sometimes been denied to Negroes. In any case, the opinions of the attorneys general carried no authority of a judicial nature. Their status was that of learned argument, not precedent.

Approaching the conclusion of this part of his opinion, Taney repeated his pronouncement excluding Negroes, free and slave, from all rights and protections guaranteed in the Constitution:

> The only two provisions which point to them and include them, treat them as property, and make it the duty of the Government to protect it; no other power, in relation to this race, is to be found in the Constitution; and as it is a Government of special, delegated powers, no authority beyond these two provisions can be constitutionally exercised. The Government of the United States had no right to interfere for any purpose but that of protecting the rights of the owner, leaving it altogether with the several States to deal with this race, whether emancipated or not, as each State may think justice, humanity, and the interests and safety of society require. The States evidently intended to reserve this power exclusively to themselves.

There, in one astounding paragraph is the proslavery Constitution, with "property" substituted for "persons," with free Negroes undifferentiated from slaves, with all antislavery "interference" proscribed and proslavery interference required. From the implied recognition of slavery in the Constitution and from the limited protection extended to the institution in the fugitive-slave clause, Taney derived a racial categorization, permanent and inflexible, that appears nowhere on the face of the document. In holding that free Negroes had no rights whatever under the Constitution, he denied them status not only as citizens but as persons. For instance, a Negro would not need to be a citizen to claim the protection of the Fifth Amendment, which declares that no *person* shall be deprived of life, liberty, or property without due process of law. Whether the Fugitive Slave Act of 1850 violated this and other procedural guarantees is a matter of controversy, but the point is that Taney proposed to settle the issue simply by excluding Negroes as a race from all constitutional rights, even those extended to *persons*. This is one more manifestation of his resolve to plug every loophole in the southern defense.

"No one, we presume, supposes," Taney continued, "that any change in public opinion or feeling, in relation to this unfortunate race . . . should induce the court to give to the words of the Constitution a more liberal construction in their favor than they were intended to bear when the instrument was framed and adopted." To do so "would abrogate the judicial character of this court, and make it the mere reflex of the popular opinion or passion of the day." The disingenuousness of this passage is too evident. Taney had repeatedly used evidence of unfavorable treatment of the Negro since 1789 to bulwark his argument, including a very recent opinion of the Attorney General. But he rejected as irrelevant any evidence of more favorable treatment after that date.

Summing up, Taney cited "the language of the Declaration of Independence and of the Articles of Confederation" (in both instances he insisted that the language did not mean what it said). He cited the "plain words of the Constitution" (which he made plain by virtual judicial amendment); the laws of Congress and state legislatures (actually, an unrepresentative selection of such laws, frequently misinterpreted); and the "uniform action" of the executive department (rendered uniform by ignoring every exception). All of these things, "concurring together," led to the same conclusion. "And," he declared in his best *ex cathedra* tone, "if anything in relation to the construction of the Constitution can be regarded as settled, it is that which we now give to the word 'citizen' and the word 'people'."

And upon a full and careful consideration of the subject,
the court is of opinion that, upon the facts stated in the plea
in abatement, Dred Scott was not a citizen of Missouri within
the meaning of the Constitution of the United States, and not
entitled as such to sue in its courts; and, consequently, that the
Circuit Court had no jurisdiction of the case, and that the
judgment on the plea in abatement is erroneous.

3

At this point, according to his critics, the Chief Justice could and
should have remanded the case to the lower court with instructions to dismiss it for want of jurisdiction. Instead, he proceeded
to take up the substantive issue of whether Dred Scott had become free by virtue of his residence in Illinois or at Fort Snelling.
Taney justified his procedure in a four-page passage (much of
which was rebuttal to Justice Curtis), arguing that he was not
going to the merits of the case but rather offering a second reason for dismissal on jurisdictional grounds.

Of course the legal justification for continuing on was not
Taney's real reason for doing so. His strategy clearly reflected
his determination to rule on the constitutionality of the Missouri
Compromise restriction. There were two questions requiring attention, he said. First, was Dred Scott free by reason of his stay
in federal territory where slavery had been forbidden? Second,
was he free by reason of his removal into a free state? "We proceed," said Taney, "to examine the first question." But Scott's
residence in Illinois, it will be remembered, had preceded his
residence at Fort Snelling. Taney was taking up the two questions in reverse chronological order and in this way avoiding a
serious problem. For if he had first considered the effect of
Scott's residence in Illinois, it would have been difficult to ex-
plain why the same reasoning should not apply to Scott's residence in the federal territory, making it unnecessary to examine
the constitutionality of the Missouri Compromise restriction.
That was precisely how Justice Nelson had fashioned his opin-

ion. But Taney, with a different purpose in mind, went directly to
the territorial issue and the storm center of controversy.

The Chief Justice began his discussion of the territorial question by dismissing as irrelevant the one clause of the Constitution in which the word "territory" appears—the part of Article
Four, Section Three, authorizing Congress "to dispose of and
make all needful rules and regulations respecting the territory or
other property belonging to the United States." A very narrow
interpretation of this passage, developed by certain Democratic
spokesmen, had been echoed in Senator Geyer's argument as
counsel for Sanford. The gist of the interpretation was that the
territory clause referred only to federal ownership and disposal
of public land, that it conferred no power to govern the territories, and that such power must be implied from some other
part of the Constitution. Taney concurred in this view but proposed to add an even more severe limitation. The clause affected
only the land already owned or claimed by the United States in
1789, he declared. In all areas subsequently acquired, such as
Louisiana, it had no force of any kind. "It was a special provision for a known and particular territory. Its purpose was "to
transfer to the new Government the property then held in common by the States . . . before their league [meaning the Con-
federation] was dissolved." All of this the Chief Justice deduced
from the language of the clause itself. He quoted no framers of
the Constitution, cited no court decisions in support of his
explication.

It is difficult to take the argument seriously. Of course the
framers of the Constitution had the existing western territory
particularly in mind when they approved Article Four, Section
Three. No doubt they also had existing states particularly in
mind when they approved the provision for regulation of interstate commerce, and they had no notion of encompassing railroad transportation to California or airplane flights to Hawaii.
To say that future acquisitions of territory could not be regulated
under the territory clause because the framers were thinking
only of territory already acquired was absurd. Such a principle,
generally applied, would have made the Constitution useless
long ago. Besides, some of the framers probably did have later

acquisitions in mind. The mouth of the Mississippi, for instance, had already become a coveted place by 1787.

According to Taney, then, the authority of Congress under the territory clause extended only as far west as the Mississippi. In any case, he maintained, it was merely an authority to dispose of public lands, not a general power to govern. The phrasing of the clause was not that "usually employed by statesmen, when they mean to give the powers of sovereignty."

> The words "rules and regulations" are usually employed in the Constitution in speaking of some particular specified power which it means to confer on the Government, and not . . . when granting general powers of legislation. As, for example, the particular and specific power "to regulate commerce"; "to establish an uniform rule of naturalization"; "to coin money and regulate the value thereof."

Actually, every power delegated to Congress by the Constitution is in some way a "specified power," whatever the exact phrasing may be. Thus the power "to establish an uniform rule of naturalization" is no more "particular" or "specific" (and no less plenary) than the power "to establish . . . uniform laws on the subject of bankruptcy." Similarly, the authority to "make all needful rules and regulations respecting the territory," a broad and untrammeled grant of power if there ever was one, is the precise equivalent of authority to "pass all needful laws respecting the territory."

The greatest weakness of the Taney argument, however, was its incompatibility with the context of historical events. For the new United States in the 1780s, the two principal western problems (aside from defense against the Indians) were land disposal and government. The first had been dealt with in the Land Ordinance of 1785; the second, in the Northwest Ordinance of July 13, 1787. In the Convention on August 18, 1787, James Madison proposed additions to the emerging Constitution empowering Congress "to dispose of the unappropriated lands of the United States" and also "to institute temporary governments for new States arising therein." It was these proposals that were converted into the territory clause, and the parallel between what

had already been done under the Articles and what was authorized under the Constitution is plain enough. Madison and the
other framers expected Congress to continue exercising the same
kind of power in the western territory that had produced the two
ordinances, and this included the power to forbid slavery. Then,
in 1789, the Northwest Ordinance, with its antislavery provision,
was re-enacted by a Congress that included many of the framers,
and there was no resistance on constitutional grounds. The conclusion is inescapable that the territory clause simply confirmed
the exercise of power in the territories equivalent to that previously exercised in the famous ordinances.

What the Chief Justice managed to do with his bizarre interpretation of the territory clause was to clear the way for invalidating the Missouri Compromise restriction without challenging
the legitimacy of the more venerable Northwest Ordinance. Under the Articles of Confederation, he asserted, "there was no
Government of the United States in existence." Instead, there
were "thirteen separate, sovereign, independent States, which
had entered into a league or confederation for their mutual protection and advantage . . . But this Confederation had none of
the attributes of sovereignty." Apparently, Taney did not regard
the power to declare war, or the power to make peace, or the
power to enter into treaties, or the power to fix the value of
coins, or the power to regulate relations with the Indians, or the
power to establish post offices, or the power to grant letters of
marque and reprisal, as constituting an "attribute of sovereignty."

The Northwest Ordinance, according to Taney, was therefore
not the work of a United States government created by the Articles of Confederation, but rather the work of the independent
sovereign states acting through the agency of Congress. "We do
not question the power of the States, by agreement among themselves, to pass this ordinance, nor its obligatory force in the Territory," he declared. In short, the Articles Congress, usually pictured as a relatively weak body, actually possessed virtually
unlimited authority because, being too weak to be classified as a
government, it constituted collective state sovereignty in action.
This theory assumed *unanimous* action by the thirteen "independent sovereignties"; Taney conveniently ignored the fact that

the Ordinance of 1787 was passed by the vote of only eight of the thirteen states. Nevertheless, in his phantasmal history of the United States, the Congress under the Articles was mightier than the Congress established by the Constitution. It could prohibit slavery and otherwise exercise "despotic and unlimited power" in the western territory, even though the Articles themselves contained no authorization; whereas a Constitutional Congress possessed no delegated power to govern the territories, in spite of the territory clause, which referred only to land disposal.

At this point, Taney inserted about four pages of rebuttal to McLean, denying that there was any conflict between his opinion and that of John Marshall in *American Insurance Company v. Canter* (1828). "Florida," Marshall had declared, "continues to be a territory of the United States, governed by virtue of that clause in the constitution which empowers congress 'to make all needful rules and regulations respecting the territory or other property belonging to the United States.'" This sentence plainly conflicted with Taney's argument that the clause did not apply to any area acquired after 1789. But Taney simply ignored the sentence and concentrated instead on Marshall's supplementary acknowledgment (made in the interest of consensus) that the right of Congress to govern the territories might be derived from any of several sources. One of these was the "inevitable consequence of the right to acquire territory." Whatever the source of the power, Marshall had added, the possession of it was "unquestioned." Taney agreed that the power itself was unquestionable, but then he closed the question that Marshall had left open. The power to govern the territories was not conferred in the territory clause but could be implied from the right to acquire territory, which in turn would have to be implied from some other power expressly delegated. Double implication was preferred to a plain reading of the Constitution.

Thus Taney took advantage of Marshall's ambiguity to obscure the fact that he was in sharp disagreement with Marshall about the meaning of the territory clause. But another sentence in Marshall's opinion was even more troublesome. Speaking of the territories, he had declared: "In legislating for them, Congress exercises the combined powers of the general, and of a

state government." Now, since no one questioned the power of a
state to prohibit slavery, it would seem that Marshall had clearly
acknowledged the power of Congress to prohibit slavery in the
territories. Not so, said Taney, for Marshall's statement applied
only to legislation regarding the territorial judiciary, which was
the matter at issue in the *American Insurance Company* case.
But it is obvious to anyone reading the passage that the sentence
quoted above was Marshall's generalization about congressional
power in the territories, *from which* he drew his specific conclusion about organization of the judiciary. Taney's interpretation is
untenable.

Having cast aside both the judicial decision and the clause of
the Constitution that seemed most relevant to his subject, the
Chief Justice then unveiled his own explanation of the source
and limits of federal power in the territories. The power to govern, he had already said, proceeded from the power to acquire.
The latter, one might think, should be derived from the power to
make war and enter into treaties. Instead, Taney declared that
the power to acquire territory stemmed solely from the power to
admit new states into the Union. This was a kind of reasoning
analogous to pumping water uphill, but what strikes one most
forcibly is the sharp contrast between Taney's strangulated interpretation of the territory clause and his expansive use of the
state-making clause.

These two clauses lie side by side in the Constitution, com-
prising the whole of Article Four, Section Three, and there can
be no doubt that in the minds of the framers they were closely
linked. Yet the territory clause, according to Taney, applied only
to land already held by the central government in 1789. The
statehood clause, in contrast, applied as well to all land that
might in the future be acquired. More than that, the statehood
clause was the sole authority for any such future acquisitions and
the sole authority for government of the territories. So it is that a
judicial decision can arbitrarily shrink one passage of the Constitution and expand another.

Thus far the Chief Justice had made but scant progress toward his goal of invalidating the Missouri Compromise restriction. He had first denied that Congress possessed any delegated

power to govern the territories, but then had acknowledged that such power nevertheless existed by implication and as a matter of necessity. Just what advantage he saw in this change of derivation is not clear, for the key question remained virtually untouched: Did the power to govern, whatever its source, include the power to prohibit slavery?

For one thing, it was obvious that the necessities of government in a territory could not be provided by Congress within the limits of the powers delegated in Article One, Section Eight. On the contrary, what a frontier community needed primarily was the means of social control ordinarily associated with police powers reserved to the states. Therefore, to say that the Constitution did not empower Congress to exclude slavery from the territories was not a forceful argument; for the same was true of a great many powers that Congress necessarily exercised in the territories.* Strict construction, whatever its utility elsewhere as a curb on congressional authority, simply would not work in the context of the territorial system.

Furthermore, strict construction is essentially a negative concept and a relatively weak foundation for the exercise of judicial review. Something more potent was needed to wipe out a legislative power that had been in use for two-thirds of a century. So Taney began moving toward the conclusion that excluding slavery from the territories was not only unauthorized by the Constitution but positively forbidden by it. The Constitution, he said, conferred no authority to establish permanent colonies in the West or to treat the people there as "mere colonists, dependent upon the will of the general government." Instead, persons migrating to federal territory retained all their constitutional rights and were in this respect "on the same footing" with residents of the various states. The Constitution, that is, followed the flag promptly and absolutely into newly acquired territory.

For example, said the Chief Justice, no one would contend that Congress, in legislating for the territories, could abridge the

---

* Such as provision for the arrest, trial, and punishment of criminals, the enforcement of contracts, the probating of wills, and the solemnizing of marriages. And Congress passed laws forbidding fornication, dueling, and gambling in the territories—so why not laws forbidding slavery?

personal liberties protected by the First Amendment. Similarly, the rights of private property were guarded against congressional invasion by the due-process clause of the Fifth Amendment. "And," Taney continued, "an act of Congress which deprives a citizen of the United States of his liberty or property, merely because he came himself or brought his property into a particular Territory of the United States, and who had committed no offense against the laws, could hardly be dignified with the name of due process of law."

With this emphatic assertion of the principle of "substantive due process," Taney had arrived at the climax of his argument but seemed unaware of the fact. Surprisingly, he did not proceed straightway to the conclusion that the Missouri Compromise restriction was in violation of the Fifth Amendment and therefore void. Instead, he went on giving examples of what Congress could not do in governing the territories, and he made no further mention of the due-process clause.

"The powers over person and property of which we speak," Taney said in summary, "are not only not granted to Congress, but are in express terms denied, and they are forbidden to exercise them." Then, in a digression of only two sentences, he struck a heavy blow at the Douglas version of popular sovereignty:

> And if Congress itself cannot do this—if it is beyond the power conferred on the federal government—it will be admitted, we presume, that it could not authorize a territorial government to exercise them. It could confer no power on any local government, established by its authority, to violate the provisions of the Constitution.

The reasoning here may well have been sound, granting the premises upon which it rested, but whether a territorial legislature could constitutionally forbid slavery was a question that had never arisen in the Dred Scott case. Whatever may be said about the rest of Taney's opinion, this passage was *obiter dictum*, pure and simple. It exemplifies, however, his determination to provide slavery with comprehensive judicial reinforcement.

The Chief Justice had used some nineteen printed pages to arrive at a position that could have been reached in two or three sentences—namely, that the Bill of Rights and other constitutional limitations on the power of Congress were operative in the territories as well as in the states. Next, however, he moved with extraordinary haste through the crucial part of his argument to a conclusion based largely upon a few flat assertions. First, he dismissed the law of nations as authority on the subject. Then there followed a paragraph of summary that requires not only quotation but a certain amount of commentary. For convenience, each sentence has been numbered:

> [1] Now, as we have already said in an earlier part of this opinion, upon a different point, the right of property in a slave is distinctly and expressly affirmed in the Constitution. [2] The right to traffic in it, like an ordinary article of merchandise and property, was guarantied to the citizens of the United States, in every State that might desire it, for twenty years. [3] And the Government in express terms is pledged to protect it in all future time, if the slave escapes from his owner. [4] This is done in plain words—too plain to be misunderstood. [5] And no word can be found in the Constitution which gives Congress a greater power over slave property, or which entitles property of that kind to less protection than property of any other description. [6] The only power conferred is the power coupled with the duty of guarding and protecting the owner in his rights.

Since the Constitution uses neither the word "slavery" nor the word "property" in connection with Negroes, the first sentence is manifestly untrue. Whatever implications may have been understood by the framers, nothing is *expressly* affirmed about slavery as a property right. The second and third sentences constitute the whole of Taney's proof for his assertion in sentence number one, and both are stated in misleading terms. The Constitution permitted, but did not guarantee, continuation of the African slave trade for twenty years. Even this temporary immunity applied only to the original thirteen states and not to the area affected by the Missouri Compromise. Insofar as the slave-trade clause did recognize a "right of property" in slaves, it likewise acknowledged the power of Congress to extinguish that right, eventually in the original states and immediately in the rest of the national domain. As for the fugitive-slave clause, it appears in the section of the Constitution devoted to interstate comity and from its text alone could have been interpreted as an obligation laid solely on the individual states (as with the rendition of fugitives from justice). There is no express "pledge" of assistance from the central government in the recovery of fugitive slaves. If the clause required such intervention, it did so only by implication. The fourth sentence is one of those superfluous reiterations that weaken credibility. It exemplifies Taney's habit of strengthening a dubious argument by declaring it to be an incontestable argument. The fifth sentence, affirming the unexceptionalness and equality of slave property, seems incompatible with the fugitive-slave and slave-trade clauses, which, if they treat slaves as property, treat them as a unique kind of property. The sixth sentence may or may not have been intended merely as an elaboration of sentence number three, on the fugitive-slave clause, but the effect of its broad phrasing was to endorse subsequent southern demands for a comprehensive federal slave code in the territories.

Together, the fifth and sixth sentences of this paragraph constituted a return to the strict-construction approach with which Taney had begun his discussion of the Missouri Compromise restriction. After asserting that slaves were recognized as property by the Constitution, he did not, as one might expect, invoke the due-process clause in defense of property rights against congressional interference. Instead, he contented himself with holding that Congress had been delegated no power to treat property in slaves differently from other property. Nevertheless, he was at last ready to make his historic pronouncement:

> Upon these considerations, it is the opinion of the court that the Act of Congress which prohibited a citizen from holding and owning property of this kind in the territory of the United States north of the line therein mentioned, is not warranted by the Constitution, and is therefore void; and that neither Dred Scott himself, nor any of his family, were made free by being carried into this territory; even if they had been

carried there by the owner, with the intention of becoming a permanent resident.*

"Upon these considerations . . ." What, precisely, did the Chief Justice mean? Was he referring to the preceding paragraph or to the preceding twenty pages? Did the "considerations" include, for instance, his earlier reference to the due-process clause? If so, it is strange that he should have been so unexplicit about it. For, in spite of a general impression to the contrary, Taney never did specifically declare the Missouri Compromise restriction to be a violation of the Fifth Amendment. He did not even say in his conclusion that it was "forbidden" by the Constitution. Instead, he merely held that it was "not warranted by the Constitution," thus ending on a vague note of strict construction.

Here, then, was the historic first instance of judicial invalidation of a major federal statute, with an argument weak in its law, logic, history, and factual accuracy. Taney had directed much of his effort at constriction of the territory clause, and to no purpose; for he did not deny the power of Congress to provide territorial government but instead converted it from a delegated to an implied power. Next, having perhaps realized the difficulty of applying strict construction to an implied power, he shifted from the strategy of demonstrating that Congress lacked constitutional authority over slavery in the territories to the strategy of demonstrating that the exercise of such power was forbidden by the due-process clause. In the end, however, he turned back toward his original strict construction approach, and he never said specifically why the Missouri Compromise restriction was unconstitutional.

4

After disposing of Dred Scott's claim to freedom based on his residence at Fort Snelling, Taney still needed to consider the

---

* This final clause was Taney's only reference to the important question of whether Dred Scott's half-dozen years in free territory constituted "temporary" or "permanent" residence. Taney, by implication, treated it as temporary.

claim based on Scott's two years in Illinois. Here, the Chief Justice merely cited his opinion in *Strader v. Graham,* insisting that everything in that opinion was authoritative and ignoring all the differences between it and the Dred Scott case.

> The slaves had been taken from Kentucky to Ohio, with the consent of the owner, and afterwards brought back to Kentucky. And this court held that their *status* . . . depended upon the laws of Kentucky, when they were brought back into that State, and not of Ohio; and that this court had no jurisdiction to revise the judgment of a State court upon its own laws. This was the point directly before the court, and the decision that this court had not jurisdiction, turned upon it, as will be seen by the report of the case.
>
> So in this case. As Scott was a slave when taken into the State of Illinois by his owner, and was there held as such, and brought back in that character, his *status*, as free or slave, depended on the laws of Missouri, and not of Illinois.

Taney, it will be noted, first restated the doctrine of reversion, and then, perhaps in answer to Justice McLean,* he declared that enunciation of that doctrine in the *Strader* case had been a necessary preliminary to reaching the decision that the Supreme Court had no jurisdiction. But this was untrue. Let us begin with the absurd statement that the Supreme Court "had no jurisdiction to revise the judgment of a State court upon its own laws." Such revising of state court judgments was precisely the work often required of the Supreme Court under the twenty-fifth section of the Judiciary Act of 1789, as exemplified in *McCulloch v. Maryland, Cohens v. Virginia,* and many other leading decisions. The judgment of the Kentucky court in the *Strader* case was indeed immune from revision, but *only* because there was no federal question to give the Supreme Court jurisdiction. Taney, however, transposed cause and effect in order to justify his *Strader* dictum. That is, in reality the decision of the state court proved to be final because the Supreme Court discovered that it had no jurisdiction; but in Taney's looking-glass world,

---

* McLean, in both his *Strader* and *Dred Scott* opinions, said that most of Taney's *Strader* opinion was dictum.

the Supreme Court had no jurisdiction because the state court's decision was final.

Still, whatever the value of the *Strader* decision as precedent, the doctrine of reversion could stand firmly by itself, based as it was upon the principle of state sovereignty and the authority of Story's *Conflict of Laws*. The Chief Justice, it appears, did not say more on the subject because he regarded Nelson's opinion, which was limited to the comity issue, as a kind of supplement to his own.

The opinion concluded with a denunciation of the manner in which the case had come before the Supreme Court. This passage had not been a part of the opinion read orally on March 6. Taney added it later to the page proof. Dred Scott, he said, had brought a similar suit in the Missouri courts, had carried it to the state supreme court, and had lost it there. After that, Scott's only legal recourse was to take the case directly to the United States Supreme Court by writ of error. If he had done so, the writ would have been dismissed for want of jurisdiction—because of the *Strader* precedent and because "the language of the 25th section of the Act of 1789 is too clear and precise to admit of controversy." The plaintiff, Taney continued, did not "pursue the mode prescribed by law," but instead turned to the federal court system and as a consequence was now bringing before the Supreme Court "the same case from the Circuit Court, which the law would not have permitted him to bring directly from the State court."

> And if this court takes jurisdiction in this form, the result . . . is in every respect substantially the same as if it had, in open violation of law, entertained jurisdiction over the judgment of the State court. . . . It would ill become this court to sanction such an attempt to evade the law, or to exercise an appellate power in this circuitous way which it is forbidden to exercise in the direct and regular and invariable forms of judicial proceedings.

Taney's complaint about *Scott v. Sandford* undoubtedly had merit, for the suit amounted to taking an appeal from the highest court of Missouri to the Supreme Court by way of a lower

federal court. Much less plausible, however, and indeed astonishing in some of its implications, was the rationale of his assertion that the Supreme Court would have dismissed an appeal of
Scott v. Emerson.

The law, said the Chief Justice, "would not have permitted"
Scott to bring his suit up directly from the state court. But further than that, the Supreme Court would have been "in open violation of law" if it had entertained jurisdiction in such an appeal. Still further, it was actually "forbidden" to exercise its
appellate power in this manner. Now, what "law," precisely, did
Taney have in mind? Not his own words in *Strader v. Graham,*
one would think; for even if one were to concede their authorita-
tiveness, there is nothing *illegal* about a court's reviewing and
even reversing its previous decisions. Was he referring, then, to
the Judiciary Act of 1789? If so, it all came to the same thing;
for that statute was phrased in the language of authorization,
rather than of prohibition, and only the peculiar gloss of *Strader*
could give it the meaning and force indicated by Taney. The
circular effect of the whole argument is fascinating. The Court
was "forbidden by law" to accept jurisdiction in any case resembling *Strader v. Graham.* Forbidden by what law? Why, by the
Judiciary Act of 1789 as interpreted in *Strader v. Graham!* A few
years later, there would be much discussion in Congress of adding an "unamendable amendment" to the Constitution. Here, in
a sense, was an effort to make a Court decision unreviewable.

According to Taney, then, the federal courts generally had no
power to hear *Scott v. Sandford* because it was an illegitimate
substitute for appealing *Scott v. Emerson;* but at the same time,
the Supreme Court would have had no power (in fact, was "forbidden") to hear *Scott v. Emerson.* For Dred Scott, then, there
was no legitimate access to the Supreme Court, even though his
claim to freedom, unlike that of the slaves in the *Strader* case,
rested in part on federal law.

The excessiveness of the argument and language in this curious addendum may be explained in part by the fact that the
paragraphs were written in the midst of public reaction to the
decision as announced in Taney's oral opinion on March 6. The
abuse heaped upon him would have severely tested anyone's

self-restraint. It would be a mistake to conclude, however, that passion entered the Dred Scott affair at this point. For the fierceness of the northern outcry against Taney's opinion was no more intense than the passionateness with which it had been written. As a historical document, it can be fully understood only if one senses the anger that simmered just below the surface of its flat judicial prose.

Concurrence, Dissent,
and Public Reaction

Except, perhaps, for the dissent of Justice Curtis, which won wide acceptance in Republican circles as the official rejoinder to Taney, none of the other opinions delivered in the Dred Scott case had a significant effect on the course of events. Yet each in its own way reveals something about the nature of the sectional conflict, and, taken together, they exemplify the subtle variations possible in American constitutional thought.

The order in which the opinions were published in Howard's *Reports* did not follow the order of their oral delivery on March 6 and 7, but rather was carefully specified by Taney. First, after his own, he placed Wayne's brief and unqualified concurrence. Then came the Nelson opinion, presumably because it supplemented Taney's with a more extensive treatment of the issue presented by Scott's residence in Illinois. Written as the opinion of the Court and then demoted, it concurred with Taney's opinion on only one major point. Yet the Chief Justice was obviously pleased with what amounted to an emphatic reaffirmation of his *Strader* decision.

The Nelson opinion, holding simply that Dred Scott's status depended entirely on the law of Missouri as interpreted by its highest court, has been treated gently by most historians and seems at first glance to reflect a degree of dispassion in the midst of sectional bitterness. Upon closer scrutiny such an impression dissolves, however. Within the limits that he had set for himself, Nelson leaned toward slavery at every opportunity.

For one thing, while supposedly avoiding the whole controversy over the validity of the Missouri Compromise restriction, Nelson nevertheless remarked in passing: "Many of the most eminent statesmen and jurists of the country entertain the opinion that this provision . . . was not authorized by any power under the Constitution." These were virtually his only words on the subject, and the effect accordingly was halfway endorsement of the proslavery doctrine. Remembering that Nelson's opinion came close to being the official opinion of the Court, one can readily imagine the confusion and excitement that might well have been inspired by this provocative but inconclusive judicial pronouncement on the most inflamed public issue of the age.

Nelson's proslavery bias was also evident in an emphatic declaration on the nature of Dred Scott's residence in Illinois:

> The removal of Dr. Emerson from Missouri to the military posts was in the discharge of his duties as surgeon in the army, and under the orders of his Government. He was liable at any moment to be recalled. . . . In such a case, the officer goes to his post for a temporary purpose, to remain there for an uncertain time, and not for the purpose of fixing his permanent abode. The question we think too plain to require argument.

Thus Nelson's opinion, if it had been the opinion of the Court, would have confirmed the right of an army officer to take a slave into a free state for an unlimited period of time.

And precisely what did Nelson mean when he said that the question of slavery belonged to the separate states, "subject only to such limitations as may be found in the Federal Constitution"? (Taney had made approximately the same statement in *Strader v. Graham*.) As a minimum, he was referring to the recovery of fugitive slaves, but the possible maximum of such limitations on state power was not easy to visualize. That it might well extend to the legitimizing of slavery in the free states would soon be suggested by Abraham Lincoln. That Nelson had more than the minimum in mind is indicated by the curiously mar-

ginal and vaguely menacing comment with which he concluded
his opinion:

> A question has been alluded to, on the argument, namely:
> the right of the master with his slave of transit into or through
> a free State, on business or commercial pursuits, or in the exer-
> cise of a Federal right, or the discharge of a Federal duty,
> being a citizen of the United States, which is not before us.
> This question depends upon different considerations and prin-
> ciples from the one in hand, and turns upon the rights and
> privileges secured to a common citizen of the republic under
> the Constitution of the United States. When that question
> arises, we shall be prepared to decide it.

These words, which may have been comment on a case then in
the New York courts,* would have had much greater impact if
they had come at the conclusion of the official decision in *Dred
Scott v. Sandford;* for they plainly cast doubt on the power of
free states to forbid or restrict any entry of slaves that might be
defined as "temporary." Nelson's opinion, then, though less inflammatory than Taney's, would have aroused anger in the North
on a number of counts if it had been presented as the opinion of
the Court.

Grier, like Wayne, really wrote no opinion. In just a few sentences that appeared fourth in Howard's *Reports,* he concurred
with Nelson's opinion and with Taney's ruling against the constitutionality of the Missouri Compromise restriction. As we have
seen, he also lent welcome support to Taney on the issue of the
plea in abatement by finding a *"prima facie* case of jurisdiction"
which required the Court to decide all questions "properly arising" in the record.

Taney perhaps set the Nelson and Grier documents close to
his own in order to stress the bisectional nature of the Court's
decision. After Grier's statement he placed the remaining opinions of southern justices—Daniel, Campbell, and Catron. Of the
three, only Daniel supported Taney on the plea in abatement.
Campbell announced that he was ignoring the issue. Catron

---

* *Lemmon v. The People* (1852-60).

flatly disagreed with the Chief Justice, and privately he maintained that the entire section of Taney's opinion dealing with Negro citizenship was dictum.

Daniel was accordingly the only one of the three to discuss the question of Negro citizenship, and he reached the same conclusion as Taney but by a shorter path: A slave, being "strictly property," could not be a citizen. Emancipation did not automatically convert a slave into a citizen; for the conferring of citizenship was an act of sovereignty which no slave-owner or other individual could perform. Hence Dred Scott, whether free or not, had never become a citizen and could not bring suit under the diverse-citizenship clause. Like Taney, Daniel was determined to proceed to the merits of the case even though he had already decided against Scott on jurisdictional grounds. He offered no technical justification for doing so, however, but instead bluntly asserted that questions of such "primary interest and magnitude," having been elaborately argued by counsel, should be considered and, if possible, "finally put to rest."

In considering the case on its merits, the three southern justices, unlike Taney, began with the issues presented by Scott's residence in Illinois. Catron was content merely to concur with Nelson, but not until he had in one sentence increased the confusion about the meaning of Nelson's opinion. Referring to the effect of Illinois law on Scott's status, he wrote: "Unless the master becomes an inhabitant of that State, the slaves he takes there do not acquire their freedom; and if they return with their master to the slave State of his domicil, they cannot assert their freedom after their return." It appears that Catron was ignoring the new proslavery radicalism of *Scott v. Emerson* and reaffirming the principles of the old tacit agreement between the sections. Domiciling a slave in a free state worked his emancipation. Temporary residence did not, and Catron regarded Scott's residence in Illinois as temporary.

Daniel and Campbell likewise seemed to treat Scott's residence in Illinois as temporary without being explicit on the point. They and Catron thus compounded the difficulty of discerning just what, if anything, the Court majority contributed to the law of interstate comity as related to slavery. Dred Scott's suit had been based upon an assumption of permanent residence in Illinois, while the principal decisions cited against him, such as *The Slave Grace* and *Strader v. Graham,* dealt with instances of temporary residence. Obviously John Emerson's tour of duty in Illinois constituted a borderline case, but *Rachel v. Walker* provided strong Missouri precedent in Scott's favor. Southern courts for some time had been using the doctrines of reversion and reattachment, largely as a basis for turning aside claims to freedom arising out of temporary residence on free soil. Beginning with *Scott v. Emerson,* however, the Missouri supreme court applied those doctrines to all suits for freedom based upon residence in free territory, no matter how permanent that residence might have been. That is, the court wiped out the distinction between domicile and sojourn, making it irrelevant in Missouri. Against this background, the stand taken by the Supreme Court majority in *Dred Scott v. Sandford* was fraught with confusion. On the one hand, five of the justices indicated a belief that Scott's residence in Illinois was temporary, though only Nelson said so clearly. On the other hand, the opinion of the Court, as delivered by Taney, reaffirmed the principle of reversion and thereby left standing the extremist doctrine of *Scott v. Emerson* as the final word on the subject. Thus there was no clear-cut ruling on whether Scott's residence in Illinois was temporary or permanent.

In their treatments of the territorial question, Daniel, Campbell, and Catron traveled different paths to the same conclusion that the Missouri Compromise restriction was unconstitutional. Daniel, the most passionate of the three in his devotion to slavery, relied partly upon the "common-property" doctrine associated with Calhoun, declaring that Congress as mere agent or trustee could not discriminate against part of the American people in its administration of the territories. Like Taney he insisted that the territory clause referred to the disposal of land and "did not extend to the personal or political rights of citizens or settlers." He went beyond the Chief Justice, however, in asserting that the antislavery clause of the Northwest Ordinance was "*ab initio* void," and that the Constitution, by giving slavery special protection, placed it on higher ground than any other kind of property. Daniel's extremism revealed itself most clearly in the intemperateness of his language, which impugned the motives and intelligence of persons supporting congressional power over slavery in the territories.

Campbell agreed substantially with Taney and Daniel in minimizing the scope and force of the territory clause. He relied heavily upon argument by analogy, stressing American hostility to British imperialism during the era of the Revolution. Americans, he said, had acknowledged British supremacy in the matter of land titles, while insisting that political power must rest on consent of the people. In other words, the distinction between land disposal, as a function of central authority, and government, as an exercise of local right, had been inherent in the very nature of the Revolution. And the Founding Fathers, having just rebelled against the British colonial system, could not possibly have intended that the territory clause should be used to establish an American colonial system. Thus Campbell's argument was based less upon the Calhoun principle of state equality than upon the Douglas principle of territorial self-government. He was the only justice besides Taney who said anything touching on the problem of whether a territorial legislature could prohibit slavery. But unlike the Chief Justice, he concluded that it was a political question: "How much municipal power may be exercised by the people of the Territory, before their admission to the Union, the courts of justice cannot decide."

Campbell made no use of the due-process clause and very little of the common-property doctrine. His principal emphasis was upon strict construction and a resulting absence of federal power. He insisted, for example, that the defining of what constituted property was a prerogative belonging exclusively to the states, and that the United States government must accordingly accept all such definitions without discriminating against any one of them. This meant that a master might take his slave anywhere in the Union without fear of federal interference. Only the sovereign authority of a state could place any impediment in his path. Congress therefore could not deny in the territories those property rights of a slaveholder which, within the states of the Union, it was bound to observe and protect.

Justice Catron was something of a maverick among the southern majority, and it is little wonder that Taney caused his opinion to be published seventh, just ahead of the two dissents. As we have seen, Catron thought that the Court had no right to review the plea in abatement. He also rejected Taney's narrow construction of the territory clause, maintaining that the clause *did* vest Congress with the power to govern in the territories. But the power to govern did not, of and by itself, include the power to prohibit slavery. What determined the extent of congressional authority within the original United States, he declared, were the terms of the land cessions made by the states. Slavery was legally abolished in the Old Northwest because Virginia assented to the Ordinance of 1787, an "engagement" which Congress could not break. But south of the Ohio River, because of the guarantees to North Carolina and Georgia, Congress had no power to legislate against slavery.

Beyond the Mississippi, Catron proceeded, congressional authority was limited by the terms of the Louisiana Purchase. There, under Spain and France, slavery had been lawful, and the treaty with France had guaranteed inhabitants "the free enjoyment of their liberty, property, and the religion which they profess." Congress could not revoke this guarantee, which stood "protected by the Constitution." The Missouri Compromise restriction was therefore void. Catron's view that the treaty of 1803 laid a permanent restriction on the legislative power of Congress was neither original with him nor sound constitutional law. Advanced without much success during the Missouri controversy, the argument would have elevated treaties above statutes virtually to the level of the Constitution. In effect, this would have made the Supreme Court the enforcer of international agreements against the two collateral branches of the federal government. In decisions handed down after the Civil War, the Court upheld the power of Congress to alter or override a treaty.

Not satisfied with just one ground for judgment, Catron also invoked the common-property doctrine as a second reason for the invalidity of the Missouri Compromise restriction. The point, he said, was "not that citizens of the United States shall have equal privileges in the Territories, but the citizen of each State shall come there in right of his State, and enjoy the common property. He secures his equality through the equality of his State." The Missouri Compromise restriction, he concluded, was therefore doubly void—as an invasion of the treaty with France and as a violation of the "most leading feature of the Constitution . . . which secures to the respective States and their citizens an entire equality of rights, privileges and immunities."

As the chart on the next page indicates, the justices who ruled against the constitutionality of the Missouri Compromise restriction produced a variety of reasons for doing so and never agreed completely on any of them. Plainly, too much emphasis has been placed upon the due-process clause. Taney alone mentioned it, and how much his argument rested upon the clause is far from clear. The justices were closer to consensus on three other lines of reasoning: (1) a narrow interpretation of the territory clause, with Catron as the principal exception; (2) Calhoun's common-property doctrine, with Campbell something of an exception; and (3) the insistence that slavery was no different from other property and had the same rights attached to it, with Daniel going further and declaring that slavery was a kind of super-property given special status by the Constitution.

2

The dissenting justices, McLean and Curtis, submitted two of the three longest opinions, constituting about 44 per cent of the total judicial wordage. As a professional performance, Curtis's contribution was more thorough, scholarly, and polished. McLean's opinion, as a consequence, and also in view of his presidential aspirations, has been taken less seriously by historians.

The two men disagreed about whether the plea in abatement was before the Court. McLean, after insisting that it was not, went ahead and discussed the issue of Negro citizenship anyway. His argument lacked coherence, but he seemed to be reaffirming the conclusion of Judge Wells that any free person domiciled in

SLAVERY IN THE TERRITORIES

	TANEY (WAYNE AND GRIER)	DANIEL	CAMPBELL	CATRON
Missouri Compromise restriction is unconstitutional	yes	yes	yes	yes
Extremely narrow interpretation of territory clause	yes	yes	yes	no
Common-property doctrine	refers to	relies on heavily	mentions	relies on partly
Slavery has same rights as other property	uses	has higher standing than other property	uses extensively	uses
Due-process clause	relies on to some extent	no mention	no mention	no mention
Missouri Compromise restriction violates treaty with France	no mention	no mention	no mention	yes
Ordinance of 1787	legal because of unanimous state consent	illegal	legal because of state and territorial consent	valid and unbreakable as a compact
Power of territorial legislature over slavery	denies	no mention	implies that it is a political question	no mention

a state was a citizen of that state for purposes of a suit in a federal court.

Curtis, as we have seen, joined Taney in maintaining that the Court could and should review the plea in abatement. But then, in an extended technical discussion, he set strict limits on the Court's authority to review the question of jurisdiction and Dred Scott's claim to citizenship. In disagreement with Taney, he held that the Court was governed by the common-law rules of pleading; that it could examine no jurisdictional matter not appearing in the plea in abatement; and that the facts presented in the plea must "of themselves" constitute a negative of the averment of citizenship. This highly formalistic line of reasoning had the effect of disqualifying any *inference* drawn from the plea in abatement, as well as any direct evidence drawn from other parts of the record showing that Scott, at the time of filing suit, had been a *slave* and therefore not a citizen (as Taney maintained). The only question before the Court, said Curtis, was that raised literally by the plea in abatement—whether the fact of Scott's African ancestry and the fact that his parents had been slaves were "inconsistent with his own citizenship in the State of Missouri, within the meaning of the Constitution and laws of the United States."

The phrasing here is important, for it indicated that Curtis did not intend to seek his answer in the constitution and laws of Missouri. Instead, he followed Taney in converting the question to one of national citizenship. He cited an opinion of the Marshall Court to the effect that "a citizen of the United States, residing in any State of the Union, is, for purposes of jurisdiction, a citizen of that State." In Curtis's clever and complicated treatment, the Marshall Court formula became a bridge connecting the law of Missouri to the law of those states that had been most favorable to Negro citizenship. His argument ran as follows:

1. According to the Marshall Court formula, nothing in the law of Missouri could deprive Dred Scott of his rights under the diverse-citizenship clause, provided that he was a citizen of the United States and a resident of Missouri at the time of bringing suit.

2. Since his residence had not been controverted, the only

question was whether Scott's African ancestry and slave parentage made him ineligible for United States citizenship.

3. If *any* person of such background could be a United States citizen, Scott had the right to claim citizenship too, since no other reason for excluding him had been advanced in the plea in abatement.

4. United States citizenship antedated the Constitution. This was indicated by the language of Article Two, Section Four, referring to "a citizen of the United States at the time of the adoption of the Constitution."

5. The Confederation was a government of severely limited authority and had been delegated no power "to act on any question of citizenship, or to make any rules in respect thereto." The matter was left entirely in the hands of the states, and thus United States citizenship was synonymous with state citizenship in 1789.

6. Under the Confederation government, free Negroes in five states, being recognized as citizens of their respective states, were also citizens of the United States.°

7. There was nothing in the Constitution which, *proprio vigore,* deprived any class of persons of citizenship possessed at the time of its adoption.

8. The Constitution in fact neither defined citizenship nor invested Congress with any authority to do so, except in regard to naturalization of aliens. Instead, all relevant clauses of the Constitution pointed to the conclusion that "persons born within the several States, who, by force of their respective constitutions and laws, are citizens of the State, are thereby citizens of the United States.

9. The plea in abatement therefore showed no facts inconsistent with Dred Scott's being a United States citizen or a resident of Missouri, entitled to bring suit in federal court.

What all this demonstrated, it should be noted, was not the citizenship of Dred Scott but merely the absence of any disproof of citizenship within the narrow confines of the plea in abate-

---

° The states named by Curtis were New Hampshire, Massachusetts, New York, New Jersey (by their constitutions), and North Carolina (by court decision in *State v. Manuel,* 1838).

ment. Other parts of the record showed clearly that Scott had *not* been born free within a state that recognized Negroes as citizens. The validity of Curtis's conclusion thus depended upon the validity of his technical argument (strenuously contested by Taney) that the Court could not pursue the question of jurisdiction beyond what appeared on the face of the plea in abatement.

Having confirmed Dred Scott's capacity to bring suit against Sanford in a federal court, the two dissenting justices then proceeded to the merits of the case, while denying the right of the Court majority to do so, and indicating an unwillingness to be bound by those parts of the majority opinion that were, in their view, "of no authority." The two men dealt with the substantive issues in different order, but their arguments, as a matter of convenience, can be treated together under three major headings.

1. *Congressional power over slavery in the territories and, specifically, the constitutionality of the Missouri Compromise restriction.* Both McLean and Curtis took the Republican position of interpreting the territory clause broadly as an express and plenary delegation of power to govern. They struck effectively, each in his own way, at the Court majority's view that the clause referred only to land and that the framers of the Constitution made no provision for temporary government of western territory, in spite of the obvious need for it and in spite of the conspicuous example of the Northwest Ordinance. Curtis, in particular, probed the weakness of this argument with an irony that was all the more effective because of its judicial coolness:

> That Congress has some power to institute temporary governments over the Territory, I believe all agree; and, if it be admitted that the necessity of some power to govern the Territory of the United States could not and did not escape the attention of the Convention and the people, and the necessity is so great that, in the absence of any express grant, it is strong enough to raise an implication of the existence of that power, it would seem to follow that it is also strong enough to afford material aid in construing an express grant of power respecting that Territory; and that they who maintain the existence of the power, without finding any words at all in which it is conveyed, should be willing to receive a reasonable interpretation

of language of the Constitution manifestly intended to relate to the Territory, and to convey to Congress some authority concerning it.

Curtis also disposed expertly of Taney's dubious contention that the territory clause had been designed only for land already in the possession of the United States when the Constitution was written. Such a clipped-off interpretation of part of a constitution intended to last indefinitely was contrary, he declared, not only to the language but also to the "nature and purpose of the instrument." Both Curtis and McLean made short work of Taney's argument that the phrase "rules and regulations" had a weaker, more limited meaning than the word "laws." The prime exhibit here was the commerce clause, by virtue of which, Curtis pointed out, Congress "regulated" the conduct of American citizens as far away as China, having "established judicatures with power to inflict even capital punishment within that country."

Of course, all of Taney's straining had come to nothing because he had been compelled to acknowledge that Congress did have the power to organize and govern the territories. The crucial question, then, seemed to be whether slavery was somehow exempt from this acknowledged authority, contrary to the established practice of more than half a century. If so, Curtis said, the exemption should derive from a specific provision of the Constitution, and not from "abstract political reasoning" such as the common-property doctrine, which, though it might well guide legislation, had no legal force in judicial proceedings. He could find just one specific provision of the Constitution alleged to have been violated by the Missouri Compromise restriction. That was the due-process clause of the Fifth Amendment. But the due-process clause, after all, had been "borrowed from Magna Charta," and the principle "existed in every political community in America in 1787." Why, then, had no one discovered at the time that the antislavery provision of the Northwest Ordinance violated Magna Carta? Furthermore, Curtis argued, congressional legislation forbidding slavery in a territory did not result in forfeit of property except as a consequence of disobedience to the law, and this kind of sanction had been common even in the slave states themselves.

2. *The effect of taking a slave into a jurisdiction where slavery was forbidden.* Both dissenters reaffirmed the principle that slavery was entirely a creation of municipal law and had no existence where such law did not give it positive protection. In some American jurisdictions, they added, there was also such a thing as positive *antislavery* law, which operated with a force sufficient to change the status of a slave brought within its reach. The effect was to dissolve completely the old relationship and "terminate the rights of the master." Curtis apparently believed that such a transformation occurred only as a result of more or less permanent residence in a free territory, but McLean seemed vaguely in favor of applying the principle to sojourners as well.

The nature of Emerson's residence in Illinois and at Fort Snelling was crucial. The Court majority, as we have seen, apparently assumed that it was temporary; McLean and Curtis found it sufficiently permanent to be classed with domicile. Neither the justices then nor historians later seem to have been fully aware of the fact, but the two sides were thus arguing from different premises and, to a considerable extent, talking past each other. Arguments and citations of the majority demonstrating that residence other than permanent in a free state or territory left a slave's status unchanged were met by the two dissenters with arguments and citations demonstrating that residence other than temporary made him forever free.

Curtis added, however, that in his opinion certain features of the Dred Scott case made it unnecessary to settle the question of domicile. For one thing, John Emerson had gone to Fort Snelling not only as a citizen but "in a public capacity in the service of the same sovereignty which made the laws." And surely the United States could "govern their own servants, residing on their own territory, over which the United States had the exclusive control." But Curtis laid even heavier emphasis on the fact that at Fort Snelling, with Emerson's consent, Dred Scott had taken a wife. The validity of the marriage could not be contested (since slavery had had no status in Wisconsin Territory), and according to international law it commanded recognition in other jurisdictions. Further than that, Curtis declared, any law of Missouri having the effect of annulling such a lawful marriage would be an impairment of the obligation of contract, forbidden to states by the Constitution. As a consequence, "the consent of the master that his slave, residing in a country which does not tolerate slavery, may enter into a lawful contract of marriage . . . is an effectual act of emancipation."

3. *The effect on Dred Scott's status of his return to Missouri, and the extent to which the law of Missouri, as interpreted by the supreme court of Missouri, was binding on the Supreme Court of the United States.* Both dissenting justices maintained that the emancipation of Scott, by virtue of his residence in a free state and a free territory, had been absolute and irrevocable. They thus rejected the principle of reattachment, and McLean perceptively noted that the principle had not been directly asserted by the Missouri supreme court in *Scott v. Emerson.* Instead, Judge Scott had asserted the doctrine of reversion in an extreme form, ruling that Dred Scott's status depended entirely on Missouri law, and that Missouri would no longer enforce foreign law against its own citizens.

McLean and Curtis denied that the Court must accept *Scott v. Emerson* as the settled law of Missouri on the subject of comity. International law, they said, required Missouri to recognize Dred Scott's change of status under the laws of Wisconsin Territory; for international law, as part of the common law, had been incorporated into the law of Missouri and could be displaced only by statute, not by mere judicial decision. Besides, *Scott v. Emerson* was a sharp departure from well-established judicial opinion in Missouri, and the Supreme Court had repeatedly held that, in reviewing state court decisions, it was not compelled to take the most recent decision as the rule.

Curtis even anticipated Taney's parting complaint about the manner in which the case had reached the Supreme Court. Some reliance, he said, had "been placed on the fact that the decision in the Supreme Court of Missouri was between these parties, and the suit there was abandoned to obtain another trial in the courts of the United States." But he cited two recent cases in which the

Taney Court had not only permitted the same procedure but also virtually overruled the state court decisions—in one instance, unanimously.

If the two dissenting opinions seem more convincing than the opinions of the Court majority, it is not merely because they were, by modern standards, on the right side. Curtis and Mc-Lean, in spite of their differing styles, displayed a fundamental agreement on the major issues that contrasted sharply with the heterogeneity of the majority's reasoning. They were in many respects the constitutional conservatives, following established precedent along a well-beaten path to their conclusions. Taney and his southern colleagues were the innovators—invalidating, for the first time in history, a major piece of federal legislation; denying to Congress a power that it had exercised for two-thirds of a century; sustaining the abrupt departure from precedent in *Scott v. Emerson;* and, in Taney's case, infusing the due-process clause with substantive meaning. And even though McLean did indulge his weakness for playing to the antislavery gallery, the southern justices were by far the more idiosyncratic and polemical.

Curtis's opinion, especially when read head-on against Taney's, is very impressive. One cannot entirely suppress the suspicion that the hostility displayed by the Chief Justice in the aftermath of the decision was partly inspired by the realization that he had been badly beaten in the argument by his much younger colleague from Massachusetts.

3

The first wave of public comment on the Dred Scott decision was in response to the newspaper summaries of the oral opinions delivered on March 6 and 7, 1857. Soon thereafter, the two dissenters filed their written opinions and released copies to the press. Thus antislavery elements for a time had better documentary ammunition along with the eruptive force of their moral outrage.

The fierceness of the attack upon the decision was reminiscent of the uprising against the Kansas-Nebraska bill three years earlier. Horace Greeley's New York *Tribune* set the pace with editorials almost every day denouncing this "atrocious," this "wicked," this "abominable" judgment and the "detestable hypocrisy," the "mean and skulking cowardice" of its author. The *Tribune* invective, though never surpassed, was matched by scores of Republican newspapers across the North, such as the Chicago *Democratic Press,* which expressed a "feeling of shame and loathing" for "this once illustrious tribunal, toiling meekly and patiently through this dirty job."

But the defending hosts had the special advantage of being able to appeal to the sanctity of the judicial system. "The decision is right, and the argument unanswerable, we presume," said the Louisville *Democrat,* "but whether or not, what this tribunal decides the Constitution to be, that it is; and all patriotic men will acquiesce." More forthright was the *Constitutionalist* of Augusta, Georgia, which declared: "Southern opinion upon the subject of southern slavery . . . is now the supreme law of the land . . . and opposition to southern opinion upon this subject is now opposition to the Constitution, and morally treason against the Government." Democrats everywhere were happy about the doctrinal effect of the decision. It was the "funeral sermon of Black Republicanism," said the Philadelphia *Pennsylvanian.* "It sweeps away every plank of their platform, and crushes into nothingness the whole theory upon which their party is founded." Similarly, the New Orleans *Picayune* assured its readers that the decision put "the whole basis of the Black Republican organization under the ban of the law."

It is doubtful that many persons really expected the new party to crawl away and die just because its cardinal principle had been pronounced unconstitutional. Republican leaders had little difficulty coping with the theoretical implications of Taney's opinion. The greater danger lay in the excessiveness of much Republican protest; for this could destroy the party's moderate image in the North and push it closer to a fatal association with abolitionism in the public mind. Democratic spokesmen hastened to picture critics of the Court as dangerous men verging on outlawry and blasphemy. The New York *Journal of Commerce* said that Republicanism was showing itself to be "only another name for revolution and anarchy," while the Richmond *Enquirer*, seeing evidence of an "epidemic of apoplexy" in radical antislavery circles, predicted, "All the insane asylums in Yankeedom will be inadequate for the accommodation of its victims." The rhetorical climax was reached in an Iowa editorial: "These daring libellers will next ascend to the Throne of the Supreme Ruler of the Universe and accuse God of partiality . . . They have the audacity of the devil . . . They hate the Constitution, the Bible and God . . . Where they will stop in their blasphemies and their treasons no mortal can tell."

A windfall in mid-March further strengthened the Democratic case; for at this point the public learned that the real owner of Dred Scott was probably not John F. A. Sanford but his sister Irene, the wife of a prominent Massachusetts Republican. The revelation apparently first appeared in the Springfield *Argus*, Democratic organ in the city where the onetime wife and widow of John Emerson now lived with her second husband, Congressman Calvin C. Chaffee. Republican embarrassment was acute, and Chaffee responded to the exposé with an emphatic disclaimer. "In the case of Dred Scott," he wrote to the Springfield *Republican*, "the defendant was and is the only person who had or has any power in the matter, and neither myself nor any member of my family were consulted in relation to, or even knew of the existence of the suit till after it was noticed for trial, when we learned it in an accidental way."

Events soon conspired to impair the credibility of this disclaimer, however. John Sanford, confined to an asylum, died on May 5, and just three weeks later out in Missouri, Taylor Blow manumitted Dred Scott and his family, having received title to them by quitclaim from the Chaffees. There are several possible explanations of the mysterious transaction, and the Chaffees' use of quitclaim suggests that they themselves may have been unsure of their legal interest in the slaves. But Democratic editors naturally preferred to believe that Congressman Chaffee had acknowledged himself a slave-owner and a liar. Certainly the Dred

Scott affair took on a peculiar odor with the revelations of the Chaffee connection, and nothing contributed more to the suspicion that it was a contrived case.

Although newspapers were the primary medium for public discussion of the Dred Scott decision, there were other channels of criticism. Some of the more zealous antislavery clergy did not hesitate to raise the subject in their churches. Montgomery Blair heard John McLean's opinion read from a pulpit on the first Sunday after it was read in court. One of the most notable performances was a series of sermons denouncing slavery and the Supreme Court by George B. Cheever, pastor of the Church of the Puritans in New York City. A master of vituperation, Cheever preached resistance even to the extreme of revolution if necessary, declaring that when sin and the Devil usurped power, it was the duty of everyone to disobey. Cheever was associated with Henry Ward Beecher and several other Congregationalist ministers in the editing of *The Independent,* a radical church weekly that equalled the New York *Tribune* in the vehemence of its attacks on the Dred Scott decision, which it called a "vain attempt to change the law by . . . Judges who have achieved only their own infamy." "If the people obey this decision, they disobey God," the paper warned.

The decision also received the attention of many official church organizations, notably the annual district conferences of the Methodist Episcopal Church, North. For example, the committee on slavery of the Providence Conference, meeting on April 1, denounced the Taney opinion as an effort at "nationalizing slavery." The New Hampshire Conference rejected the decision as contrary to religion, justice, and the Constitution. Such condemnation echoed through other religious meetings across the North and provided further basis for the already widespread conservative protest against the mixing of clergy in politics.

After full publication of the decision in Howard's *Reports,* the discussion became more substantive and technical, with members of the legal profession now offering their expert commentary. The best of these critiques were much cooler in tone than the general run of editorial comment and all the more effective as a consequence. Such was the case, for instance, with an article in *The Law Reporter* for June 1857 written by two young Bostonians, one of whom, Horace Gray, later became a member of the United States Supreme Court. Their review was essentially an endorsement of the Curtis opinion, but they were respectful in their disagreement with Taney, whom they praised as a "great magistrate." The article exemplified a general tendency of contemporary criticism and later scholarship to spend much time on questions associated with the legitimacy of the decision—whether the Chief Justice really spoke for a majority of the Court, what the Court really decided, how the justices aligned themselves on each issue, and whether the invalidation of the Missouri Compromise restriction was dictum.

Although most of the critiques were general in nature, the *New Englander* (later the *Yale Review*) carried one article undertaking to demonstrate that Justice Daniel had been wrong in his interpretation of Roman law, and another analyzing that part of Taney's opinion dealing with Negro citizenship. The latter piece, by W. A. Learned, was particularly effective in exposing the historical and logical weaknesses of the Taney argument. Learned called attention, for example, to the Chief Justice's habit of lumping free Negroes with slaves when defining their status, and he had a keen eye for the instances in which Taney seemed to draw the very opposite inference from that indicated by the facts.

Pamphlet commentaries on the decision also began to appear soon after publication of the Howard volume. One of the ablest came out of Louisville, with the author identified only as "A Kentucky Lawyer." He may have been the first to point out the aimlessness of Taney's distinction between original territories and those later acquired, since the limitations on Congress were precisely the same in each case. Especially perceptive were his remarks on Taney's use of the due-process clause; for he showed that the crucial question was not whether slaves constituted property but whether prohibition constituted deprivation.

The longest critique produced in 1857 was the work of a seventy-five-year-old man stricken with cancer. Thomas Hart Benton, in a book of 130 pages, plus a 62-page appendix, concentrated entirely on the territorial aspect of the decision. The

Court's great error, he said, was its Calhounish assumption that
the Constitution extended automatically to new territories, carrying protection of slavery with it. Benton agreed with Taney that
the territory clause referred only to disposal of public land and
that nothing in the Constitution expressly endowed Congress
with power to govern a territory. But then the theories of the
two men parted company. Congressional authority in the territories, according to Benton, was derived straight from the inherent sovereign power of the federal government, without reference to the Constitution. That document, he insisted, embraced
only the states. None of its limitations extended to the territories,
except when Congress so provided by positive enactment. Benton's doctrine, no less extreme in its way than Calhoun's, gained
considerable support later in the century, but was eventually rejected by the Supreme Court. In 1857 it had too much of an imperial flavor to win many adherents.

From the foregoing discussion it must not be inferred that
there were no writers supporting the Dred Scott decision, but
the literature of defense was less impressive in both volume and
quality. This fact is not surprising, because the Court had put
the ball in the antislavery court, so to speak, and the best defense for a decision allegedly complete and perfect was not further supportive argument but rather obeisance to the Court.
Such was the emphasis of Caleb Cushing, recently attorney general under Pierce, in a speech delivered at Newburyport, Massachusetts, on October 31 and circulated in broadside. Not satisfied
with describing the Chief Justice as "the very incarnation of judicial purity, integrity, science, and wisdom," the orotund Cushing also declared that Taney was "infirm of body, but with a
mind which seems to beam out the clearer from its frail earthly
shrine as if it had already half shaken off the dust of mortality
and begun to stand as it were transfigured into the celestial glory
and beauty of immortality." This was an eloquent way of saying
that the man had one foot in the grave, but Taney liked it and
thanked Cushing for his kind words at a time when "evil passions" ruled the hour.

Earlier in the year, Taney had also received from Samuel
Nott a copy of his pamphlet, "Slavery and the Remedy," in a

new edition containing a favorable commentary on the Dred Scott decision. Taney's letter of acknowledgment to the Massachusetts clergyman is the most revealing recorded statement of his attitude toward the Negro—"this weak and credulous race," as he put it, whose life in slavery was "usually cheerful and contented," and for whom a general and sudden emancipation would mean "absolute ruin." Many slaves had been freed in Maryland, Taney wrote. "And in the greater number of cases that have come under my observation, freedom has been a serious misfortune to the manumitted slave." He himself had freed his own slaves more than thirty years past. "And I am glad to say that none of those whom I manumitted disappointed my expectations, but have shown by their conduct that they were worthy of freedom, and knew how to use it." If Taney noticed the glaring discrepancy in his words, he offered no explanation of it.

The views of the Court majority lent support to the thriving racist anthropology of the day which defined the black race as a distinct and lower species of mankind, perhaps even the product of a separate creation. Thus, in 1859, one of the leading popularizers of the theory of polygenesis, Dr. John H. Van Evrie of New York, published a pamphlet edition of the Dred Scott decision with an introductory essay in which he declared that it was a document second in importance to the Declaration of Independence. The decision "fixed the *status* of the subordinate race *forever*," he said, and, being in accord with nature, could "never perish."

The racist implications of the decision were fiercely denounced in radical antislavery circles. For the free Negro community especially, this "judicial incarnation of wolfishness," as Frederick Douglass called it, seems to have inspired a sudden shift to a higher level of militancy. Words of defiance rang out at numerous protest meetings, and it was as a response to the Dred Scott decision that black abolitionists organized a celebration of "Crispus Attucks Day" on March 5, 1858, in Boston's cradle of liberty, Faneuil Hall. This spectacular meeting honoring the Negro killed in the Boston Massacre was "a feast of sight and sound," repeated every year until after the Civil War.

Many white critics of the decision likewise deplored its repressive effect on free Negroes, but such voices were in a minority throughout most of the North. Taney's ruling against Negro citizenship carried nothing like the same emotional charge as his ruling against the Missouri Compromise restriction. The dilemma confronting Republicans was this: The amount of racial discrimination in the North laid them open to charges of hypocrisy in their expressions of sympathy for the slave; but any words or actions tending to vindicate themselves of the charge laid them open to another and more dangerous one of advocating racial equality. In short, whenever discussion shifted from slavery to race, Republicans were in trouble, and the first half of Taney's Dred Scott opinion was concerned with race. Complaints about it were answered with variations on the theme of the mote and the beam. "Ye hypocrites," said the Louisville *Democrat,* "reform yourselves, before you preach to us." If northerners regarded the Negro as a citizen, why were so many of his rights trampled upon? How could a citizen be excluded from school, jury service, and the polls—indeed, from entire states? This tender spot was probed, of course, not only by proslavery southerners but by antislavery militants, black and white, who pointed out that the Dred Scott decision, as it applied to free Negroes, had a majoritarian ring that transcended sectional lines. "Judge Taney's decision, infamous as it is," said Susan B. Anthony, "is but the reflection of the spirit and practice of the American people, North as well as South."

In its primary effect, the decision meant the exclusion of Negroes from access to the federal courts in civil cases, but the potential ramifications were more numerous and complex than anyone realized at the time. For one thing, there was the problem of definition. Could an Ohio quadroon, white according to the law of his state, bring a federal suit against a white person in Tennessee, where quadroons were legally black? Would the same definition apply in the federal courts of both states? Clearly, either Congress or the Supreme Court would some day have to say who was and who was not a Negro.

The executive branch of the federal government, which, over the years, had not been entirely consistent about it, could now proceed with authority to deny blacks all privileges associated with United States citizenship, such as passports for travel abroad and eligibility for pre-emption of federal land. The decision likewise lent support to the discriminatory laws of state governments and encouraged further assaults upon the already limited freedom and security of the nonslave black population. In Arkansas, for instance, a proposal to enslave all free Negroes who did not leave the state within a year had recently failed, owing in part to constitutional scruples. The Dred Scott decision breathed new life into the movement, and the legislature passed the expulsion act in 1859, with the result that most free Negroes hastily fled the state. At the same time, the decision posed a threat to black suffrage in the few states allowing it; for the franchise was in each case limited to United States citizens. Had Taney's opinion, then, made Negro voting unconstitutional? The legislature of Maine laid this question before the state supreme court, which returned a negative reply based primarily on the dissenting opinion of Justice Curtis.

There was, in fact, a strong reaction to the decision in a number of northern state legislatures during the spring of 1857, but in some states the reaction itself had repercussions unfavorable to the black population. For instance, the Ohio legislature, which was under Republican control in 1857, approved resolutions condemning the Dred Scott decision and also passed laws to prevent slaveholding and kidnapping in the state (meaning prohibition of sojourning and increased interference with enforcement of the Fugitive Slave Act). Ohio held an election in the fall of 1857, with both the legislature and the governorship at stake. The Republican state convention denounced *Dred Scott* as "anti-constitutional, anti-republican, anti-democratic, incompatible with State rights and destructive of personal security." The Democrats stressed the white supremacy aspects of the decision. They assembled quotations from various radical Republican statements and published them as the "Congo Creed." Although Salmon P. Chase won re-election as governor by a very narrow margin, the Democrats captured control of the legislature. They then not only repealed some of the antislavery legislation of the previous session but, citing the Dred Scott decision, they also passed the "visible admixture law," which, in effect, disfranchised persons of mixed blood between white and mulatto.

In New York there was a similar sequence of advance and retreat on the racial front. Republican setbacks in the New York and Ohio elections of 1857 cannot be attributed solely, perhaps not even primarily, to a racist backlash against the more radical attacks on the Dred Scott decision. The financial panic that began in late summer no doubt disposed many men to vote for a change of management, and Ohio Republicans were further handicapped by an embezzlement of public funds in the Chase administration. Nevertheless, the remarkable capacity of the Democratic party to survive through years of adversity after 1860 may have been owing in part to a deep-seated feeling that it was "right" on the race question. No one can say for sure that large numbers of northern votes were determined or heavily influenced in the late 1850s by Democratic appeals to racism, but Republicans believed that such was the case. Abraham Lincoln had come to that bitter conclusion after the defeat of Frémont for the presidency in 1856. Speaking at Chicago, just six days before the Dred Scott decision, he complained, "We were constantly charged with seeking an amalgamation of the white and black races; and thousands turned from us, not believing the charge . . . but *fearing* to face it themselves."

Yet Lincoln himself increasingly evinced the same fear. His first public comment on *Dred Scott* had a schizoid quality. With elaborate but moving metaphor he argued, in direct contradiction of Taney, that the condition of the Negro in America had worsened over the years and "never appeared so hopeless" as in the 1850s, when "all the powers of earth" seemed to be combining against him. But then Lincoln's sympathies seemed to shift abruptly from the black race to the white, and he used his strongest language ever on the subject when he said that there was a "natural disgust in the minds of nearly all white people, to the idea of an indiscriminate amalgamation of the white and black races." It was at about this time that he began to use census statistics to show miscegenation as a by-product of slavery, and it was at this point that he introduced the rhetorical flourish of disclaiming any wish to have a Negro woman either for a slave or for a wife. A year later, under heavy pounding from Douglas, he would awkwardly back off from criticizing the first half of Taney's opinion and declare his opposition to Negro citizenship. Various other Republican leaders joined in the scramble to dissociate themselves from the unpopular doctrine of racial equality. Horace Greeley protested that too many Republicans thought they "must be as harsh, and cruel, and tyrannical, toward the unfortunate blacks as possible, in order to prove themselves 'the white man's party.'"

The race question tended to unite Democrats and divide Republicans, whereas the slavery question tended to divide Democrats and unite Republicans, who could agree especially in opposing further extension of the institution on both pro-Negro and anti-Negro grounds. Republican politicians therefore concentrated their attacks on the second half of Taney's opinion, which, after all, was the part that struck directly at the foundations of their party. To be sure, the invalidation of a law already substantially repealed seemed unlikely to make any great difference in the territories themselves, but Republicans could point with alarm to certain broader implications of the decision. Slavery, previously considered legal only where authorized by positive local law, had been made legal throughout the country, except where forbidden by positive local law. Worse, however, was the ominous possibility that the power of local law to prohibit slavery had been seriously impaired and would be further eroded. In its report on the Dred Scott decision, a joint committee of the New York legislature declared:

> It follows as a direct consequence of this doctrine, that a master may take his slave into a free State without dissolving the relation of master and slave; and your committee cannot but be alarmed and shocked at the apprehension that some future decision of the pro-slavery majority of the supreme court will authorise a slave driver, as threatened by the devotees of slavery, to call the roll of his manacled gang at the foot of the monument on Bunker Hill, reared and consecrated to freedom.

This warning that *Dred Scott* constituted a long step toward the nationalization of slavery rang out many times throughout the North before Lincoln took it up in his House-Divided speech of June 16, 1858. It was a dramatic way of holding the emphasis of the discussion to slavery, rather than race, and of countering the emotional impact of the "racial equality" outcry coming from the Democrats. Yet expansion of federal protection for slavery within the free states was at most a potential danger. Meanwhile, the Republican party faced the immediate problem of having had its principal objective pronounced unconstitutional. "With all of your outrage, what are you going to *do* about it?" the Democrats gleefully demanded. Republican editors and other spokesmen frequently replied, "We intend to get the decision overruled." Even under the most favorable circumstances, however, such a reversal obviously could not be achieved for a number of years. It did not solve the problem of how Republicans could reject the decision without defying the law. But Taney, by trying to cover too much ground in his defense of slavery, provided them with the solution. The opportunity to challenge the legitimacy of the decision was, in the words of David M. Potter, a "psychological godsend."

Accordingly, *"obiter dictum"* became the Republican battle-cry in the war upon the Dred Scott decision. The Court's invalidation of the Missouri Compromise restriction should some day be formally overruled, but until then it could simply be ignored as without authority. Both dissenting justices had said so, and their views were emphatically endorsed in the professional criticism of the case emanating from the northern bar. Historians of the next half-century would generally echo those same views. And, as we shall see, the decision would be virtually nullified by disregard in the administration of Abraham Lincoln. The *obiter dictum* argument served Republican needs not only by vindicating the legality of the party platform but also by helping to pull attention away from the race issue in *Dred Scott*.

Some Republicans went further and set forth a narrow definition of the Court's authority vis-à-vis the other branches of government. This was, after all, the first time that the American people had to consider the meaning and consequences of judicial review actually exerted at the level of federal law.* Over the years between the *Marbury* and *Dred Scott* cases, judicial review had won substantial acceptance in theory and practice, though primarily in respect to state law. So Taney in 1857, unlike John Marshall in 1803, felt no need to justify exercise of the power and said nothing whatever on the subject.‡ The critical question was not whether the Supreme Court could declare a law of Congress unconstitutional, but rather, what were the total effects of such a declaration. What did *Dred Scott v. Sandford* mean beyond the judgment that Scott was still a slave? Did the decision, as a New Hampshire editor asserted, immediately become a part of the supreme law of the land and thus fully binding on all federal and state officials?

It was one thing to say that the Supreme Court might refuse to enforce a law plainly in conflict with a specific provision of the Constitution. It was another thing to say that the Court was the final, authoritative arbiter of all questions involving interpretation of the Constitution. The distinction is between the institution of judicial review, narrowly defined, and the doctrine of judicial supremacy or judicial sovereignty, which did not become settled American dogma until the twentieth century. The issue had been debated many times before William Cullen Bryant's New York *Evening Post* on March 14, 1857, accused the Supreme Court of "judicial impertinence" in assuming the power to "act as the interpreter of the Constitution for the other branches of the government." Thomas Jefferson and Andrew Jackson were but the two most prominent names on a long list of American statesmen who had insisted that Congress and the President were co-equals with the Court in this respect. Taney himself had taken precisely the same position as attorney general under Jackson.

---

* *Marbury v. Madison* had been in a sense self-liquidating. It required no enforcement by the executive branch and did not in any significant way inhibit the power of the legislative branch.

‡ Two years later in *Ableman v. Booth,* where it was not relevant to the issues before the Court, Taney affirmed the power, perhaps in answer to Republican comment on *Dred Scott:* "And as the Constitution is the fundamental and supreme law, if it appears that an act of Congress is not pursuant to, and within the limits of, the power assigned to the Federal Government, it is the duty of the courts of the United States to declare it unconstitutional and void."

Here is what he had written in 1832: "Whatever may be the force of the decision of the Supreme Court in binding the parties and settling their rights in the particular case before them, I am not prepared to admit that a construction given to the constitution by the Supreme Court in deciding in any one or more cases fixes of itself irrevokably and permanently its construction in that particular and binds the states and the Legislative and executive branches of the General government, forever afterwards to conform to it and adopt it in every other case as the true reading of the instrument although all of them may unite in believing it erroneous."

Lincoln, who made no use of the *obiter dictum* argument in criticizing the Dred Scott decision, followed the Jefferson-Jackson line of limiting the scope and denying the finality of the decision. He did so, however, with a sophisticated realism that amounted to neither a full acceptance nor a complete rejection of the doctrine of judicial supremacy. In his first public comment on the case, he conceded the Supreme Court some measure of pre-eminence as constitutional authority. Republicans, he said, thought that "its decisions on Constitutional questions, when fully settled, should control, not only particular cases decided, but the general policy of the country, subject to be disturbed only by amendments of the Constitution as provided in that instrument itself." The phrase "when fully settled" governs the rest of the sentence, and Lincoln insisted that this condition had not yet been met in the Dred Scott case:

> If this important decision had been made by the unanimous concurrence of the judges, and without any apparent partisan bias, and in accordance with legal public expectation, and with the steady practice of the departments throughout our history, and had been in no part, based on assumed historical facts which are not really true; or, if wanting in some of these, it had been before the court more than once, and had there been affirmed and re-affirmed through a course of years, it then might be . . . factious, nay, even revolutionary, to not acquiesce in it as a precedent.
>
> But when, as it is true we find it wanting in all these claims to the public confidence, it is not resistance, it is not factious, it

is not even disrespectful, to treat it as not having yet quite established a settled doctrine for the country.

Thus the Dred Scott decision as of June 1857, according to Lincoln, was in an intermediate phase between promulgation and legitimation. Its doctrines were not yet the accepted law of the land and not compelling as a "political rule." The Republicans, knowing that the Court had more than once overruled its own previous decisions, intended to work for such a reversal in this case. Neither was the decision, at its present stage, binding on the coordinate branches of the federal government. "If I were in Congress," Lincoln said a year later, "and a vote should come up on a question whether slavery should be prohibited in a new territory, in spite of that Dred Scott decision, I would vote that it should."

Lincoln regarded the unqualified doctrine of judicial supremacy as incompatible with the principle of self-government and would say so publicly at the very moment of entering the presidency. Meanwhile, the great advocate of popular sovereignty, Stephen A. Douglas, for his own political reasons, was paying solemn lip service to judicial supremacy and describing the conflict raging over Taney's opinion as a "naked issue between the friends and the enemies of the Constitution." It would not be entirely wrong to say that the meaning of the Dred Scott decision became the heart of the matter in the famous debates of 1858.

⊱ 9 ⊰

The
Lecompton and Freeport
Connections

The tangible significance of the Dred Scott decision was far from clear in the spring and summer of 1857. It had no immediate legal effect of any importance except on the status of free Negroes. Unlike the Fugitive Slave and Kansas-Nebraska acts, it provoked no violent aftermath, presented no problem of enforcement, inspired no political upheaval. Whether the Court's action had shifted the sectional balance of power remained to be seen. After the great Republican triumph in 1860 and the ensuing disruption of the Union, it was only natural to look back on the decision as one of the critical factors in a political revolution. No one could have been more emphatic about it than Charles Warren, historian of the Supreme Court. "It may fairly be said," he wrote, "that Chief Justice Taney elected Abraham Lincoln to the Presidency." What Warren had in mind primarily was the effect of Taney's decision on the unity of the Democratic party.

At this point, we must begin to come to grips with one of the more familiar stories in American political history—how the Dred Scott decision and Lincoln's shrewd exploitation of it in the Freeport debate compelled Douglas to take a stand that alienated the South, disrupted the Democratic party, and thus cleared the way for a Republican victory in 1860. The supporting evidence seems to carry conviction. Taney's opinion, as we have seen, did declare that since Congress had no power to prohibit slavery in the territories, it could not authorize a territorial government to do so. This was dictum, of course, but it seemed a logical corollary to his major conclusion. Furthermore, Douglas, in an effort to salvage the principle of popular sovereignty, did undercut the Taney dictum with his own "Freeport doctrine," and southern Democrats did reject that doctrine so vehemently as to split their party along sectional lines.

But when the chronology of these developments is examined in detail, some curious discrepancies emerge to view. The Dred Scott decision did not at first split the Democrats but instead drew them closer together in defense of the Supreme Court against Republican censure. Northern Democrats strongly approved of Taney's ruling against Negro citizenship, and, having long maintained that congressional regulation of slavery in the territories was bad policy, they found it easy to accept the verdict that such regulation was also unconstitutional. The Democrats, in short, did not, as a direct result of the Dred Scott decision, suffer the kind of acute internal disagreement over slavery which had racked their party in 1846-50 and in 1854. To be sure, there remained a "difference of opinion," as James Buchanan had phrased it, about the "point of time" when a territorial government could establish or prohibit slavery. Southerners insisted that Taney had settled the issue in their favor, and the President agreed. But for northern Democrats, acquiescence meant renouncing popular sovereignty in favor of Calhounism, and this would have placed them at a serious disadvantage in their struggle with the Republicans.

Had Taney's dictum put an end to the strategy of the Benjamin formula, whereby northern and southern Democrats agreed to disagree about the power of territorial legislatures over slavery? Douglas faced up to the problem in a major political address at Springfield, Illinois, on June 12, 1857. Seeking to undercut the dictum without expressly repudiating it, Douglas in effect carried an appeal from the formalities of constitutional law to the realities of American political life. Acknowledging that the right to take slaves into a territory was fully guaranteed by the Constitution and could not be alienated by act of Congress, he added:

It necessarily remains a barren and a worthless right, unless
sustained, protected and enforced by appropriate police regulations and local legislation . . . These regulations and remedies must necessarily depend entirely upon the will and wishes
of the people of the Territory . . . Hence the great principle of
popular sovereignty and self-government is sustained and
firmly established by the authority of this decision.

Here was the essence of the "Freeport doctrine" articulated more
than a year in advance of the Freeport debate. Perhaps better
designated the principle of "residual popular sovereignty," it
amounted to little more than a special application of the truism
that unpopular law is difficult to enforce. Douglas had used the
argument in 1850 to minimize the historical significance of the
Northwest Ordinance. More recently, it had been taken up by
several southern congressmen who wanted to demonstrate that
granting their section its constitutional rights did not mean forcing slavery on an unwilling people. Thus Lawrence O. Branch
of North Carolina declared on December 18, 1856, "Every one
knows that if the majority of the Legislature are opposed to slavery, there are a multitude of ways in which the slaveholder may
be harassed and kept out by hostile legislation, and by a failure
to provide remedies for the protection of his rights. Practically,
the institution can only be introduced and sustained where the
majority are willing to tolerate it." Similar statements were made
by other southerners at about the same time.

Douglas, however, had discreetly avoided such argument during the campaign year 1856, asserting repeatedly that the extent
of territorial power over slavery must be left to judicial determination. Thus he had virtually pledged to accept a Supreme Court
decision on the constitutionality of his "great principle" and appeared to be reneging on that pledge at Springfield. One might
therefore expect to find the Springfield speech attacked in the
southern press, but, on the contrary, it was generally praised. The
Washington *Union,* which would lead the attack on the Freeport
doctrine in 1858, said that the speech deserved unqualified com-
mendation for its "lucid statements, vigorous thoughts, and powerful arguments."

In 1857, then, the Dred Scott decision did not cause any kind of crisis within the Democratic party, and Douglas affirmed the principle of residual popular sovereignty without incurring southern censure. Yet, in 1858, Douglas came under fierce southern attack for saying virtually the same thing he had said at Springfield in 1857. And by 1859, southern insistence upon full acknowledgment of slaveholding rights under the Dred Scott decision was widening an already dangerous breach in the Democratic party. Clearly, the decision by itself did not have a convulsive effect on party politics, but it became one of the elements in an explosive compound. In order to understand how the decision contributed to the disruption of the Union, one must study its relationship to a new crisis arising in Congress over the Lecompton constitution for Kansas.

The struggle for Kansas entered a new phase in February 1857 when the proslavery territorial legislature, convinced that there was no hope of an enabling act from Congress, initiated a statehood movement of its own. It passed legislation providing for election of delegates to a constitutional convention. The free-state forces, now a majority of the population by a wide margin, refused to participate on the grounds that the arrangements were unfair. As a consequence, a convention of strictly proslavery sentiment was elected. It convened in the autumn of 1857 at Lecompton, the territorial capital, and drafted the notorious "Lecompton constitution."

The tone of the document was set in the first section of an article devoted entirely to slavery. Probably reflecting the influence of the Dred Scott decision, it proclaimed: "The right of property is before and higher than any constitutional sanction, and the right of the owner of a slave to such slave and its increase is the same and as inviolable as the right of the owner of any property whatever." Here, imbedded in a prospective state constitution was a proslavery version of the "higher law" doctrine. Other sections of the article spelled out in some detail the establishment of slavery in Kansas. The constitution as a whole was not submitted to the Kansas electorate. Instead, voters were offered a choice between the "Constitution with slavery" and the "Constitution without slavery," but the decision could affect only the *further* introduction of slaves into Kansas. Thus "without slavery" actually meant *with* slavery to some extent. About two hundred slaves already held within the territory would continue in bondage, and so too would any children born to them. More important, the fundamental law of Kansas would be that of a slave state, and it could not be amended for seven years. Furthermore, the convention placed administration of the referendum in the hands of its own presiding officer. This arrangement strengthened the conviction of free-staters that the Lecompton movement was a fraud from beginning to end, and they accordingly determined to boycott the election. It appeared that the constitution "with slavery" would triumph by default.

Meanwhile, the free-state faction had captured control of the territorial legislature, and that body promptly passed an act submitting the entire Lecompton constitution to the voters. The outcome of both contests was predictable. On December 21, as the free-staters persisted in their refusal to participate, 6,226 votes were cast for the constitution *with* slavery (many of them apparently fraudulent), and 569 for the constitution *without* slavery. On January 4, with the proslavery element now abstaining, there were 138 votes for the constitution *with* slavery, 24 for the constitution *without* slavery, and 10,226 against the constitution as a whole. What the majority of Kansans wanted had been made unmistakably clear.

Long before these results were known, the outlines of another sectional crisis had begun to emerge. Many northern Democrats joined the Republicans in condemning the "Lecompton swindle," while southerners, though not without considerable doubt and some open dissent, showed a strong disposition to close ranks in militant support of the document. Buchanan, after having wavered for several months, came down firmly on the southern side. In what may have been the most important single presidential decision of the 1850s, he resolved to support the Lecompton constitution. The stage was thus set for the spectacular revolt of Stephen A. Douglas as leader of the anti-Lecompton Democrats, a development that split the party, confused the Republican opposition, and sent a shock wave through the South.

The predominant influence on Douglas appears to have been the surge of anti-Lecompton feeling in Illinois and the knowledge that his seat in the Senate was at stake in the coming legislative election. A defeat in that contest might well ruin his presidential chances in 1860, and the outlook was far from encouraging. The Republicans had captured the governorship in 1856 and now expected to reap additional gains from the new Kansas controversy. Illinois Democrats desperately needed to dissociate themselves from southern ultraism and, if possible, even steal some antislavery thunder from the Republicans. Douglas dramatically provided the means of doing so. His anti-Lecompton heroics, which to Buchanan and many southerners seemed unreasonable and disloyal, were a response to stark political necessity in Illinois. "You have adopted the only course that could save the Northern Democracy from annihilation at the next election," wrote one of his correspondents.

For southerners, even though many of them might understand the political pressures on Douglas in his home state, it was nevertheless a dark hour when he launched his attack on the Lecompton constitution and accused the administration of proposing to force it down the throats of the people of Kansas. "This defection of Douglas," wrote a South Carolinian, "has done more than all else to shake my confidence in Northern men on the slavery issue, for I have long regarded him as one of our safest and most reliable friends." For southerners, the greatest offense of the Little Giant consisted not so much in disagreeing with Democrats as in cooperating with the hated Republicans. "With indecent haste," a Mississippi editor later wrote, "Douglas placed himself at the head of the Black column and gave the word of command." Thereby, he became "stained with the dishonor of treachery without a parallel in the political history of the country."

Undeterred by the threat of disruption within his party, Buchanan transmitted the Lecompton constitution to Congress on February 2, 1858, with a special message recommending admission of Kansas as the sixteenth slaveholding state. Kansas at that moment, he declared, was already "as much a slave State as Georgia or South Carolina." Insisting that the Lecompton movement had been scrupulously legal from beginning to end, that the free-state faction was "in a state of rebellion against the government," and that the referendum of January 4 had no legal force, he promised "domestic peace" if the constitution were accepted and predicted that "disasters" might follow its rejection.

The thirty-fifth Congress was safely Democratic and under firm southern control. In the Senate, there were 37 Democrats, 20 Republicans, and 5 Native Americans (all southerners); in the House of Representatives, there were 128 Democrats, 92 Republicans, and 14 Native Americans (all southerners). Within the Democratic party, southerners outnumbered northerners 25 to 12 in the Senate, and 75 to 53 in the House. The South controlled the Democratic caucuses and thus the organization of Congress. In both houses, the presiding officers and most of the important committee chairmen were southerners. It soon became evident that in the Senate, only two or three Democrats would join the Douglas revolt. The House was a different matter. There, more than twenty northern Democrats, together with a handful of southern Americans, aligned themselves with the Republicans to form a narrow anti-Lecompton majority.

The closeness of the contest in the House encouraged administration leaders to believe that with extra effort they could drive the Lecompton constitution through Congress. Buchanan undertook to check the rebellion within his party by ruthless use of federal patronage, removing many postmasters and other appointees who persisted in their support of Douglas. These tactics greatly increased the rancor of the struggle, and Douglas became convinced that the chief aim of the administration was his political destruction. He emerged from the Lecompton controversy deeply resentful of the southern Democratic leadership, which sought to expel him from the party for one act of dissent in a long record of strenuous efforts to accommodate the South.

The lengthy congressional debate on the Lecompton question ranged over the whole turbulent history of territorial Kansas and recapitulated all the earlier phases of the slavery controversy. The Dred Scott decision, though not directly relevant to the issue at hand, was obviously much on men's minds and came often into the discussion. In fact, Republicans frequently seized any opportunity to attack the decision, no matter what subject might be under discussion. One of the most vehement denunciations, for instance, was delivered with complete irrelevance during a debate on filibustering in Nicaragua. Many speakers linked *Dred Scott* with Lecompton in a general pattern of proslavery aggression. Thus Senator John P. Hale of New Hampshire closed a long speech on both subjects by declaring: "Sir, you are now proposing to carry out this Dred Scott decision by forcing upon the people of Kansas a constitution against which they have remonstrated, and to which . . . a very large portion of them are opposed. . . . if you persevere in that attempt, I think, I hope the men of Kansas will fight. I hope they will resist to blood and to death."

Sharpest of the many attacks on the Supreme Court was one delivered as part of an elaborate anti-Lecompton speech by Senator William H. Seward of New York. The Dred Scott decision, Seward charged, had been manufactured by the Court at the instigation of the President, both forgetting "that judicial usurpation is more odious and intolerable than any other among the manifold practices of tyranny." The "whisperings" between Buchanan and Taney at the inauguration thus confirmed an agreement already reached to hang "the millstone of slavery" on the people of Kansas. The next day, the President received the justices "as graciously as Charles I did the judges who had, at his instance, subverted the statutes of English liberty." Then, on the following day, the Court rendered its decision, and the President, "having organized this formidable judicial battery at the Capitol," was now ready to begin the work of subduing Kansas through the "fraudulent" agency of the Lecompton convention.

Evidence not made public until much later lends some support, as we have seen, to Seward's charge of collusion between Buchanan and the Court, but much of what he said was untrue or at least grossly inaccurate. To southerners, the speech, like that of Charles Sumner two years earlier, seemed doubly offensive because it had been so carefully prepared and was in fact put into print before being delivered. Reverdy Johnson, counsel in the case and a personal friend of the Chief Justice, promptly denounced the "mad and reckless" oratory of the New York senator, who, he said, had subjected the Supreme Court to "as calumnious an attack as ever dishonored human lips." Taney himself

appears to have resented the speech deeply. He later told his official biographer that if Seward had been elected President in 1860,
he, Taney, would have refused to administer the oath of office.

The principal southern response to Seward came from Judah
P. Benjamin, who spoke for several hours in defense of Taney,
the Court, and the Dred Scott decision. He devoted about two-
thirds of his speech to the main theoretical issue arising out of
Taney's opinion—whether slavery in Anglo-American law was the
rule or the exception. And so, in the midst of debate on the
Lecompton constitution, Benjamin's senatorial audience heard
once again about the Royal African Company and the partici-
pation of the British crown in the slave trade; about the *Somerset*
case and the case of *The Slave Grace;* about the clauses in the
Constitution recognizing the right of property in slaves; and
about the reaffirmation of that right by the Supreme Court in
Prigg v. Pennsylvania.

Everywhere in the United States, said Benjamin, slaves were
property under common law and by virtue of the Constitution.
A master taking a slave into a free state did not forfeit *title* to
his property; he merely placed himself in a position of having no
"*remedy* or *process* for the assertion of his title." This meant in
effect that the law of a state liberating slaves brought illegally
within its boundaries had no legal effect outside its boundaries.
But Benjamin went further and declared that such liberation,
like a refusal to protect patents and copyrights, constituted a
violation of the "principles of eternal justice." His argument as
a whole reveals certain proslavery potentialities of the Dred Scott
decision which, because of the intervention of the Civil War,
were never fully explored.

Those members of Congress who, as a group, said the least
about the Dred Scott case were the northern Democrats, for
whom it had been an embarrassment from the beginning. Douglas in particular displayed remarkable prudence whenever the
subject arose, having apparently resolved not to give the administration additional reason for charging him with apostasy.
During debate on the Lecompton constitution in early February,
Lyman Trumbull posed virtually the same question that Lincoln
would ask at Freeport—namely, what remained of popular sover-

eignty in the wake of the Dred Scott decision? Douglas simply declared his unwillingness to discuss the matter at that time. Never once throughout the session did he reiterate the principle of residual popular sovereignty that had figured so prominently in his Springfield speech of the preceding year. Thus, while cooperating with the Republicans in the fight against the Lecompton constitution, he carefully dissociated himself from their attacks on the Dred Scott decision.

On March 23, the Senate took final action on the proposal to admit Kansas with the Lecompton constitution. John J. Crittenden of Kentucky offered a substitute measure requiring that the constitution first be resubmitted to the voters of the territory. It failed, 34 to 24, and then the main bill was passed, 33 to 25. Four northern Democrats (including Douglas) and two southern Whig-Americans joined the Republican opposition. In the House, however, the Republicans and their allies defeated the bill, 120 to 112, by substituting the proposal for resubmission (now called the "Crittenden-Montgomery" amendment). The Senate again rejected the Crittenden plan, and both houses agreed to the formation of a conference committee. Administration forces accordingly had one more chance to avoid total defeat. Their influence lay behind the committee's report of a compromise bill on April 23, although the measure was ostensibly the work of William H. English, a lukewarm anti-Lecompton Democrat from Indiana.

The "English compromise" was designed to give the administration and the South a procedural victory masking its substantive defeat. It proposed admission of Kansas with the Lecompton constitution intact, provided that the voters of the territory first approved the standard grant of federal land specified for the new state. If the land grant were disapproved in the referendum, Kansas could not again be considered for admission until its population equaled the current federal ratio for one representative in Congress, something more than 90,000. In short, rejection of the land grant would mean the end of the Lecompton constitution and postponement of statehood for several years.

There seemed to be little doubt that the Kansans, given such an opportunity, would bury the "Lecompton fraud" under an overwhelmingly negative vote. The primary effect, then, would be much the same as if the Crittenden-Montgomery substitute had passed. Yet nearly everyone who had voted for the Crittenden plan now voted against the English bill, and vice versa. The principal exception was a group of anti-Lecompton Democrats in the House who were coaxed and coerced back into the comfortable circle of party regularity. At last the administration forces had the majorities they needed. On the last day of April, the compromise passed the Senate, 31 to 22, and the House, 112 to 103.

Douglas, after almost agreeing to support the English bill, cast his vote against it, thereby convincing many southerners that he was still in league with the "black" Republicans. There was merit in his view of the bill as a shabby piece of legislation that promised Kansas immediate admission as a slaveholding state but punished her with delay if she preferred to be a free state. Yet the measure did seem to constitute the kind of pragmatic adjustment of sectional disputes that he had often promoted, and it did also seem likely to bring about a restoration of Democratic party unity. Douglas as a bitter-ender on the anti-slavery side of an issue was an unfamiliar sight, but intransigence in Washington translated into expedience in Illinois. Douglas apparently decided that accepting the English compromise would look too much like caving in under administration pressure. With his contest for re-election drawing near, mail from home strongly reinforced the conclusion that he must "yield not one inch."

The opposition of Douglas probably facilitated passage of the English bill, making it look more attractive to southern militants who had pledged themselves against anything resembling resubmission. The compromise was in fact a blessing for such men, even for those aiming at disunion, because it enabled them to crawl back off a shaky limb. Threats of secession were numerous during the controversy. Often their tone was that of a letter to Senator James H. Hammond from one of his South Carolinian constituents: "Save the Union, if you can. But rather than have Kansas refused admission under the Lecompton Constitution, let it perish in blood and fire." The ultimatum "Lecompton or disunion" reverberated in the halls of Congress, in the southern press, and in southern legislatures. With Alabama leading the way, contingent steps toward secession were officially taken by several states.

At the same time, many southerners realized that the Lecompton bill, with its disreputable background, constituted a very dubious basis for a sectional ultimatum. The issue was not sufficiently clear-cut to make a good test case. Governor Joseph E. Brown of Georgia, who took an aggressive stance, nevertheless later admitted that an outright defeat of the Lecompton bill would have produced "great confusion" in his state and that the Democratic party there would have been "divided and distracted." In other words, outright defeat would have placed militant southerners in the position of having to choose between launching a secession movement that seemed likely to fail and backing down from their threats to a chorus of northern jeers. It is therefore not surprising that the English compromise should have been welcomed throughout the South with far more praise than its substance warranted. There were dissenting voices, to be sure, and a good deal of hairsplitting explanation was necessary, but southern Democrats for the most part embraced the fiction that the English bill provided a complete vindication of southern rights.

Of course just about everyone knew that the South had squandered another round of disunion rhetoric to gain nothing more than the veneer of technical victory over real defeat. The English bill, in effect, killed the Lecompton constitution but turned the carcass over to the people of Kansas for final disposal. On August 2, they performed the task convincingly by a vote of 11,300 to 1,788. The secession movement of 1858 and the alacrity with which it was abandoned lent reinforcement to the widespread northern conviction that disunion maneuvers in the South were largely blackmail and bluff. Thus, the *Ohio State Journal* at Columbus, which often spoke for Governor Salmon P. Chase, said that defeat of the Lecompton bill had provided a test and exposed the emptiness of "the miserable threats" of disunion. And the *Illinois State Journal* at Springfield, which often spoke for Abraham Lincoln, said that "secession would be killed by ridicule, as nullification was by force."

The English bill, although it put only a temporary damper on talk of secession, did remove Kansas permanently from the center of sectional controversy. Yet, being an ill-favored thing as compromises go, it left an unusually large residue of dissatisfaction and resentment. This time, for example, efforts to repair the split in the Democratic party proved unsuccessful. The administration continued its patronage reprisals against anti-Lecompton Democrats, and in Illinois it sponsored the formation of a rival party organization to challenge Douglas's leadership. On the Senate floor, Douglas angrily denounced this "conspiracy against the unity and integrity of the Democratic party . . . in Illinois." Various peacemakers began working strenuously to patch up a truce, and when Congress adjourned, there was good reason to believe that they were succeeding. "From what I learn," Buchanan wrote on June 30, "Douglas has determined to come back to the party with a bound and to acquiesce cordially . . . in the English bill." But the Little Giant, taking the measure of northern opinion on a roundabout journey home to Illinois, found hostility to the administration running high and made his decision accordingly. Given a hero's welcome by an enthusiastic crowd in Chicago on July 9, he responded with a slashing attack on the Lecompton constitution and the English bill in a speech that amounted to a renewal of civil war within the Democratic party.

Coming as a great shock after persistent reports of a reconciliation, this Chicago speech was probably the point of no return in the process of Douglas's alienation from the South. Of course the South never approached unanimity on any major issue, and Douglas continued to have supporters in every southern state right down to 1860. One is nevertheless struck by the volume and intensity of southern editorial attacks upon him in the period following the Chicago speech. No abolitionist had ever been more fiercely denounced, but then abolitionists could not be accused of treason to the South. "Douglas was with us," the indictment ran, "until the time of trial came; then he deceived and betrayed us." Now he was the South's worst enemy, guilty of "flagrant inconsistency and patent double dealing," covered with the "filth of his defiant recreancy." A generation must die out and new issues cover the past before he could purge the guilt of his vile alliance with the Republicans. "He must be forgotten before he can be forgiven."

On all sides there had been tremendous emotional investment in the Lecompton struggle. The English compromise formally disposed of the Kansas issue but drained off little of its emotional content. Anger remained—and went in search of other issues. In retrospect it is now clear that the critical question facing the nation in the summer of 1858 was whether the Democratic party could pull itself together sufficiently to prevent a Republican victory in the next presidential election. The paramount issue keeping Democrats divided after the English compromise was the person of Stephen A. Douglas, accused party traitor with designs on the presidency. Southern hatred for him had taken on a life of its own, and yet it could not feed indefinitely on the record of his past transgressions—not in view of the obvious practical need to close ranks against the Republicans. Additional reasons for continuing to anathematize him were required, and so, some eighteen months after its promulgation, the Dred Scott decision became a disruptive issue within the Democratic party.

2

At Chicago on July 9, 1858, when he dramatically renewed his quarrel with the Buchanan administration, Douglas also took notice of the "kind, amiable, and intelligent gentleman" who had become his official opponent in the approaching senatorial contest. Several weeks earlier, Illinois Republicans in their state convention at Springfield had designated Abraham Lincoln as their "first and only choice . . . for the United States Senate, as the successor of Stephen A. Douglas." Lincoln responded to the nomination with his carefully prepared House-Divided speech, and the memorable campaign of 1858 was under way.

The staccato sentences and muscular phrasing of the speech produced a bold effect, and its argument seemed to move Lincoln toward the radical side of Republicanism. A house divided against itself, he said, could not stand; the government could not

endure permanently half slave and half free; he did not expect
the Union to be dissolved but expected rather that it would cease
to be divided; slavery would either be put in course of ultimate
extinction or be legalized everywhere in the United States; the
tendency was in the latter direction and had been ever since passage of the Kansas-Nebraska Act; the Dred Scott decision was
the last step but one in a plan for the nationalization of slavery
designed by Douglas, Pierce, Taney, and Buchanan; coming next
and probably soon, another judicial decision would declare that
no state had the power to exclude slavery from its limits. Illinois
would awake one day to find itself a slave state.

The House-Divided speech embodied a political strategy
shaped in response to recent political developments. Lincoln had
uneasily watched the emergence of Douglas as a party rebel,
much admired even in certain Republican circles. If any sizable
number of Illinois Republicans were captivated by the Little
Giant's new antislavery image, his re-election to the Senate
would be ensured. Somehow, then, Lincoln had to minimize the
significance of the Lecompton split in the Democratic party and
maximize the distance, in matters of principle, between Douglas
and the Republican party. He therefore dismissed the Lecompton controversy as a mere "squabble" and took up the charge that
Democratic leaders, including Douglas, were engaged in a plot
to nationalize slavery. Douglas's primary function in the plot, one
that he continued to perform in spite of his anti-Lecompton
stand, was the undermining of northern resistance to slavery by
inculcating a doctrine of moral indifference under the deceptive
label of "popular sovereignty." When Douglas had won enough
northerners to his philosophy of not caring whether slavery expanded or not, the scene would be fully set for the "second Dred
Scott decision" holding slavery to be lawful everywhere in the
Union. What claim, then, could such a man have upon Republican support? "Our cause," Lincoln insisted, "must be intrusted to,
and conducted by its own undoubted friends—those whose hands
are free, whose hearts are in the work—who *do care* for the
result."

Not surprisingly, Lincoln in the House-Divided speech made
only passing reference to the conflict between Taney's Dred

Scott opinion and the Douglas version of popular sovereignty. The strategy of the speech, after all, was to emphasize the affinities, not the differences, between Douglas and the slaveholding South. In other words, the Freeport question did not really fit into Lincoln's battle plan. As the campaign proceeded, however, neither man hesitated to exploit any weakness in his opponent's argument. And so, with Douglas praising popular sovereignty and defending the Dred Scott decision, Lincoln was bound to raise the question of their incongruity. Speaking at Chicago on July 10 in reply to the Douglas speech of the previous evening, he asked: "What is popular sovereignty? . . . What has become of it? Can you get anybody to tell you now that the people of a territory have any authority to govern themselves, in regard to this mooted question of slavery, before they form a state constitution?" No, he continued, the Supreme Court had denied that the territories could rightfully exclude slavery. "When that is so, how much is left of this vast matter of squatter sovereignty I should like to know?" A voice from the audience answered, "It has all gone."

Here was the substance of the Freeport question, put rhetorically but forcefully almost seven weeks before the debate at Freeport. Douglas, in his speeches at Bloomington and Springfield on July 16 and 17, accordingly revived the concept of residual popular sovereignty, which he had not used in public since the preceding summer. "If the people of a territory want slavery they will have it," he declared, "and if they do not want it they will drive it out, and you cannot force it on them. Slavery cannot exist a day in the midst of an unfriendly people and unfriendly laws." Thus, six weeks before the debate at Freeport, Douglas clearly set forth the Freeport doctrine of "unfriendly legislation," doing so in response to questions from his opponent.

Lincoln did not immediately pursue the matter further. The Dred Scott decision nevertheless received considerable attention from both speakers during the course of their first formal debate at Ottawa on August 21. Lincoln reiterated his conspiracy charge, for instance, and Douglas pronounced it an "infamous lie." Douglas declared that Lincoln opposed the Dred Scott decision primarily because it denied citizenship to Negroes; Lincoln responded with an emphatic disavowal of racial equality. Douglas condemned Lincoln's "warfare on the Supreme Court"; Lincoln asked how Republican criticism of the Dred Scott decision was any worse than the Democratic party's continued repudiation (in its official platform) of the Supreme Court decision upholding the constitutionality of a national bank.

During the Ottawa debate also, Douglas fired a volley of seven questions at Lincoln, who cautiously put off answering them until the next debate at Freeport six days later. Meanwhile, some of Lincoln's advisers decided that he had kept too much on the defensive at Ottawa and must become more aggressive. And so, at Freeport, Lincoln not only answered Douglas's seven questions but countered with four of his own. There is no contemporary evidence that he regarded any one question as more important than the others. Two of them, the second and third, were directly related to the Dred Scott decision, but only the latter conformed to the campaign strategy adopted in the House-Divided speech.

This third question pressed the issue of a conspiracy to nationalize slavery: "If the Supreme Court of the United States shall decide that States can not exclude slavery from their limits, are you in favor of acquiescing in, adopting and following such decision as a rule of political action?" Douglas, who had been insisting that any decision of the Supreme Court must be accepted as the law of the land, prudently chose to ridicule the query instead of answering it. "Such a thing is not possible," he said. "It would be an act of moral treason that no man on the bench would ever descend to." It "amazed" him that anyone should ask such a question. A schoolboy would know better than to do so. Lincoln might as well ask whether, if he stole a horse, Douglas would condone it.

Lincoln renewed the question in later debates, noting that there had been no response except sneers. The essence of the Dred Scott decision, he declared, was compressed into one Taney sentence: "The right of property in a slave is distinctly and expressly affirmed in the Constitution." If this premise were accepted as true, said Lincoln, and if it were combined with the supremacy clause of the Constitution, the result would be a syllogism with the inevitable conclusion that nothing in the constitution or laws of any state could "destroy the right of property in a slave." Thus the logical basis for the second Dred Scott decision had been fully laid.

But Douglas steadfastly refused to consider even the possibility of a decision "so ridiculous" as to declare that Illinois and other free states could not prohibit slavery within their own boundaries. It was "an insult to men's understanding, and a gross calumny on the court" to suggest such a thing, he asserted. And there, in spite of some further needling by Lincoln, the matter rested.

If the Lincoln-Douglas debates are viewed properly as a representative event in the struggle between Republicans and northern Democrats for public favor in the free states, this vision of a "second Dred Scott decision" becomes a matter of considerable importance. For it was in some respects a rhetorical device used to express a widespread and deepening suspicion of southern motives that had begun to affect even Douglas's political outlook. This growing northern hostility to the slaveholding South, as distinguished from hostility to southern slavery, may be the key to Republican success in 1860. If so, then Lincoln's third query at Freeport is perhaps the most significant of the lot. But of course it was the second question that had the more visible consequences and that became in retrospect one of those decisive moments on which destiny turns.

Once Lincoln decided to fire back some questions of his own at Freeport, it was almost automatic to include one pointing up the contradiction between the Dred Scott decision and the Douglas version of popular sovereignty.* Republicans had been asking

---

* Second Freeport question and answer:

"Can the people of a United States Territory, in any lawful way, against the wish of any citizen of the United States, exclude slavery from its limits prior to the formation of a State Constitution?"

"I answer emphatically, as Mr. Lincoln has heard me answer a hundred times from every stump in Illinois, that in my opinion the people of a territory can, by lawful means, exclude slavery from their limits prior to the formation of a State Constitution. . . . It matters not what way the Supreme Court may hereafter decide as to the abstract question whether slavery may or may not go into a territory under the constitution, the

it in one way or another for more than a year: Congressional prohibition having been voided by the Supreme Court, could a territorial legislature legally prohibit slavery? Douglas, it should be noted, actually returned two answers—one a carefully phrased implication, the other an emphatic assertion. He implied that the Court had not yet decided the question of territorial power over slavery, thereby treating the relevant passage in Taney's opinion as dictum. This maneuver left room for a possible revival of the old leave-it-to-the-Court formula that had served the Democratic party so well in the past. It was thus a strategy looking forward to the presidential contest of 1860.

For the senatorial campaign in progress, however, something more forceful was needed. So Douglas answered Lincoln's second question by reiterating the principle of residual popular sovereignty, which at this point became known as the "Freeport doctrine." But whatever practical wisdom there may have been in the argument that slavery could never survive where it was not wanted, the constitutional foundations of the Freeport doctrine were weak. Lincoln, seeing an opportunity to score forensic points against his adversary, pursued the matter vigorously in subsequent debates and speeches. He reminded Illinoisans that Douglas, when asked the same question on the Senate floor in 1856, had labeled it a judicial issue. Now that the Supreme Court had decided the question, however, Douglas was shifting his ground, maintaining in effect that a territorial legislature could nullify a judicially recognized constitutional right. "Why this," said Lincoln, "is a *monstrous* sort of talk . . . There has never been as outlandish or lawless a doctrine from the mouth of any respectable man on earth." And it was a doctrine, he added, that would also justify open resistance to the Fugitive Slave Law.

At Jonesboro on September 15, Lincoln added an important

---

people have the lawful means to introduce it or exclude it as they please, for the reason that slavery cannot exist a day or an hour anywhere, unless it is supported by local police regulations. Those police regulations can only be established by the local legislature, and if the people are opposed to slavery they will elect representatives to that body who will by unfriendly legislation effectually prevent the introduction of it into their midst."

corollary to the second Freeport question when he confronted Douglas with this "fifth interrogatory":

> If the slaveholding citizens of a United States Territory should need and demand Congressional legislation for the protection of their slave property in such Territory, would you, as a member of Congress, vote for or against such legislation?

Douglas responded by reaffirming the principle of nonintervention and in a later debate stated more explicitly that he would oppose any effort to establish a congressional slave code for the territories.

With this question Lincoln anticipated the most significant southern response to the Freeport doctrine. Indeed, even as the Jonesboro debate took place, the Washington *Union* and the Richmond *Enquirer* were arguing over whether Douglas had done the South a service by pointing up the need for a territorial slave code. In general, however, the Freeport doctrine provoked no great new explosion of southern anger—certainly nothing to compare with southern reaction to Douglas's Chicago speech of July 17 and to his earlier anti-Lecompton speeches in the Senate. It was the whole pattern of his behavior beginning in December 1857, and not the Freeport doctrine alone, that ruined his political standing in the South.

3

If United States senators had been elected then as now by popular vote, instead of by state legislatures, history might well record that Lincoln defeated Douglas in a close contest. But the Illinois Democrats, having more holdover senate seats and a slight advantage in the legislative apportionment, won narrow control of both houses at Springfield and a joint majority of 54 to 46. By that margin, Douglas was re-elected on January 6, 1859. The party also won five out of the state's nine congressional races, thereby holding its own against the Republicans in the House of Representatives.

Elsewhere, however, the midterm congressional elections added up to defeat for the northern wing of the Democratic party. Its fifty-three seats in the House of Representatives were reduced to thirty-one, and this remnant included at least a dozen anti-Lecompton Democrats, a majority of whom refused even to caucus with their party. Some of the party's losses in the North probably resulted from fusion of Republican and Know-Nothing forces that had supported separate tickets in 1856, allowing Democratic candidates to win with pluralities. Other losses in 1858 have been attributed to party in-fighting, especially over patronage. Still, even with such qualifications, the election results seem to indicate a strong northern reaction against the administration and its Kansas policy. Of the fifty-three northern Democrats in the House of Representatives, twenty-six had been consistently pro-Lecompton, and eleven had been consistently anti-Lecompton to the extent of opposing even the English compromise. Twenty-three of the twenty-six loyalists sought re-election, but only six were successful. Of the eleven insurgents, four did not run for re-election but were replaced by anti-Lecompton Democrats; seven sought re-election, and six did so successfully. Thus 86 per cent of the insurgents and only 26 percent of the loyalists running for re-election won the approval of the voters.

The election returns of 1858 therefore reflected two important political changes growing out of the Lecompton controversy. One was the split in the Democratic party—a split not strictly along sectional lines, but having a definite sectional tendency none the less. The other was a substantial decline of Democratic strength at the polls in certain crucial northern states—a decline which, if not reversed, could mean nothing other than the election of a Republican president in 1860.

Rumors of a reconciliation between Douglas and Buchanan began to circulate soon after the results of the Illinois election were known, but then, on December 9, 1858, there came a dramatic renewal of hostilities. The news flashed out of Washington that the Democratic caucus was removing Douglas from the chairmanship of the Senate committee on territories, a position that he had held for eleven years. It was a petty act of revenge, obviously carrying the stamp of administration approval, and it set the tone of a rancorous session.

Official Washington gave the Little Giant a cold reception upon his return to the Senate. Many of his colleagues ungraciously ignored him. When the Douglases staged a "grand ball" at their residence, issuing some 1200 invitations, every member of the cabinet sent his regrets. The President, meanwhile, continued to operate his "guillotine" by making anti-Douglas appointments in Illinois. Douglas, moreover, quickly fell into a series of personal quarrels with three senators who supported the administration. In one case, the adversaries exchanged notes and appointed intermediaries, before reaching an awkward, unfriendly adjustment. These incidents lent credence to talk of a plot to force Douglas into a duel. "The war of the roses," wrote a New York *Times* correspondent, "is evidently just beginning."

In the face of such hostility, Douglas displayed considerable restraint, and the feud within the Democratic party continued merely to sputter viciously without a major confrontation as the thirty-fifth Congress entered its final weeks. Then, on February 23, 1859, Senator Albert G. Brown of Mississippi launched an attack on Douglas and a demand for federal legislation protecting slavery in the territories. "We demand it and we mean to have it," Brown said. If the protection were denied, he would recommend secession. The debate that followed lasted ten hours or more and constituted a milestone in the history of the slavery controversy; for at this point the more theoretical implications of the Dred Scott decision replaced the practical problem of territorial Kansas as the storm center of sectional conflict.

Douglas, in responding to Brown's attack, significantly made no use of the "unfriendly legislation" formula. Instead, he argued that slave property in the territories was entitled to the same amount of protection given other kinds of property, and no more; that the extent to which a territorial government might interfere with any property right, including slaveholding, was a judicial question; and that congressional imposition of a slave code in the territories would be a violation of the principle of nonintervention. In his answer to the second Freeport question, it will be remembered, Douglas had already implied that the limits of territorial power remained undetermined, thus ignoring Taney's dictum on the subject. But he had then gone on to declare that it did not matter *what* the Supreme Court might "hereafter decide"; that if the people of a territory wanted to exclude slavery, they would find the legal means of doing so. His southern critics were therefore little impressed when he now revived the familiar refrain, "Take it to the Supreme Court." For he was recommending a cure that he had already labeled futile.

Brown and his Mississippi colleague, Jefferson Davis, replied that judicial remedies alone would not be sufficient to protect slave property against a hostile territorial legislature. Thus they agreed with Douglas's Freeport diagnosis but refused to accept his conclusion that nothing further could be done. "What the Government owes to person and property is adequate protection," Davis insisted. "If . . . constitutional rights are violated by the inhabitants of a Territory, or anybody else, it is the duty of Congress to interpose, with whatever power it possesses, to make that protection adequate."

With some justification, Douglas could now claim to be defending the principle of nonintervention against Republican and southern interventionists alike. Pressed hard by Davis in the debate, he stated categorically: "I will vote against any law by Congress attempting to interfere with a regulation made by the Territories, with respect to any kind of property whatever." Even more emphatic was George E. Pugh of Ohio, who had supported the Lecompton bill and voted for the English compromise. Vigorously denying that the principle of popular sovereignty had been ruled unconstitutional, he said, "The court decided no such thing . . . In the whole Dred Scott case there was no act of a Territorial Legislature before them in any shape or form." And to southern insistence on a federal slave code for the territories, he responded, "Never; while I live, never! I consider it a monstrous demand."

What the long day's debate clearly revealed was the persistence of an irrepressible conflict within the Democratic party. Ostensibly, it had now become a conflict over the meaning of the Dred Scott decision, but behind that lay the bitter memory of the Lecompton struggle, and just ahead loomed the contest for the presidency. Southerners in large numbers had already announced what they would do if a Republican were elected to that office. Now the debate of February 23 made it plain that southern Democratic leaders would not accept Douglas as the nominee of their party. A prime purpose of the slave code issue was to demonstrate his unacceptability. As Douglas himself complained, the southerners neither hoped nor attempted to get a territorial slave code enacted into law. What they wanted instead was to make it a test of party loyalty and a plank in the Democratic platform. If they succeeded, Douglas would no doubt be driven into another revolt; if they failed there would be adequate reason for a southern withdrawal from the national convention. Either way, the demand for congressional protection of slavery in the territories promised to disrupt the Democratic party.

The South, though increasingly a minority section, had continued to exercise enormous power in national politics. Southerners, at the beginning of the Buchanan administration, dominated the Supreme Court, dominated presidential counsels, and, through the caucus system, controlled both houses of Congress. This had all been possible because of a kind of holding-company arrangement, in which the South was the majority section within the Democratic party, and the Democrats were the majority party of the nation. Thus the critical task of southerners endeavoring to protect slavery within the confines of the Union was to maintain the majority status of the Democratic party. In the past, this had meant tolerating some measure of internal sectional disagreement and camouflaging it at election time with vague or ambiguous planks in the party platform. Good sense would seem to have required a continuation of such strategy in the late 1850s. What southern Democrats needed most of all from their northern allies were election victories. What they demanded instead was orthodoxy, as they themselves defined it.

In studying southern motives at this point, it is difficult to distinguish calculation from miscalculation, and both, in turn, from irrationality. Certainly there were avowed secessionists working openly to disrupt the Democratic party as a step toward disunion. Covertly or subconsciously allied with these bold spirits was a larger group of southerners who continued to describe secession as a last resort while conducting themselves in a way that tended to eliminate other choices. Their "conditional Unionism" with impossible conditions amounted to secessionism in the end. Jefferson Davis exemplifies the latter category, but whether he calculated or miscalculated the consequences of the slave code movement is difficult to determine. He may have done both in that agony of ambivalence with which some southern leaders contemplated the prospect of disunion. Warnings against pressing the demand for a territorial slave code were issued in great profusion, not only by Douglas and his supporters but also by many prominent southerners. Yet the Brown-Davis strategy seemed likely to prevail. In effect, the strategy gave the suppression of internal dissent priority over the defeat of the Republican enemy—a preference justified with the argument that Douglas's "squatter sovereignty" was as bad as the Wilmot Proviso and perhaps even worse. "It adds insult to injury," said the Memphis *Avalanche,* "for it mocks and derides the just claim of the slaveholder . . . It is a snare and a swindle, full of mean cunning, rank injustice and insolence." This sense of being cheated out of their judicial victory rankled southerners deeply and no doubt helps account for the unreasoning persistence with which so many of them pursued the slave code issue. Like the fight to prevent resubmission of the Lecompton constitution, it became a "point of honor" to invest the Dred Scott decision with some semblance of political effectiveness. With Kansas pushed into the background, the struggle for southern rights now seemed concentrated in the effort to defend the decision, not only against direct attack but also against the erosive effect of the Freeport doctrine. "The Dred Scott decision," said one Republican senator, "is the only Democratic platform that now exists. . . . It is the party test."

4

Now fully determined to seek the presidential nomination, even though he issued perfunctory disclaimers from time to time,

Douglas felt the irrepressible urge to strike back at his southern critics and to define his own position in forceful terms. "I do not intend to make peace with my enemies, nor to make a concession of one iota of principle," he confided to one of his Illinois lieutenants. Soon after the adjournment of Congress, he set to work preparing a comprehensive statement of his views on the territorial question. Arrangements were made to publish it in the September issue of *Harper's Magazine* under the title, "The Dividing Line Between Federal and Local Authority: Popular Sovereignty in the Territories." Anyone who now plods through this long and often tedious article is likely to wonder how it could have stirred up so much excitement. Yet its publication proved to be one of the most important political events of the year.

Harper's Magazine, besieged with Republican and southern proposals to answer Douglas, turned them all down, but newspaper columns and hastily printed pamphlets provided ample battleground for the clangorous war of words. Reverdy Johnson and George T. Curtis, two of the four attorneys in the Dred Scott case, each published an extensive commentary. So did Horace Greeley. Buchanan requested his attorney general, Jeremiah S. Black, to prepare a rebuttal, and Black complied with such speed that his unsigned pamphlet appeared scarcely two weeks after publication of the *Harper's* essay. A restatement of standard proslavery doctrine, it was offensive in tone, heaping sarcasm and ridicule, not only on Douglas's argument but also on his literary style.

Douglas, meanwhile, had begun a short speaking tour of Ohio, where the Democrats needed help in the biennial state election. At Wooster on September 16, 1859, he replied angrily to Black, calling the latter a "calumniator" who would "prostitute a high government office by writing deliberate falsehoods to mislead the American people." Lincoln, who had followed his old adversary into Ohio, spoke at Columbus on the same day and devoted most of his time to a critique of the *Harper's* essay, which was, he said, "the most maturely considered" of Douglas's "explanations explanatory of explanations explained." But the battle at this point was primarily between Douglas and the administration. Soon Black published an "Appendix" in answer to the Wooster speech. Douglas countered with another pamphlet. Black again replied, and Douglas, in still another pamphlet, had the final word. By then it was past the middle of November, and public attention had long since shifted to John Brown, now convicted and awaiting execution at Charlestown, Virginia. Most people had, in any case, grown weary of the repetitious, ill-tempered exchange between Black and Douglas. It remained to be seen whether they might have silenced the territorial issue by talking it to death.

The argument presented by Douglas was highly vulnerable to criticism, partly because he claimed a consistency that his record did not confirm, and partly because of his determination to justify constitutionally a policy that was sounder in practice than in theory. Having begun to defend his brand of popular sovereignty on constitutional grounds in 1856, he now undertook the more difficult enterprise of providing a constitutional defense for residual popular sovereignty—the Freeport doctrine—in the face of the Dred Scott decision. That slavery could not prosper against the will of the majority in any locality had been acknowledged as an extralegal fact of life by various southerners. But it was a different matter to have the acknowledgment thrown back at them as a constitutional principle by the man already widely accused of betraying the South. Furthermore, Douglas had previously resorted to the Freeport doctrine primarily as local campaign strategy in Illinois. The *Harper's* essay, published with so much flourish in the nation's leading magazine, seemed far more deliberately anti-southern—almost like a declaration of war.

What Douglas set out to prove in the essay was that territorial legislatures possessed the legal right to establish or prohibit slavery, even though Congress did not. There were essentially two ways of arriving at such a conclusion, and Douglas with characteristic flexibility followed both, even though they were incompatible. One way was to derive territorial power from congressional authority (in spite of the Dred Scott decision) by drawing a distinction between what Congress could itself *do* and what it could *authorize* other agencies of government to do. Thus, Douglas argued, Congress could establish judicial and executive bodies, conferring upon them powers that Congress could not itself exercise. Similarly, "Congress may also confer upon the legislative department of the Territory certain legislative powers which it cannot itself exercise."

The other way was to derive territorial power directly from the text of the Constitution or from the natural right of self-government, without any reference to congressional authority. Douglas gave primary attention to this line of argument and the crux of it was his assertion that in the early Republic, western territories had been regarded as incipient states, possessing as much control over their domestic affairs as the thirteen original states of the Union. In evidence, he quoted extensively from Jefferson's Ordinance of 1784 with its generous provisions for the erection of "additional states" in the West. He failed to mention that the ordinance had never been put into operation, and he completely ignored the highly paternalistic Ordinance of 1787, which scarcely would have lent support to his case. Ignoring, indeed, even the official title, "An Ordinance for the government of the Territory of the United States north-west of the River Ohio," Douglas maintained that the founders' generation had always used the word "states" to designate new political communities in the West, and the word "territory" to designate public land in the West. The territory clause of the Constitution, he reiterated in harmony with Taney, had no bearing on the slavery question. Temporary governments in the West were created by Congress under its constitutional authority to admit "new states," and no state, however incipient, could be denied control over its own domestic institutions.

By identifying territorial power absolutely with state sovereignty, Douglas was led to an argument astonishingly similar to the principal theme of Lincoln's House-Divided speech:

> If the Constitution does establish slavery in Kansas or any other Territory beyond the power of the people to control it by law, how can the conclusion be resisted that slavery is established in like manner and by the same authority in all the States of the Union? And if it be the imperative duty of Congress to provide by law for the protection of slave property in the Territories . . . why is it not also the duty of Congress . . . to provide similar protection to slave property in all the

States of the Union, when the Legislatures fail to furnish such protection?

In short, if southern Democrats were right about the meaning of the Dred Scott decision, then Republicans were right in viewing the decision as a fateful step toward the nationalization of slavery. Douglas, as Judah P. Benjamin later charged on the Senate floor, had appropriated notorious Republican doctrine.

With good reason, then, the Richmond *Enquirer* labeled the *Harper's* essay "an incendiary document." Its reverberations, to be sure, were momentarily drowned out in mid-October by news of the John Brown raid on Harpers Ferry. But Brown's startling adventure and Douglas's aggressive manifesto were both incorporated by many southerners into a nightmarish vision of the southern future within the Union. For the Harpers Ferry raid seemed to dramatize the rising, implacable strength of their enemies, while the *Harper's* essay seemed to confirm the dwindling numbers and increasing unreliability of their northern friends.

❧ 10 ❧

Not Peace
but a Sword

The new thirty-sixth Congress assembled on December 5, 1859, a few weeks after Douglas published his final rejoinder to the Attorney General and just three days after John Brown died on the gallows in Virginia. Less than five months ahead lay the Democratic national convention, scheduled to meet at Charleston, of all places. Any lingering hope that the President might try to reunite the divided party was dispelled by his third annual message. Buchanan's previous messages had contained only passing references to the Dred Scott case. Now, almost three years after the Court's decision, he proceeded to "congratulate" the American people on the "final settlement" of the territorial issue:

> The right has been established of every citizen to take his property of any kind, including slaves, into the common Territories belonging equally to all the States of the Confederacy, and to have it protected there under the Federal Constitution. Neither Congress nor a Territorial legislature nor any human power has any authority to annul or impair this vested right. . . .
>
> Thus has the status of a Territory during the intermediate period from its first settlement until it shall become a State been irrevocably fixed by the final decision of the Supreme Court. Fortunate has this been for the prosperity of the Territories, as well as the tranquillity of the States.

Here, straight from a Pennsylvanian in the White House, was proslavery doctrine pure enough to have satisfied John C. Calhoun, including even an acknowledgment that the territories belonged to the states, rather than to the nation. Here too was the Dred Scott decision stamped "irrevocable" and Taney's dictum against popular sovereignty accepted as authoritative. Furthermore, Buchanan added a flat endorsement of the southern demand for congressional protection of slavery in the territories whenever such protection should be needed.

The need seemed likely to materialize soon; for the Kansas legislature had already passed a bill abolishing slavery in the territory, only to have it killed by the governor's pocket veto. There would surely be enough antislavery strength to override a veto when the effort was made again in 1860. And a similar movement had begun in Nebraska Territory, despite the fact that there were no slaves in residence there. The testing of Douglas's Freeport doctrine was plainly under way.

Southern congressional leaders still had no desire to press for immediate slave-code legislation, however. What they wanted instead was an anti-Douglas platform for Charleston, phrased in such a way as to maximize southern solidarity. Jefferson Davis accordingly came forward on February 2, 1860, with a set of resolutions that sounded like "Calhoun brought up to date." Endorsed by the President and approved with some minor revisions by the Democratic caucus in the Senate, they became the focus of sectional debate over slavery for the rest of the session. The critical resolutions were those numbered four to six, as follows:

4. That neither Congress nor a Territorial Legislature, whether by direct legislation or legislation of an indirect and unfriendly character, possesses power to annul or impair the constitutional right of any citizen of the United States to take his slave property into the common Territories, and there hold and enjoy the same while the territorial condition remains.

5. That if experience should at any time prove that the judiciary and executive authority do not possess means to insure adequate protection to constitutional rights in a Territory, and

if the territorial government shall fail or refuse to provide the
necessary remedies for that purpose, it will be the duty of Congress to supply such deficiency.

6. That the inhabitants of a Territory of the United States,
when they rightfully form a constitution to be admitted as a
State into the Union, may then, for the first time . . . decide
for themselves whether slavery as a domestic institution shall
be maintained or prohibited within their jurisdiction.

The fourth and sixth resolutions, it will be seen, amounted to a
categorical rejection of Douglas, popular sovereignty, and the
Freeport doctrine. The fifth resolution was likewise aimed at
Douglas, but its bland and contingent terms made it something
of a farce because a new bill abolishing slavery had just been
hastily passed in the Kansas legislature and repassed over the
governor's veto. The time for congressional intervention had
therefore already arrived, said the Jackson *Mississippian.* "We
invoke the guardians of the people's rights at Washington to
come at once to the rescue." Albert G. Brown promptly introduced a bill to "punish offenses against slave property" in Kansas, but it was buried in committee. Judah P. Benjamin later
admitted that legislation for the protection of slavery in Kansas
would be a waste of time. "We want a recognition of our right,
because it is denied," he said, "but we do not want to exercise it
now, because there is no occasion for exercising it now."

The interminable debate in the Senate over the Davis resolutions was echoed in the House of Representatives, in newspaper
columns, in many state legislatures, and in the local and state
conventions of the Democratic party which were at work choosing delegates to send to Charleston. With Illinois leading the
way, the conventions in the Old Northwest lined up unanimously
behind Douglas. Although his support in the other northern
states was less solid, it became increasingly clear that he had no
pre-eminent rival for the presidential nomination and could expect to receive a majority of the votes on the first ballot. But a
convention rule dating back to 1832 required a two-thirds majority to nominate, and that was a different matter. Douglas

would need some southern help to win; yet the state conventions
in the South, one by one, turned their faces against him and endorsed the principles of the Davis resolutions.

So the Charleston convention assembled on April 23 in a condition of virtual stalemate, the Douglas delegates being numerous
enough to dictate a platform but not to nominate their candidate.
Southerners had reason to believe that by holding out firmly
against Douglas they could force him to withdraw from the contest. Douglas men, at the same time, could see two ways of
increasing their percentage of the total vote. By making concessions on the platform they might recruit some moderate southerners to their ranks. On the other hand, by rejecting demands
for an explicitly proslavery platform they might provoke enough
southern walkouts to leave themselves a two-thirds majority of
the delegates remaining in the hall.

In a rare moment of consensus, the delegates voted to con-
struct their platform first. The platform committee consisted of
thirty-three members, one from each state. The delegates from
Oregon and California joined the fifteen southerners to present a
majority report denying territorial power over slavery and calling for federal protection of the institution whenever it might be
needed. The minority report simply reaffirmed the indistinct
Cincinnati platform of 1856 and referred the question of territorial power to the Supreme Court. There was no insistence on
the Douglas version of popular sovereignty, no reiteration of the
Freeport doctrine.

The crisis came when these reports were presented to the
convention. The Douglas forces, with their superior numbers,
adopted the minority report. As one last gesture of compromise,
however, they eliminated the resolution referring the territorial
question to the Supreme Court. This left a platform that said
nothing about slavery beyond reaffirming the Cincinnati platform. It was an inoffensive rejection of southern demands, but a
rejection none the less, and when the voting ended, the Alabama
delegation announced its withdrawal from the convention, followed by the delegates from Mississippi, Louisiana, South Carolina, Florida, Texas, and Arkansas. The Georgia delegates took

their departure the next day. With the exception of Arkansas, these were the same states that, after Lincoln's election, would secede from the Union and form the Southern Confederacy. Their delegations withdrew, it should be emphasized, rather than accept the party platform of 1856 and out of hostility to the man whom they had supported overwhelmingly for the nomination just four years earlier.* Such was the revolutionary change of attitude in the deep South, wrought primarily by the Lecompton controversy, the Dred Scott decision, and the Harpers Ferry raid.

The withdrawal of fifty-one southern delegates did not bring success for Douglas. After two days of balloting without a nomination, the delegates approved a proposal that they adjourn and reassemble at Baltimore on June 18. There followed an interval of consultation and maneuver in preparation for resumption of the struggle. Meanwhile, the Republican convention assembled at Chicago in mid-May and surprised everyone by nominating Abraham Lincoln instead of the odds-on favorite, William H. Seward. A week earlier, delegates from the Whig-American remnant had likewise gathered in convention. Calling themselves the "Constitutional Union Party," they nominated the elderly Tennessee Whig, John Bell, on a platform of having no platform other than "the Constitution of the Country, the Union of the States, and the Enforcement of the Laws."

Congress remained in session, and the Senate resumed its discussion of the Davis resolutions until they were finally approved in late May. The central point at issue was still the meaning of the Dred Scott decision. Republicans continued to deny its legitimacy. Douglas Democrats continued to circumscribe its import by denying that it had settled the question of territorial power, though they promised to acquiesce in any future judicial ruling on that subject. Southerners continued to insist that the decision had settled all outstanding territorial issues in their favor—that both the Republicans and the Douglas Democrats

---

* On the early ballots at Cincinnati in 1856, Douglas received all the votes of South Carolina, Alabama, Mississippi, Florida, Texas, and Arkansas, as well as most of the Georgia votes. Only Louisiana supported Buchanan.

were trying to cheat them of a clear-cut victory in the courts. Nothing in the debate justified any hope of a Democratic reconciliation at Baltimore.

The platform battle was never renewed at Baltimore; for a crisis developed immediately over the seating of rival delegations, and another southern walkout ensued. The shocked but resolute delegates remaining in the hall then nominated Douglas for the presidency. The seceders hastened to convene elsewhere in Baltimore, declaring themselves to be the true national convention of the Democratic party. As their candidate for the presidency, they nominated Vice President John C. Breckinridge of Kentucky.

As a party platform, the Breckinridge convention simply adopted the majority report of the resolutions committee at Charleston, with its denial of territorial power over slavery and its demand for federal protection whenever needed. The Douglas convention had left itself at Charleston with a mere reaffirmation of the Cincinnati platform. During the Baltimore proceedings, however, an additional resolution was approved:

> That it is in accordance with the interpretation of the Cincinnati platform, that during the existence of the Territorial Governments the measure of restriction, whatever it may be, imposed by the Federal Constitution on the power of the Territorial Legislature over the subject of the domestic relations, as the same has been or shall hereafter be finally determined by the Supreme Court of the United States, should be respected by all good citizens, and enforced with promptness and fidelity by every branch of the General Government.

This diffuse formulation surrendered much of what Douglas had presumably been contending for. It acknowledged that popular sovereignty might be unconstitutional and that the Supreme Court might already have declared it so. More than that, the resolution virtually embraced the principle of congressional intervention, declaring that "every branch" of the federal government must enforce whatever judicial determination there had been, or might be, regarding slavery in the territories.

The Douglas and Breckinridge platforms were very nearly

identical, except in their interpretations of the Dred Scott decision, and by no means diametrically opposed even on that subject. The bolters had bolted at Charleston after failing to get
everything they wanted in the platform, and at Baltimore after
failing to get everything they wanted in the seating of delegates.
Back of all this intransigence there was an *ad hominem* resolve.
When it came to the test, a majority of Democrats from the deep
South preferred to break up their party rather than accept the
nomination of Douglas, just as they had already determined to
break up the Union rather than accept the election of a Republican President. In this respect, the Democratic conventions were
rehearsals for secession.

The nomination of Lincoln astonished most of the country,
but his election in November took no one by surprise. Separately, neither Breckinridge nor Bell nor Douglas had any chance
of winning, and efforts to form an anti-Republican coalition succeeded in only a few states. The best hope was that Lincoln
might somehow be denied an electoral majority, whereupon the
election would be cast into the House of Representatives. Few
southerners were sanguine, however. "The result of the Presidential struggle is no longer one of much doubt or uncertainty,"
said the Columbia *South Carolinian* more than three months before election day. "Take State by State, and make whatever
calculations we may, . . . we can arrive at no other conclusion
than that Lincoln is to be the next President of the United
States."

Their early recognition of the likelihood of defeat gave southerners abundant time before the election to consider what a Republican presidency would mean for the South and what ought
to be done about it. On both questions there was disagreement
along a wide spectrum; for the southern consensus on slavery
never translated into a consensus on disunion. In the deep South,
however, the emotional advantage was on the side of the immediate secessionists, who predicted the disruption, sooner or
later, of slaveholding society if the southern people submitted
meekly to Republican rule.

Southern political leaders and editors favoring secession, or
leaning toward it, developed a scenario for the future of the

South under a Republican administration. Of course, they said, there would probably be no overt acts of aggression in the beginning. Instead, the Republicans would set about consolidating their power in the North and insidiously dividing the South. Their energy and public appeal further enhanced by capture of the presidency, they would seize control of the House of Representatives and, with the admission of additional free states, soon become masters of the Senate. Furthermore, it was only a matter of time until the presidential power of appointment would place an antislavery majority on the Supreme Court. Then, in full command of the federal government, the Republicans could "plunder the South" with a protective tariff, repeal or emasculate the Fugitive Slave Act, abolish slavery in the territories, and prohibit the interstate slave trade. The South, at the same time, would be losing its ability to resist such aggression. Federal offices would furnish the basis for a southern abolitionist party. Then, said the New Orleans *Delta,* "the armies of our enemies will be recruited from our own forces." And everywhere the uninhibited circulation of abolitionist propaganda and the emboldened invasions of abolitionist agitators would inspire chronic servile rebellion and thus accelerate the destruction of slave society from within.

With the election of Lincoln, because of what it seemed to signify, the sectional conflict far overran the issue of slavery in the territories. Then the secession movement precipitated a new national crisis and presented a set of new national issues even more remote from the territorial question. Yet, in the final efforts to save the Union by engineering another great compromise, the territorial question, despite its questionable relevance, once again became the center of attention. Compromise leaders seemed pathetically convinced that if they could somehow solve this most troublesome of old problems, all the terrible new ones would go away.

The major sectional crises of the past had been susceptible of compromise in Congress because they had arisen in Congress and were more or less within congressional control. The crisis of 1860-61 was of a different order; for it resulted from a decision of the American people at the polls, and that decision could not in itself be reversed or modified by congressional action. Compromise leaders could only try to cushion the shock of Lincoln's election by obtaining legislation that would to some degree meet southern demands for security and sectional parity within the Union. They had to contend, moreover, not only with the momentum of a secession movement briskly in progress but also with growing sentiment in the North against any concessions extorted by threat of disunion. Congress, in short, had little control over the crisis of 1860-61, but historical tradition and public expectation required that it go through the familiar motions of legislative compromise.

Public attention was directed especially to the Senate, which had long been the matrix of sectional compromise, and the Senate responded in the spirit of 1850 by creating a special Committee of Thirteen to consider remedies for the "agitated and distracted condition of the country." The leader of the committee (though not its official chairman) was John J. Crittenden of Kentucky, who held the seat once occupied by Henry Clay. Crittenden put together his own "omnibus" of Union-saving measures. Consisting of six constitutional amendments and four supplementary resolutions, it was largely proslavery in character. It promised to settle once and for all the longstanding argument over whether slavery was an institution sanctioned by the federal Constitution or strictly a creature of state and local law. The words "slave" and "slavery," never used in the Constitution itself, appeared fifteen times in the text of the six amendments.

The most critical item in the Crittenden package was a constitutional amendment restoring the Missouri Compromise line and extending it to the Pacific coast. Slavery was prohibited north of 36° 30′ and "recognized as existing" to the south. Crittenden thus proposed to revive a territorial solution that antislavery men had long been unwilling to accept and that southerners had grown accustomed to denouncing as a gross injustice to their section. Other amendments in the package forbade abolition of slavery on federal property within slaveholding states; forbade abolition in the District of Columbia as long as slavery continued to exist in Virginia or Maryland; prohibited federal interference with interstate transportation of slaves; and required Congress to provide for the compensation of any slaveholder who was prevented by force from or intimidation from recovering a fugitive slave. Crittenden's sixth amendment, designed to place a double lock on southern security, provided that the other five amendments should never be subject to future amendment. It extended the same immunity to the three-fifths clause and the fugitive-slave clause. It also forbade any amendment authorizing Congress to "abolish or interfere" with slavery in states where it was permitted by law. As a consequence, all parts of the Constitution related directly to slavery would have been made unamendable—a privileged status accorded permanently to no other clause of the Constitution, except the guarantee of equal state representation in the Senate.*

The Crittenden omnibus was defeated in the Committee of Thirteen and defeated again when brought independently to the floor of the Senate. Adopted with some changes by the Washington Peace Conference in February 1861 and presented to Congress on the eve of adjournment, it was again rejected, this time by both houses. The plan failed primarily because of overwhelming Republican opposition, and the principal sticking point was the amendment restoring and extending the 36° 30′ line. On this issue, the President-elect declared himself "inflexible" and urged members of Congress to "entertain no proposition for a compromise in regard to the *extension* of slavery." In the dire circumstances such inflexibility seemed irrational and unconscionable to supporters of compromise. "What," asked a Douglas newspaper in upper New York, "would the North lose, then, by this Compromise line? Nothing. What would the South gain by it? We answer again, nothing . . . . The quarrel, after all, is about an unsubstantial right—a mere abstraction."

Obviously, this was an argument that could have been directed with equal relevance to both sections. Indeed, what perhaps needs explaining most is the extent to which southerners insisted upon the 36° 30′ amendment as a *sine qua non* of compromise. For in a way, the amendment appeared to be a substantial concession to antislavery sentiment, rather than to the

---

* Article V made two clauses unamendable before 1808 (foreign slave trade and prohibition on direct taxes) and declared that no state without its own consent could be deprived of "its equal suffrage in the Senate."

slaveholding interest. That is, it virtually nullified the Dred Scott decision in three-fourths of the existing western territory and imposed the Republican principle of federal exclusion there. So this, it seemed, was an opportunity for advocates of free soil to gain back much of what had been lost in the 1850s. Yet Republican members of Congress were united in their opposition to the amendment, while a great many southerners, especially in the border states, regarded it as the most essential element in a compromise program that just might satisfy the minimal demands of the deep South and thus prepare the way for a swift reconstruction of the Union.

One may with good reason doubt that the momentum of secession could have been arrested by congressional approval of a constitutional amendment which had little practical significance and was unlikely ever to be ratified.* Yet there is also good reason to consider why this worn-out solution to a disappearing problem should have become laden with so much hope in the winter of 1860-61 and why it should have been rejected with so much passion. The answer obviously lies, not in what the amendment was designed to accomplish, but rather in what it was assumed to signify.

Southern fear of Republican power could be substantially diminished only by a substantial renunciation of Republican purpose. "The crisis," said Albert G. Brown, "can only be met in one way effectually, . . . and that is, for the northern people to review and reverse their whole policy upon the subject of slavery." By the terms of Crittenden's 36° 30′ amendment, in contrast with the old Missouri Compromise restriction, slavery would have been not just silently permitted in part of the federal territory

---

* The Crittenden amendments, even if passed by the required two-thirds majority in the Senate and House of Representatives, would then have had to win the approval of 52 legislative chambers in 26 states. The odds against such an achievement were forbidding enough in themselves, and the progress of secession made them enormous. By February 1, seven states had seceded and only 27 remained in the Union. Yet the number required for ratification could not be reduced below 26 without acknowledging secession as a legal right and an accomplished fact—something that most Republicans and many northern Democrats were unwilling to do. All of which meant that the opposition of two states—say, Maine and Vermont—would have been sufficient to block ratification.

but given positive constitutional protection there. Thus Republican acceptance of the amendment would have constituted at least a partial renunciation of the Republican purpose—a signal of semi-surrender to southern demands. In this perspective, it appears that both sides may have understood clearly what southerners were asking and Republicans refusing in 1861—understood the critical symbolic meaning of their last, ostensibly empty quarrel over slavery in the territories.

2

Roger B. Taney had watched the presidential campaign of 1860 with great anxiety. By mid-October, the results of several important gubernatorial contests had clearly foreshadowed a Republican victory, and his deepening pessimism became apocalyptic. Characteristically, he said nothing in public, but he unburdened himself in a letter to his son-in-law. "I am satisfied," he wrote, "that there are true men enough in the free states to have elected Breckinridge. But how could they be expected to quarrel with their neighbors for Southern rights while the South was everywhere quarreling among themselves . . . at a moment when the knife of the assassin is at their throats." Taney agreed with his son-in-law that the South faced an imminent danger (unspecified but obviously a widespread slave insurrection), and he thought that it might "burst out" with the news of Lincoln's election. "I am old enough to remember the horrors of St. Domingo," he wrote, "and a few days will determine whether anything like it is to be visited upon any portion of our own Southern countrymen. I can only pray that it may be averted and that my fears may prove to be nothing more than the timidity of an old man."

On December 3, with Lincoln elected and the crisis deepening in Washington, the Supreme Court opened its new term. The justices also paid their customary courtesy visit to the White House. There is no evidence that James Buchanan sought Taney's advice during this period, but their attitudes toward the impending national emergency were similar. Both men placed the blame for the crisis on northern antislavery agitators, and both regarded secession as an illegal act but maintained that the federal government had no power to suppress it by force of arms.

Buchanan's views were presented to Congress and the nation in his last annual message. It was about two months later that Taney, in the midst of a busy Court schedule, took time to put his thoughts on paper. By then, secession had become a reality in six states. The purpose of this memorandum is not indicated. It may never have progressed beyond the rough draft, only part of which survives as a manuscript of eight consecutive pages with neither a beginning nor an ending. The fragment begins with Taney arguing that slavery had a firm legal foundation in the international law of Europe and that the free states of the Union were doubly obligated to respect the institution because they had also "bound themselves by the social compact of the Constitution to uphold it." Yet, said Taney, men were now violating their contractual obligation and talking about a "higher law" to justify their fanaticism against slavery—a fanaticism of the same kind that had produced the bloody excesses of the French Revolution.

Next, Taney traced the progress of "free state aggression" through the crises of 1820 and 1850; the passage of state laws defying the Fugitive Slave Act; the use of churches and schools for dissemination of antislavery propaganda; and the publication of a novel "well calculated to rouse the morbid thought of fanatics, which portrayed in pictures of exaggeration the evils of slavery." Finally, a party "educated by this means" was about to take possession of the federal government. The party had rejected all terms of conciliation and proclaimed an irrepressible conflict between free labor and slave labor. Its onward march to power left southerners convinced that Republicanism was "at best abolitionism in disguise." This apprehension had already driven six states from the Union, and more were ready to leave unless they received "guarantees against wrongs for the future."*

The South, Taney continued, was mistaken in claiming a con-

---

* The sixth and seventh states to secede were Louisiana on January 26 and Texas on February 1. Hence the writing of the fragment can be dated within a few days.

stitutional right to secede; for secession was revolutionary and "only morally competent, like war, upon failure of justice." At the same time, federal laws could be enforced within a state only by its own citizens, and federal military power could enter a state only at the request of state officials. Consequently, there was "no rightful power to bring back by force the states into the Union."

These were the views of the Chief Justice who, on March 4, 1861, administered the oath of office to the incoming President, and his feelings on that occasion are not difficult to imagine. He must have listened unhappily to Lincoln's inaugural address, especially during several disagreeable moments when he found himself virtually the target of an attack on judicial review. After having acknowledged the binding effect of a judgment by the Supreme Court in any specific case brought before it, Lincoln, with *Dred Scott* obviously in mind, went on to declare: "If the policy of the government . . . is to be irrevocably fixed by decisions of the Supreme Court, the instant they are made, in ordinary litigation between parties, in personal actions, the people will have ceased to be their own rulers, having, to that extent, practically resigned their government into the hands of that eminent tribunal." For Taney, the passage could only have served to confirm his low opinion of the new President.

Before long, the Chief Justice was watching his own state of Maryland become the scene of mob action, conspiracy, sabotage, and military repression. Then, three months after the inauguration, he clashed head on with the new administration and suffered defeat. His writ of habeas corpus ordering the release of a Marylander, John Merryman, was defied by military authorities, and his sensational opinion declaring presidential suspension of the writ unconstitutional was in effect overruled by the Attorney General. This bitter experience convinced Taney that the President was establishing a military tyranny, and he clung to the conviction as long as he lived. "The supremacy of the military power over the civil seems to be established," he lamented in 1863, "and the public mind has acquiesced in it and sanctioned it." In performing his wartime official duties, Taney opposed the Lincoln administration at every opportunity. His sympathies remained with the South. When the grandson of an old friend called upon him before leaving to join the Confederate army, the Chief Justice reportedly said: "The circumstances under which you are going are not unlike those under which your grandfather went into the Revolutionary War."

What rivets attention in Taney's private views on the sectional crisis is not so much the substance of his thought as the intensity of his feelings. A pro-southern bias could be read easily enough in his public record, but from all except a few close friends he concealed the fierceness of his hostility to the antislavery movement. This hostility, moreover, was not caused but merely aggravated by the flood of abuse that descended upon him after the Dred Scott decision. His attitudes were firmly set before that time, as he revealed in a letter to his son-in-law during the campaign of 1856:

> The South is doomed to sink to a state of inferiority, and the power of the North will be exercised to gratify their cupidity and their evil passions, without the slightest regard to the principles of the Constitution. . . . It is my deliberate opinion that . . . nothing but a firm united action, nearly unanimous in every state, can check Northern insult and Northern aggression.

Such, of course, had been the urgent message of Calhoun in his later years—that southerners must unite as a people or die as a civilization at the hands of an implacable enemy.

Taney's personal life had been torn apart in 1855 when his wife and youngest daughter died just a few hours apart. This tragedy, says his biographer, Carl B. Swisher, may have "deprived him of the emotional reserves necessary to preserve the judicial balance for which he had hitherto received credit and led to the taking of more and more extreme positions." Yet it also seems possible that Taney's growing extremism in the late 1850s was primarily a response to ominous changes in the political environment—notably the rise of the Know Nothings, whom he regarded as ugly bigots, and the rise of the Republicans, whom he regarded as dangerous fanatics. What needs to be emphasized in any case is that his Dred Scott opinion was written with an emotional commitment so intense that it made perception and logic utterly subservient. The extraordinary cumulation of error, inconsistency, and misrepresentation, dispensed with such pontifical self-assurance, becomes more understandable with the realization that the opinion was essentially visceral in origin—that law and history were distorted to serve a passionate purpose. Taney's real commitment, one must also emphasize, was not to slavery itself, for which he had no great affection, but rather to southern life and values, which seemed organically linked to the peculiar institution and unpreservable without it. He used the Dred Scott case to reinforce the institution of slavery at every possible point of attack, not because he had once been a slaveholder but because he remained, to the end of his life, a southern gentleman.

The strong feelings that governed him were no doubt a mixture. Love for the South and pride in his own southern heritage mingled with emotions of a negative sort, such as fear—fear of slave uprisings—and indignation at northern critics of slavery. Taney, above all in the late 1850s, was fiercely anti-antislavery. We must not be misled by his physical weakness or his gentle mien. Wrath, says an ancient Greek poet, is the last thing in a man to grow old. The Dred Scott opinion, defensive in substance but aggressive in temper, was the work of an *angry* southern gentleman.

From a study of Taney's private emotional responses to the sectional controversy, one can learn something about the coming of the Civil War. Like the Chief Justice, a majority of southerners had no significant economic stake in the institution of slavery, but they did have a vital stake in the preservation of southern social order and southern self-respect. With increasing frequency and bitterness as the years passed, southerners protested that they were being degraded by northern sanctimony. In the end, it may have been the assault on their self-respect—the very language of the antislavery crusade—that drove many of them over the edge. Taney's Dred Scott decision, viewed in this context, is a document of great revelatory value. In the very unreasonableness of its argument one finds a measure of southern desperation.

3

Aside from its revelatory significance, the Dred Scott decision was also a public act that had important public consequences. The chief reason for the prominence of the decision in American historical writing is the belief that it became a major causal link between the general forces of national disruption and the final crisis of the Union in 1860-61. Scholars have been emphatic in affirming the connection but vague about its mechanics. The Dred Scott decision, we are told, "helped precipitate" or "did much to precipitate" or "helped to bring about" the Civil War. But there is never much explanation of just how the cause contributed to producing the effect.

Of course the historian should take into account all discernible causal relationships, including those of such a general nature that they may be too vague to isolate and measure. One must duly consider, for instance, the ways in which the Dred Scott decision altered the formal argument over slavery; for secession was a highly formal public act as well as a highly emotional one. And no doubt the decision contributed heavily to the general accumulation of sectional animosity that made some kind of national crisis increasingly difficult to avoid. Still, since there were many other causes of the hostility between North and South, it is difficult to imagine a dissipation of the gathering storm if only Justice Nelson had been allowed to speak for the Court, as originally planned, in his less controversial Dred Scott opinion. Most historians would probably agree that the sectional conflict was already deep-seated and pervasive before 1857. But what turned a chronic struggle into a secession crisis was the outcome of the presidential election in 1860. Accordingly, if one wishes to go beyond the unverifiable general impression or conviction that the Dred Scott decision, like *Uncle Tom's Cabin* and the Harpers Ferry raid, somehow helped to "bring about" the Civil War, it becomes necessary to test the accuracy of Charles Warren's assertion that Taney "elected Abraham Lincoln to the Presidency."

There were two principal ways in which the Dred Scott decision could have had a critical influence on the election of 1860. One was by contributing significantly to the split in the Democratic party; the other was by contributing significantly to the growth of the Republican party. The disruption of the Democrats, because of its dramatic climax at Charleston and its association with the famous Lincoln-Douglas exchange at Freeport, has received the primary emphasis in historical writing. Yet, as we have seen, the Dred Scott decision did not at first put any serious strains on Democratic unity, and Douglas enunciated the Freeport doctrine in 1857 without incurring the slightest adverse criticism from southern Democrats. Only after the Lecompton struggle had done its irreparable damage did the Dred Scott decision and the Freeport doctrine become a divisive influence within the party. Furthermore, the election statistics indicate that Lincoln would have won in 1860 even against a consolidated opposition; for he carried fifteen of the eighteen free states with popular majorities, and they were enough to give him an electoral majority. The argument of certain historians that a reunited Democratic party (that is, a party approved and to some extent controlled by its southern wing) would somehow have attracted additional votes in the North remains a highly dubious speculation. In summary, the Dred Scott decision was at most a secondary factor in the division of the Democratic party, and that division in any case probably did not determine the outcome of the presidential election.

There remains the question of whether the Dred Scott decision had a significant influence on the Republican upsurge that gave Lincoln 98 per cent of the northern electoral vote. The difference between defeat in 1856 and victory in 1860 was a half-million additional Republican voters in the free states, including three hundred thousand more than the party's proportionate share of the increase in the voting population. Approximately 70 per cent of the three-hundred-thousand-vote gain was made in the five crucial free states that the Democrats had carried in 1856. The sixty-two electoral votes of New Jersey, Pennsylvania, Indiana, Illinois, and California had all gone to Buchanan in 1856; Lincoln won fifty-nine of them in 1860.

REPUBLICAN PERCENTAGES OF THE POPULAR VOTE

	N.J.	PENN.	IND.	ILL.	COMBINED*
1856	28.5	32.0	40.1	40.2	35.4
1858	52.5**	53.7	51.7	49.8	52.1
1860	48.2	56.1	51.1	50.7	52.7

* California, which had only four electoral votes, is omitted from the table because the mixing of Republican and anti-Lecompton votes in 1858 makes it impossible to measure Republican strength for that year. The Republicans carried 18.8 per cent of the state's vote in 1856 and 33 per cent in 1860.

** The New Jersey percentage for 1858 is somewhat inflated because in two congressional districts the Republicans supported anti-Lecompton Democrats.

This political revolution, moreover, was largely completed in the midterm elections of 1858, as the preceding table shows. It therefore seems chronologically sound to infer a causal connection between the Dred Scott decision and the Republican surge to power. Yet there are also considerations that militate against such an inference. For one thing, voting behavior in the late 1850s was of course affected by other influences besides the slavery issue. The economic depression that struck the country in 1857 undoubtedly had political repercussions, for instance, and in any case, it has been well demonstrated that many voters were not decisively oriented to issue politics.

In addition, the Republican gains in the late 1850s can be explained to a large extent by the collapse of the Know-Nothing movement in the North and the resulting shift of many Whig-Americans into Republican ranks. Throughout the northern tier of free states from New England to Wisconsin, this Republican absorption of political nativism had begun in 1856, when large numbers of Know-Nothings supported Frémont instead of Fillmore. In the lower North, including the states that voted for Buchanan, the major change occurred after 1856. Pennsylvania's sixteen strongest Know-Nothing counties, for example, gave Frémont only 12 per cent of their total vote in the presidential election of 1856, but gave the Republican ticket 54 per cent in

REPUBLICAN PERCENTAGES
OF TOTAL VOTE

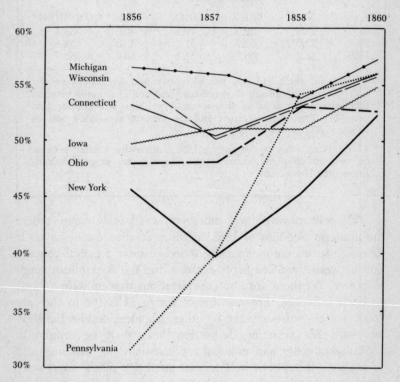

1858 and Lincoln 53 per cent in 1860. The important question that cannot be answered with any precision is whether the mass movement of Fillmore Americans into the Republican camp in 1857-58 was heavily influenced by the Dred Scott decision and other aspects of the sectional conflict, or whether the movement was virtually a necessity in any case because of the lack of satisfactory alternatives.

Aside from the knotty problem of the relationship between *Dred Scott* and Republican absorption of the Fillmore vote, there is also the difficulty of distinguishing between the political effects of the Dred Scott decision and the political effects of the Lecompton controversy. It is essential to draw this distinction

DEMOCRATIC PERCENTAGES
OF TOTAL VOTE

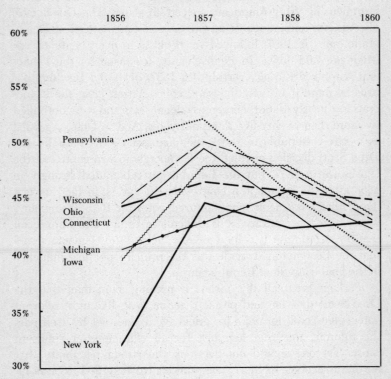

because both events took place during the two-year period of the Republican party's final surge to political dominance in the free states. One means of doing so is to examine the election results in seven northern states that held statewide elections in 1857 as well as in 1858. The pattern that emerges from such an examination is remarkably coherent. If the Dred Scott decision did improve the chances of Republican victory in 1860, one would expect to find that it had a similar effect on the elections of 1857, when the shock of the decision was still new. Instead, as the preceding charts show, the Republicans generally lost ground that year. The exceptions were states—most notably, Pennsylvania—where the influx of Fillmore men offset other losses. For

1857, the Republican chart is affected one way by a general decline of party strength and the other way by the continuing recruitment of Whig-Americans in certain states. The Democratic chart is less ambiguous. It reveals a consistent pattern of Democratic gains in 1857, followed by declines in every state except Michigan and Iowa. In Pennsylvania, for instance, the Democrats captured the governorship in 1857, defeating the Republicans by more than forty thousand votes. A year later, the Democrats lost nearly all of their congressional seats and were outpolled by more than twenty-five thousand votes. And in Ohio, regarded as a safely Republican state, the race issue stirred up by the Dred Scott decision enabled the Democrats to win control of the legislature in 1857, but the Republicans rebounded strongly in 1858 after the Lecompton controversy. There is, in fact, no evidence that *Dred Scott* manufactured votes for Republicans anywhere. On the contrary, it is difficult to escape the impression that the decision, if it helped anyone, helped the Democrats, and that the Lecompton struggle was the primary political influence in the final triumph of Republicanism.

Perhaps what all this means is nothing more than that the Dred Scott decision and public reaction to it, like most relevant antecedent conditions of a historical event, does not by itself pass the rigorous *sine qua non* test for an efficacious or sufficient cause. Yet one should not overlook the strong possibility that northern reaction to the Lecompton controversy in 1858 was intensified by the fresh memory of Taney's proslavery ruling in 1857. A clustering of events in the late 1850s induced nightmarish visions of conspiracy among northerners and southerners alike. The Dred Scott decision by itself apparently caused no significant number of changes in political allegiance. Yet it was a conspicuous and perhaps integral part of a configuration of events and conditions that did produce enough changes of allegiance to make a political revolution and enough intensity of feeling to make that revolution violent.

❧ 11 ❧

In the Stream of History

Dred Scott, after his eleven-year struggle for freedom, lived only sixteen months as a free man. He and his family were transferred by the Chaffees to Taylor Blow in May 1857 and promptly manumitted. The Scotts remained in St. Louis, Dred working as a hotel porter and his wife Harriet, as a laundress. According to newspaper reports, Eliza and Lizzie ran away for a time but had returned home by 1858. A local newspaper described Scott as "a small, pleasant-looking negro," with a moustache and "imperial" beard, dressed in a suit of "seedy black," and looking "somewhat the worse for wear and tear." Missouri law required that Dred and Harriet post bond of $1000 for good behavior in order to continue living in the state. This they did on May 4, 1858, with Taylor Blow acting as security. Soon, however, Dred was stricken with consumption, and he died on September 17. Press accounts of his death were generally brief, but some editors took time to reflect on the fame that had enveloped this obscure black man and on the significance of his day in court. "In ages yet to come," said the New York *Herald*, "Dred Scott and the decision which bears his name will be familiar words in the mouth of the ranting demagogue in rostrum and pulpit, and of the student of political history."

Scott was buried in the St. Louis Wesleyan Cemetery, which within a decade became a casualty of urban expansion and was abandoned. Taylor Blow arranged for removal of the remains to Calvary Cemetery in 1867. Ninety years later, as part of a centennial observance of the Dred Scott decision, the grave was marked with a granite headstone provided by a granddaughter of Taylor Blow. There seems to be no solid evidence of what happened to Dred's family after his death. It is said that Harriet and Eliza survived him only a few years. A woman claiming to be his other daughter, Lizzie, married Henry Madison of St. Louis, and several of her descendants attended the centennial observances in 1957.

The *Dred Scott* Court was no longer intact when the Civil War began. Curtis resigned in 1858. Daniel died in 1860 and McLean, in April 1861. After the attack on Fort Sumter, Campbell resigned to return to Alabama and serve the Confederacy. Of the three remaining southern justices, Wayne and Catron quickly revealed themselves to be staunch Unionists. Taney alone remained unrepentant and unredeemed, as it were, and Taney alone was responsible for *Ex parte Merryman*, a proceedings at chambers with which the rest of the Court had nothing to do. The often venomous hostility of many radical Republicans followed the Chief Justice into his grave, but one should not make the mistake of assuming that it was directed at the Supreme Court as a whole.

Taney gave no serious thought to resigning. He needed his salary to live on and support two daughters, one of whom was a semi-invalid. So he remained on duty in wartime Washington, an isolated, decrepit figure, still treated with respect and affection by professional associates but publicly detested as a man who drew his pay from the federal government while lending sympathy to its enemies. It seems likely that the Dred Scott decision would have been at least partly forgiven if Taney had taken a Jacksonian stand against secession. Instead, as Senator Henry Wilson bitterly and accurately complained, he "never gave one cheering word nor performed one act to protect or save" the Union. The Chief Justice, in plain words, was a copperhead, and ever more strongly so as the war progressed. If it had been possible, he would have invalidated many of the administration's principal war measures, including conscription, emancipation, and the currency program.

The fact that Taney remained chief justice until his death, without any serious threat of removal, was testimony, perhaps, to the stability of the American constitutional system. Actually, his continuance in office may have given the Lincoln administration more freedom than it otherwise would have enjoyed; for a Supreme Court headed by Taney was a court without enough influence to restrain executive or congressional power. Administration leaders nevertheless preferred to avoid direct confrontation with the Chief Justice, insofar as that was possible. For the most part, they simply ignored him, refusing even to answer his communications.

Congress likewise ignored the Dred Scott decision while defying its most memorable ruling. In June 1862, by overwhelming votes, the Senate and House passed a bill abolishing slavery in the federal territories. Opponents of the measure raised various objections, but no one mentioned the Dred Scott decision during the debate. The New York *Tribune* hailed the end of a controversy which had begun with Jefferson's Ordinance of 1784. "Champions of Freedom and Justice for All," it exclaimed, "thank God that you have lived to see this day." But the *Tribune*, like Congress, said nothing about the Dred Scott decision.

Attorney General Edward Bates struck another blow at the decision in November of the same year when he issued an official opinion holding that free men of color born in the United States were citizens of the United States. Near the end of the opinion, he took due note of *Dred Scott* but dismissed it as irrelevant, declaring that Taney's ruling applied only to full-blooded African negroes who were demonstrably descended from slave ancestors. Of course, not everyone was willing to accept the opinion as definitive. For instance, during discussion early in 1864 of a bill organizing Montana Territory, Senator Reverdy Johnson insisted that Taney's *Dred Scott* ruling against Negro citizenship was "conclusive" until reversed by the Supreme Court itself. That set off a sharp exchange between Johnson and Charles Sumner, who said that the Dred Scott decision had "disgraced the country" and ought to be "expelled from its jurisprudence," while Johnson responded with an eloquent defense of Taney and the Court.

In spite of Taney's unpopularity, the Supreme Court itself was never in any serious danger during the Civil War. Congress, at Lincoln's urging, passed a judicial reorganization act in 1862, but it was eminently moderate and designed primarily to bring the circuit court system into adjustment with recent population changes. The Court, moreover, did nothing during the war to invite Republican attack. Presented only a few opportunities to review wartime legislation and executive orders, it generally upheld administration policies, or at least acquiesced in them. Furthermore, Lincoln's appointees to the Court (five within three years) made it increasingly respectable in Republican eyes, the climax coming when Salmon P. Chase succeeded Taney as chief justice in December 1864.

Taney's death on October 12, 1864, put an end to the anomaly of a nation's fighting a war with its highest judicial officer bound in sympathy to the enemy. "The temple of the man-stealers," said the Chicago *Tribune,* "has been rent from foundation to roof, and the ancient High Priest lies cold at the altar." New Yorker George Templeton Strong wrote more pungently in his diary, "The Hon. old Roger B. Taney has earned the gratitude of his country by dying at last. Better late than never." The theme of "good riddance" was softened in many Republican newspapers by due acknowledgment of Taney's private virtues, professional skill, and good intentions, but all editorial comment led in the end to *Dred Scott.* "That decision itself, wrong as it was," said the New York *Times,* "did not spring from a corrupt or malignant heart. It came, we have the charity to believe, from a sincere desire to compose, rather than exacerbate, sectional discord. But yet it was nonetheless an act of supreme folly, and its shadow will ever rest on his memory."

Dred Scott v. Sandford has been called "the most frequently overturned decision in history." The Thirteenth Amendment, ratified late in 1865, made Taney's opinion totally obsolete in so far as it had been concerned with the institution of slavery. But emancipation only magnified, without resolving, the other major issue treated in the opinion—the status of the free Negro population, now suddenly increased from half a million to nearly five million. There the overturning process proved to be far more complex and prolonged. To be sure, Taney's ruling against Negro citizenship was reversed soon enough—first by the Civil Rights Act of 1866 and then more conclusively by the Fourteenth Amendment, which passed Congress the same year and was ratified in 1868. The opening sentence of the amendment declared: "All persons born or naturalized in the United States, and subject to the jurisdiction thereof, are citizens of the United States and of the State wherein they reside." This definition certainly resolved the specific issue presented in the Dred Scott case. No longer could Negroes be denied access to federal courts under the diverse-citizenship clause. But what else did the confirmed possession of citizenship imply? What rights did a Negro now have that a white man was bound to respect?

The answer was provided piecemeal in the Civil Rights acts of 1866 and 1875, in the Fourteenth and Fifteenth amendments, and in certain other Reconstruction measures. Blacks were expressly guaranteed equal rights before the law and placed on a level of equality with white persons in regard to contracts, litigation, property-holding, inheritance, and access to facilities used by the public (such as railroads, inns, and theaters). In more indirect language, blacks were also made eligible to vote and participate in jury service; their privileges and immunities as citizens of the United States were protected against impairment by state governments; and they were presumably intended to be principal beneficiaries of the famous clause forbidding states to deprive any person of life, liberty, or property without due process of law.

Taken all together, and viewed against the background of the predominant racial attitudes of the time, the Reconstruction program constituted a blueprint for a social revolution of remarkable proportions. But like the antislavery movement that accompanied the birth of the Republic a century earlier, it was a revolution that became abortive. No doubt there were many reasons for the failure of Radical Reconstruction. One of them was a widespread and tenacious resistance to the federal inter-

ventionism embodied in the program. That is, the employment of
national power to prevent white southerners from using their
state governments to mistreat black southerners not only offended
racial sensitivities but also clashed with traditional conceptions
of the American federal system. Among those leading the resistance to the expansion of national authority required by the
Radical program was the federal Supreme Court. In a series of
decisions extending from the 1870s to the end of the century, the
Court virtually stripped the Negro of federal protection against
private acts of oppression and against public discrimination in-
directly imposed. It upheld laws and procedures that effectively
disfranchised him and excluded him from jury service. It also
placed a federal stamp of approval upon segregation as public
policy. So, although the principal rulings of the Dred Scott decision were, strictly speaking, overturned by the Thirteenth and
Fourteenth amendments, the Court later breathed new life into
Taney's racial doctrine and did not officially repudiate it until
the middle of the twentieth century. In a broader sense, as federal judge John Minor Wisdom declared in 1968, it was *Brown
v. Board of Education* in 1954 that "erased *Dred Scott.*"

Yet the Supreme Court decisions of the late nineteenth century that contributed so heavily to the support of institutionalized racism were neither justified in racial terms nor primarily
motivated by racial considerations. The Court, after all, was
merely implementing the semi-tacit "Compromise of 1877," which
returned the race problem to the states so that the American nation could get on with other matters, such as economic expansion, that seemed more important. In race-related decisions the
Court therefore made little use of the *Dred Scott* precedent, with
its explicit racist doctrine. But *Dred Scott* had ranged over much
other ground, as we have seen, and on a number of subjects it
continued to be cited as authority. For example, the Fourteenth
Amendment did not wipe out everything that Taney had said on
the subject of citizenship. In so far as his Dred Scott opinion
supported the concept of dual citizenship, it survived and was
reinforced by Justice Samuel F. Miller in the *Slaughterhouse
Cases.* As late as 1946, a Wisconsin judge remarked that Ta-

ney's holding on dual citizenship had "never been overruled or modified."

The Dred Scott decision was most influential as precedent, however, in cases calling for judicial elucidation of the source, nature, and limits of congressional power in the territories. With the passing of slavery, to be sure, territorial government had lost much of its prominence as a public issue, but the constitutional perplexities of the system became, if anything, more pronounced in its later years, especially after the acquisition of an island empire in 1898.

As far as the *source* of congressional power was concerned, the Court showed considerable respect for Taney's assertion that it derived from the implied power to acquire territory, rather than from the territorial clause in Article Four. For instance, in 1901, Justice Henry B. Brown declared: "Whatever be the source of this power, its uninterrupted exercise by Congress for a century, and the repeated declarations of this court, have settled the law that the right to acquire territory involves the right to govern and dispose of it. That was stated by Chief Justice Taney in the *Dred Scott* case." In later years, however, the Court pushed aside the Taney interpretation. Chief Justice Harlan F. Stone said in 1945: "It is no longer doubted that the United States may acquire territory by conquest or by treaty, and may govern it through the exercise of the power of Congress conferred by section 3 of Article IV of the Constitution."

In defining the *nature* of congressional authority over the territories, the post-Civil-War Court ignored Taney's strict-constructionist argument and returned to the Marshall doctrine of plenary power. That is, it reaffirmed that Congress, in legislating for the territories, exercised the combined sovereign power of the federal government and a state government. But the Court at the same time agreed substantially with Taney that congressional power in the territories was limited by the negative provisions of the Constitution. Congress, for example, might deviate from Article Three in establishing a territorial judicial system, but it could not impose *ex post facto* legislation anywhere—not in the territories any more than in the states.

This problem of constitutional *limits* arose most notably in the *Insular Cases* of 1901, involving the status of the island possessions acquired three years earlier. The Dred Scott decision was cited and discussed by counsel on both sides, as well as by several of the justices. Delivering the nominal opinion of the Court, Justice Brown acknowledged that if Taney's Dred Scott opinion were taken at full value, it would be decisive in favor of the plaintiff. But then he went on to suggest that the Taney ruling on territories had been dictum, and he added that the Civil War had "produced such changes in judicial, as well as public sentiment, as to seriously impair the authority of this case." This was perhaps as close as the Supreme Court ever came to declaring the Dred Scott decision overruled. Brown was a Republican from Michigan. Justice Edward D. White, a Louisiana Democrat who had served in the Confederate army, objected to Brown's criticism of the Dred Scott decision, calling it "unwarranted." White, speaking for two of his colleagues, endorsed Taney's principle of constitutional limitation but nevertheless concurred in the pro-expansionist judgment of the Court as announced by Brown. He did so by inventing the distinction between "incorporated" and "unincorporated" territories which the Court later came to accept as true doctrine. In unincorporated territories, according to the White formula, the Constitution followed the American flag *ex proprio vigore* in some respects, but only by act of Congress in others. White thus circumvented *Dred Scott* while continuing to pay it lip service. But Chief Justice Melville Fuller, an Illinois Democrat speaking for himself and several other dissenting justices, quoted Taney as authority for his contention that legislation for the new territories was immediately subject to all the restraints of the Constitution.

The triumph of expansionism and colonialism amounted to a rejection of Taney's territorial doctrine, but it was in harmony with the racial theory of his Dred Scott opinion. Indeed, as C. Vann Woodward has pointed out, "At the very time that imperialism was sweeping the country, the doctrine of racism reached a crest of acceptability and popularity among respectable scholarly and intellectual circles." The racial attitudes of the early twentieth century were one of several conditions favorable to a restoration of Taney's reputation and even to some defense or at least extenuation of the Dred Scott decision.

The first book-length study of the decision since the 1850s appeared in 1909. The author, a southern lawyer named Elbert W. R. Ewing, stoutly defended every part of Taney's Dred Scott opinion. Perhaps the most impressive chapter is one arguing that the Chief Justice, throughout his opinion, did indeed speak for a majority of the Court. But the work contains too much misinformation and special pleading to be taken very seriously as scholarship. More influential was an article by Edward S. Corwin, published in the *American Historical Review* for October 1911. Corwin, then just beginning his distinguished career as a teacher and scholar in the field of American constitutional law, had no admiration for the substance of the Dred Scott decision, which he called "a gross abuse of trust by the body which rendered it." But at the same time he presented a strong case for the legitimacy of Taney's opinion, denying that any part of it was *obiter dictum*. The effect was to call in question the principal argument upon which critics of the decision had been relying for over half a century.

Other defenses of *Dred Scott* came out from time to time, but even the most eloquent ones failed to carry conviction. It remained, in the orthodox view, a "ghastly error" and a "ruinous decision." Yet the reconstruction of Taney's judicial reputation continued, gaining strength from the pro-Jacksonian bias of Progressive historians and from an anti-abolitionist trend in the historiography of the Civil War. The rehabilitation reached its climax during the 1930s. In September 1931, Chief Justice Charles Evans Hughes, son of an abolitionist minister, unveiled a bust of Taney at Frederick, Maryland, and praised him lavishly. It was unfortunate, Hughes said, that the estimate of Taney's career should have been so heavily influenced by the Dred Scott decision, rather than by the whole of his "arduous service nobly rendered." Viewing the Dred Scott decision as a well-intentioned mistake, Hughes admitted that it had seriously impaired the prestige of the Court but "chiefly because of the un-

bridled criticism induced by the temper of the times." Taney, he
concluded,, was a man of "invincible spirit" and a "great Chief
Justice."

Four years later, Carl B. Swisher published his sympathetic
but not uncritical biography of Taney in which the Dred Scott
decision, as one event in a long life and long judicial career, took
up only one of twenty-seven chapters. Swisher did not deny that
a sectional purpose animated the Dred Scott decision. He also
recognized that Taney was at heart a secessionist who nevertheless considered secession impractical because of chronic southern
disunity. The South's best hope instead seemed to lie in discred-
iting the antislavery crusade and thereby relieving the pressure
of sectional conflict. Thus Taney and his southern colleagues on
the Court "planned to defeat the abolitionists and avoid disaster." The purpose of the decision, in short, was to help protect
the South and its culture from northern subjugation.

The Swisher biography was followed the next year, 1936, by
a laudatory study of Taney's jurisprudence. Charles V. Smith,
Jr., in his *Roger B. Taney: Jacksonian Jurist,* declared that Taney
"regarded slavery as an evil institution, but one which would
have to be abolished gradually."* On the bench, said Smith, Taney generally acted impartially in dealing with slavery. The
Dred Scott opinion furnished evidence that Taney "was a firm
believer in individual rights." Admittedly a political mistake, it

---

* The curious notion that Taney was at heart an antislavery man has a long
history and retains a surprising vitality. The Cincinnati *Enquirer* in 1857
declared: "Mr. Taney, personally, is opposed to slavery in principle and
practice." According to Walker Lewis in a 1965 biography, "Slavery violated his conscience. His opposition to abolition was not because he wished
to perpetuate slavery but because he believed the abolitionists misguided."
In 1971, Robert M. Spector wrote: "From the standpoint of morality he
hated slavery as much as any abolitionist." This legend of the antislavery
Taney rests almost entirely upon two actions taken nearly forty years before
the Dred Scott decision. In 1818, he served as defense attorney for an abolitionist minister and in the process denounced slavery as an evil that must
in time be "gradually wiped away." Beginning the same year, Taney emancipated his own slaves to the number at least of eight. Whatever moral conviction may have encouraged these actions, it does not appear again in his
public record or his private correspondence. His attitude on the bench was
consistently and solicitously proslavery. By 1857 he had become as resolute
in his determination to protect the institution as Garrison was in his determination to destroy it.

was nevertheless an effort "to save the Union by protecting property rights guaranteed in the Constitution."

The Swisher and Smith books were published at a time of constitutional crisis over the Supreme Court's repeated invalidation of New Deal legislation. To some critics of the Court, Taney appeared as an attractive historical figure (setting aside the Dred Scott decision, of course) because of his association with the doctrine of judicial self-restraint. This was especially true in the case of Felix Frankfurter, the Harvard law professor who would soon be appointed to the "Roosevelt Court." During the presidential campaign of 1936, Frankfurter delivered a series of lectures later published as *The Commerce Clause Under Marshall, Taney and Waite*. He demonstrated that Taney, while disagreeing with Marshall in certain important respects, did not undertake "a wholesale reversal of Marshall's doctrines." He denied that Taney was a proslavery man "in any invidious sense." Eventually, Frankfurter hoped, it would become "intellectually disreputable" to see Taney predominantly as the judicial defender of slavery. He concluded by placing Taney "second only to Marshall in the constitutional history of our country."

Other scholars also contributed to the highly favorable estimate of Taney's career that was well established as historical orthodoxy by the end of the 1930s. Later, as a consequence of the great revolution in civil rights, the abolitionist point of view regained respectability, and extenuation of the Dred Scott decision went out of fashion. Yet Taney's reputation did not suffer severely in the changed climate of opinion. In 1972, the *American Bar Association Journal* published the results of a poll in which sixty-five professors of law, political science, and history were asked to rate the performances of all members of the Supreme Court since its establishment in 1789. Taney's name appeared in the top category of twelve "great" justices, only four of whom served before 1900.

Thus the twentieth-century rehabilitation of Roger B. Taney remains more or less intact. It rests primarily upon a proper appreciation of his entire judicial career, but it also draws strength from several dubious historical traditions that tend to mitigate his responsibility for the Dred Scott decision. These include as-

sertions that Taney was privately opposed to slavery; that the
two dissenting justices forced the Court majority to render a
broad decision; that Taney's Dred Scott opinion was an "aberration" from his habitual devotion to judicial self-restraint; and
that the worst consequences of *Dred Scott* were produced, not
so much by the substance of the decision itself, as by the violent
and unjust Republican attack upon it.

In 1957, the year of racial crisis in the schools of Little Rock,
the New York *Times* noted that the centenary of the Dred Scott
decision had arrived at a time when national unities were "again
imperiled by a Supreme Court judgment." It was inevitable that
Brown v. Board of Education, the historic desegregation decision
of 1954, should be viewed as a kind of Dred Scott decision in
reverse—with Negroes now the beneficiaries instead of the victims of judicial activism, and with sectional attitudes toward the
Court directly contrary to what they had been in 1857. This
time, to be sure, wrote Fred Rodell of the Yale Law School, the
sectional controversy would not end in civil war; for the American nation had "grown up a little since 1857." But it had not
grown up enough, he feared, to distinguish clearly and treat
separately the two basic issues in both the *Dred Scott* and the
Brown cases—namely, the status of the Negro in American life
and the amount of political power to be vested in the Supreme
Court. Neither issue was resolved in the years that followed, as
the racial struggle continued and the Court under the leadership
of Earl Warren carried judicial intervention in the making of
public policy to a new level of boldness and achievement. The
Dred Scott decision accordingly lost none of its relevance. It had,
in fact, long since become a standard part of the nation's historical and legal vocabulary.

In 1974 the *American Bar Association Journal* invited its
readers to determine by ballot what "milestones" of legal history
should be celebrated in a proposed Bicentennial volume. The
lawyers, judges, and law professors taking part in the voting paid
due respect to the formative work of the Marshall Court but
otherwise tended to be present-minded in their selections. The
twenty milestones chosen included fourteen specific Supreme
Court decisions, of which only *Dred Scott v. Sandford* was

drawn from the 115 years between 1819 and 1935. Having, in the words of Charles Evans Hughes, a "negligible influence" on modern constitutional jurisprudence, *Dred Scott* nevertheless ranked fifth among the fourteen decisions selected as legal milestones. The balloting placed it right behind *Brown v. Board of Education* and ahead of every Marshall decision except *Marbury v. Madison.*

The importance thus attached to the Dred Scott decision by members of the American legal profession in the late twentieth century is extraordinary enough to inspire some reflection on the reasons for it. No doubt the heavy vote for *Dred Scott* was partly tribute to a familiar legend. No doubt it was inspired to some degree by exaggerated estimates of *Dred Scott* influence on the disruption of the Union, on the prestige of the Supreme Court, and on the emergence of substantive due process of law. No doubt it reflected the persistence of racial troubles in modern America and the central place of the Civil War in American historical consciousness. But in the long run, Taney's decision will probably be most significant as an epoch in the growth of American judicial power.

It was Alexis de Tocqueville who wrote long ago: "Scarcely any political question arises in the United States that is not resolved, sooner or later, into a judicial question." But in Tocqueville's time and for more than a century thereafter, the political power of the judiciary was primarily a restraining force, reactive instead of innovative, holding legislation and executive action within constitutional bounds. The revolution that took place during the chief justiceship of Earl Warren was one in which the Supreme Court undertook to make public policy on a vast scale, and judicial activism as a consequence became a major channel of social change. Court decisions on desegregation, legislative apportionment, and the rights of accused persons had far-reaching effects and infused new meaning into the phrase, "government by judiciary." In 1967, two years before Warren's retirement, Adolf A. Berle opened a series of lectures at Columbia University with the startling statement that "ultimate legislative power in the United States has come to rest in the Supreme Court."

The work of the Warren Court dominated the list of "milestones" selected in 1974, and the leading Warren cases all involved judicial review of state rather than federal law. Yet the members of the American Bar Association in their balloting ignored *Fletcher v. Peck*, the earliest case in which the Court invalidated a state law on the ground that it conflicted with the federal Constitution. At the same time, they gave the largest number of votes to *Marbury v. Madison*, thereby placing it right next to the Declaration of Independence and the Constitution as an American legal landmark. This seems inconsistent, but the high rating of the *Marbury* decision reflected a clear understanding that the Warren Court had by no means tested the farthest limits of judicial power; for those limits depend upon the extent to which the Supreme Court achieves ascendancy, not over the state governments, but over Congress and the presidency. It remains to be seen whether Berle's pronouncement in 1967 was hyperbole or sound prophecy—whether the United States has or has not begun to replace representative government with the Platonic elitism of a "guardian democracy." But the conduct of the Court in recent years suggests that we have yet to comprehend the full meaning of *Marbury v. Madison* and of the Dred Scott decision as well. We have yet to glimpse the ultimate potential of judicial sovereignty, a theory of power set forth by John Marshall in 1803 but first put to significant use by his successor on March 6, 1857.

Selected Books for Further Reading

Ira Berlin, *Slaves Without Masters: The Free Negro in the Ante-Bellum South* (New York, 1974).

William J. Cooper, Jr., *The South and the Politics of Slavery, 1828-1856* (Baton Rouge, La., 1978).

Robert M. Cover, *Justice Accused: Antislavery and the Judicial Process* (New Haven, Conn., 1975).

Avery O. Craven, *The Growth of Southern Nationalism, 1848-1861* (Baton Rouge, La., 1953).

David Brion Davis, *The Problem of Slavery in the Age of Revolution, 1770-1823* (Ithaca, N.Y., 1975).

Walter Ehrlich, *They Have No Rights: Dred Scott's Struggle for Freedom* (Westport, Conn., 1979).

Don E. Fehrenbacher, *Prelude to Greatness: Lincoln in the 1850's* (Stanford, Calif., 1962).

Louis Filler, *The Crusade Against Slavery, 1830-1860* (New York, 1960).

Eric Foner, *Free Soil, Free Labor, Free Men: The Ideology of the Republican Party before the Civil War* (New York, 1970).

George M. Fredrickson, *The Black Image in the White Mind: The Debate on Afro-American Character and Destiny, 1817-1914* (New York, 1971).

Holman Hamilton, *Prologue to Conflict: The Crisis and Compromise of 1850* (Lexington, Ky., 1964).

Richard Allen Heckman, *Lincoln v. Douglas: The Great Debates Campaign* (Washington, D.C., 1967).

Michael F. Holt, *The Political Crisis of the 1850's* (New York, 1978).

Harry V. Jaffa, *Crisis of the House Divided: An Interpretation of the Issues in the Lincoln-Douglas Debates* (Garden City, N.Y., 1959).

Robert W. Johannsen, *Stephen A. Douglas* (New York, 1973).

Winthrop D. Jordan, *White Over Black: American Attitudes toward the Negro, 1550-1812* (Chapel Hill, N.C., 1968).

James H. Kettner, *The Development of American Citizenship, 1608-1870* (Chapel Hill, N.C., 1978).

Stanley I. Kutler, ed., *The Dred Scott Decision: Law or Politics?* (New York, 1967).

Stanley I. Kutler, *Judicial Power and Reconstruction Politics* (Chicago, 1968).

Walker Lewis, *Without Fear or Favor: A Biography of Chief Justice Roger Brooke Taney* (Boston, 1965).

Leon F. Litwack, *North of Slavery: The Negro in the Free States, 1790-1860* (Chicago, 1961).

John Chester Miller, *The Wolf by the Ears: Thomas Jefferson and Slavery* (New York, 1977).

Loren Miller, *The Petitioners: The Story of the Supreme Court of the United States and the Negro* (New York, 1966).

Glover Moore, *The Missouri Controversy, 1819-1821* (Lexington, Ky., 1953).

Thomas D. Morris, *Free Men All: The Personal Liberty Laws of the North, 1780-1861* (Baltimore, 1974).

Chaplain W. Morrison, *Democratic Politics and Sectionalism: The Wilmot Proviso Controversy* (Chapel Hill, 1967).

Allan Nevins, *Ordeal of the Union* (2 vols.; New York, 1947).

Allan Nevins, *The Emergence of Lincoln* (2 vols.; New York, 1950).

Roy Franklin Nichols, *The Disruption of American Democracy* (New York, 1948).

David M. Potter, *The Impending Crisis, 1848-1861*, completed and edited by Don E. Fehrenbacher (New York, 1976).

James A. Rawley, *Race and Politics: "Bleeding Kansas" and the Coming of the Civil War* (Philadelphia, 1969).

Donald L. Robinson, *Slavery in the Structure of American Politics, 1765-1820* (New York, 1971).

Robert R. Russel, *Critical Studies in Antebellum Sectionalism: Essays in American Political and Economic History* (Westport, Conn., 1972).

Richard H. Sewell, *Ballots for Freedom: Antislavery Politics in the United States, 1837-1860* (New York, 1976).

Elbert B. Smith, *The Presidency of James Buchanan* (Lawrence, Kans., 1975).

Kenneth M. Stampp, *The Peculiar Institution: Slavery in the Ante-Bellum South* (New York, 1956).

James Brewer Stewart, *Holy Warriors: The Abolitionists and American Slavery* (New York, 1976).

Carl B. Swisher, *Roger B. Taney* (New York, 1936).

Carl B. Swisher, *The Taney Period, 1836-1864,* Volume V of the Oliver Wendell Holmes Devise *History of the Supreme Court of the United States* (New York, 1974).

William M. Wiecek, *The Sources of Antislavery Constitutionalism in America, 1760-1848* (Ithaca, N.Y., 1977).

Index

Ableman v. Booth, 241
Abolitionism and abolitionists, 17, 24, 56-57, 58, 67
Adams, John Quincy, 18-19, 53
African Colonization Society, 55
African slave trade. *See* Slave trade, foreign
Alabama: contingent secession movement in (1858), 255
American Bar Association Journal, 305, 306-307
American Insurance Company v. Canter, 69, 173, 203-204
American party. *See* Know-Nothings
Amistad, slave ship, 19
Anthony, Susan B., 236
Anti-Nebraska movement, 90, 151. *See also* Republican party
Antislavery: origins of, 8-9; as sentiment and interest, 15, 90. *See also* Abolitionism and abolitionists; Republican party; Wilmot Proviso
Arkansas: slave law of, 16; expels free Negroes, 237

Arkansas Territory: and Missouri controversy, 49-51; conceded to slavery, 55
Articles of Confederation: and slavery, 9; on citizenship, 34, 35, 188, 224; and western land cessions, 42-43; Taney on, 195, 198, 202-203
Augusta (Ga.) *Constitutionalist,* 230

Bailey, Gamaliel, 147
Bainbridge, Henry, 125, 128
Baltimore convention (Dem., 1860), 278-79
Bank of Augusta v. Earle, 159
Bank of the United States, 113, 118
Bankruptcy clause, 106, 201
Banks, Nathaniel P., 92
Bates, Edward, 134, 297
Bay, Samuel M., 130
Beecher, Henry Ward, 232
Bell, John, 277, 279
Benjamin, Judah P., 95-96, 252, 272, 275

Benjamin formula, 96-97, 99, 100, 101, 245

Benton, Thomas Hart, 133, 148, 233-34

Berle, Adolf A., 308, 309

Berlin, Ira, 33

Berrien, John M., 38, 39

Birch, James H., 134

Black, Jeremiah S., 269-70

Blacks. *See* Negroes, free

Blair, Francis Preston, 147

Blair, Montgomery, 147-48, 152-53, 155-61, 184, 232

Blow, Elizabeth, 121

Blow, Peter, 121-22, 123

Blow, Taylor, 122, 142, 231, 295, 296

Branch, Lawrence O., 246

Breckinridge, John C., 278, 279, 284

Brooks, Preston, 97

Brown, Albert G., 265-66, 275, 283

Brown, Henry B., 301, 302

Brown, John, 91, 97, 270, 272, 273

Brown, Joseph E., 255

Brown v. Board of Education, 300, 306, 307

Brunson, Alfred, 125

Bryant, William Cullen, 241

Buchanan, James, 19, 39, 64, 84, 245, 258; nominated for President, 97, 154; elected, 155; corresponds with justices on DS case, 164, 166, 167-68; inauguration, 168-69, 251; and Lecompton controversy, 248-50; quarrels with Douglas, 250, 256, 264-65, 269; praises DS decision, 273-74; and secession, 284-85

Butler, Andrew P., 75, 76

Calhoun, John C., 57, 66, 78, 133, 218, 287; on Missouri

Compromise, 53; proslavery resolutions of, 58, 62-63; constitutional theories of, 58, 63, 66-67, 70, 77, 81, 161; his "Southern Address," 76-77

California, 59, 63; gold rush, 72; proposals for government of, 73, 76, 78; statehood movement in, 78; admission of, 79, 80, 81, 83

Campbell, John A., 119, 149, 166, 167, 296; and substance of DS decision, 175, 179, 181; DS opinion, 216-19, 221, 222

Carroll, William T., 170

Cass, Lewis, 64, 72, 96, 100; territorial doctrine of, 68-69, 70, 82, 85, 93

Catron, John, 119, 149, 296; corresponds with Buchanan on DS case, 164-65, 166, 167, 169; DS opinion, 169, 184, 216-18, 220-21, 222; and substance of DS decision, 175, 177-79, 181

Chaffee, Calvin C., 140, 142-43, 231-32, 295

Chaffee, Mrs. Calvin C. *See* Emerson, Mrs. John

Charles River Bridge v. Warren Bridge, 114, 115

Charleston convention (Dem., 1860), 275-77, 279, 290

Chase, Salmon P., 68, 87, 98, 237, 255, 298

Cheever, George B., 232

Chicago convention (Rep., 1860), 277

Chicago *Democratic Press,* 230

Chicago *Tribune,* 298

Cincinnati: enforcement of black laws in, 33

Cincinnati convention (Dem., 1856), 97, 277

Cincinnati *Enquirer,* 304

Citizenship, 34, 35, 194, 300-301.
    See also Negro citizenship
Civil Rights acts, 299
Civil War: effect of, on DS deci-
    sion, 5, 297-98; DS decision
    and coming of, 289-94
Clay, Henry, 37, 59, 60, 113; and
    Compromise of 1850, 79, 81,
    82
Clayton, John M., 73
Clayton compromise, 73-75
Cobb, Howell, 79
Cohens v. Virginia, 111, 210
Columbia *South Carolinian,* 279
Comity, interstate. *See* Conflict of
    laws; Scott, Dred, in Illinois;
    Slaves, status of, in free
    territory
Common-law tradition, 102-103,
    104
Common-property doctrine, 58,
    62, 83; in DS opinions, 218,
    219, 220-21, 222, 226
Compromise of 1850, 133; en-
    acted, 79-84; public reaction
    to, 84-85; influence of, on
    Kansas-Nebraska Act, 86-
    87
Conflict of laws, 28, 137-38; in
    DS v. Sandford, 158-59, 165,
    184, 211, 217. *See also* Scott,
    Dred, in Illinois; Slaves,
    status of, in free territory
Connecticut: supreme court of,
    30; laws of, 104, 191
Constitution, U.S.: on slavery, 13-
    15; and racial discrimination,
    33; and Negro citizenship, 34,
    192-93, 198, 224; and federal-
    ism, 105-106; as law, 107-108.
    See also Constitutional Con-
    vention (1787); and specific
    clauses and cases
Constitutional Convention
    (1787): slavery issues in, 10-
    15, 21, 24; and territories, 43-

44; and judicial review, 105;
    and federal structure, 106-108
Constitutionalism, 104, 105
Constitutional Union party, 277
Corporations: and citizenship,
    39-40
Corwin, Edward S., 303
Craig v. Missouri, 111
Crawford, William H., 37
Creole, slave ship, 19
Crittenden, John J., 253, 281
Crittenden compromise, 281-84
Crittenden-Montgomery amend-
    ment, 253, 254
Curtis, Benjamin R., 118, 119,
    149, 153-54, 164, 173;
    blamed for enlarged DS deci-
    sion, 166-67; DS opinion, 169,
    184-85, 214, 221-29, 237;
    quarrels with Taney, 170-72,
    199; resigns from Court, 172,
    296; and substance of DS
    decision, 175, 177-81
Curtis, George T., 155, 156, 160-
    61, 269
Cushing, Caleb, 197, 234

Dallas, George M., 64
Daniel, Peter V., 119, 149, 163,
    170, 296; DS opinion, 167,
    184, 216-19, 221, 222, 233;
    and substance of DS decision,
    175, 178, 179, 181
Dartmouth College v. Woodward,
    111, 114
Davis, Jefferson, 81, 266, 268;
    resolutions of, 274-75, 276,
    277
Davis, John, 62
Davis, Woodbury, 177
Declaration of Independence, 46;
    and slavery, 8; Taney on, 192,
    198; DS decision compared
    to, 235
Delaware: manumission in, 8

Democratic party, 56, 90; effect of Kansas-Nebraska Act on, 89, 92; and interpretation of Kansas-Nebraska Act, 94-96; and judicial intervention, 100-101; effect of DS decision on, 230-32, 245-47, 290; and race question, 238, 239; split in, over Lecompton issue, 248-50, 256-57, 264, 265; southern control of, 267. *See also* Elections; and specific legislation

District of Columbia: slavery in, 18, 58, 85; racial discrimination in, 33; slave trade in, 76, 79, 80

Diverse-citizenship clause, 39-40, 144, 194

Domicile. *See* Slaves, status of, in free territory; Scott, Dred, in Illinois

Dorr War, 117-18

Douglas, Stephen A., 72, 76, 79, 97, 277; doctrine of popular sovereignty, 69, 70, 71, 82; and Kansas-Nebraska Act, 85-88; and debate on Kansas, 93-96, 99-100; on DS decision, 243; and Freeport doctrine, 244-47; and Lecompton controversy, 248-50, 252-53, 254, 256-58; and South, 249, 256-57, 267-68, 274-75; Lincoln on, 258-59; and debates with Lincoln, 259-63, 290; re-elected, 263; removed from committee chairmanship, 264-65; in debate on slave code, 265-68; *Harper's Magazine* article by, 269-72; in election of 1860, 275-79

Douglass, Frederick, 235

Dred Scott v. Sandford: delivery of, 3-4, 169; public reaction to, 4, 229-36; and judicial re-view, 5; influence of, on coming of Civil War, 5, 289-94; complexity of, 6; anticipated in Missouri Compromise debates, 49; comes before Supreme Court, 92, 146-47, 150, 151-52; in Court conference phase, 97, 153-54, 163-64, 165-68; as aberration, 116, 119; principal issues in, 119-20; origins of, 140-44; in trial court, 144-46; argued before Supreme Court, 152-53, 155-63; publication of, 169-70; analysis of substance of, 174-82; opinion of the Court (Taney), 183-213; concurring opinions, 214-21; dissenting opinions, 221-29; consequences of, 235-37, 241-43, 244-45, 289-94; Lincoln on, 238; and slavery conspiracy charge, 239-40, 258; and 1858 Lincoln-Douglas campaign, 244, 258-63; effect of, on Democratic party, 245-47, 257, 268, 276-77, 290; and Lecompton controversy, 250-53; replaces Kansas as principal sectional issue, 265, 268; and debate on slave code, 266; in Douglas-Black debate, 270-72; praised by Buchanan, 273-74; subject of 1860 congressional debate, 274-75, 277; and 1860 party platforms, 278-79; and Crittenden compromise, 283; and Lincoln's inaugural, 286; defied during Civil War, 297; reversal of, 298-300, as precedent, 300-302; historical treatment of, 303-306; ranked among "milestones," 306-307; as epoch in growth of judicial power, 308. *See also* Taney,

Roger B.: Opinion in *DS v. Sandford*

Due-process clause: Calhoun on, 58; invoked by antislavery radicals, 67-68; Republicans on, 98; Taney and, 198, 205-206, 209, 222, 229, 233; in concurring and dissenting opinions, 219, 221, 222, 226

Elections: *1844*, 60; *1848*, 63-64, 72, 75-76; *1852*, 84; *1854*, 89; *1856*, 97-98, 154-55, 291-94; *1857*, 237-38, 292-94; *1858*, 263-64, 291-94; *1860*, 275-79, 284, 290-94
Ellsworth, Oliver, 109
Emancipation. *See* Manumission, private; Slavery
Emerson, Henrietta, 127
Emerson, John, 121-22, 123-27, 227
Emerson, Mrs. John (Eliza Irene Sanford; Mrs. Calvin C. Chaffee), 125-27, 132, 142-43; as defendant, 129-31, 132-33, 137-38; and ownership of DS, 140, 231-32
English, William H., 253
English compromise, 253-54, 255-56, 257
Ewing, Elbert W. R., 303
Ex parte Merryman, 286, 296

Federal government: and slavery, 18-25; and racial discrimination, 33-34, 236-37
Federalism, principle of, 105-106
Federalist, The, 42, 104
Federalist party, 47, 50, 90
Field, Alexander P., 132, 139, 143
Field, Roswell M., 140, 143, 145, 146, 147, 152

Fifteenth Amendment, 299
Fillmore, Millard, 79, 97, 155
Fletcher v. Peck, 111, 308
Florida: acquisition of, 55, 59
Florida Territory, 55, 203
Fort Armstrong, Ill., 121-22, 123-24
Fort Jesup, La., 124-25, 128
Fort Snelling, Minn., 124, 125, 126
Fourteenth Amendment, 299
Frankfurter, Felix, 305
Franklin, Benjamin, 9
Freedom, suits for, 31
Freeport, Ill.: Lincoln-Douglas debate at, 244, 260, 290
Freeport doctrine, 244-45, 265, 274, 275, 276, 290; Douglas anticipates, 245-46; Douglas enunciates, 261-63; Douglas defends, 270
Freeport question: second, 252, 261-62, 265-66; corollary to second, 262-63; third, 260-61
Free Soil party, 68, 90
Frémont, John C., 97, 155, 238, 291
Fugitive Slave Act (1850), 24, 84, 152, 193, 237; passage of, 79, 80, 85, 198, 262
Fugitive-slave clause, 21, 192, 197, 207-208, 282; in Constitutional Convention, 13, 14; significance of, 23-24. See also *Prigg v. Pennsylvania*
Fugitive slave law of 1793, 20-21, 22-23
Fuller, Melville W., 302

Gag rule, 58
Gamble, Hamilton R., 137, 138, 153
Garland, Hugh, 132, 143
Garrison, William Lloyd, 56, 57

Georgia: slave law of, 16, 32-33; law of, concerning free Negroes, 40; western land cession by, 46, 220; and Yazoo land fraud, 111
Georgia platform, 84-85
Gerry, Elbridge, 105
Geyer, Henry S., 134, 148, 153, 156, 159-61, 200
Gibbons v. Ogden, 111
Goode, George W., 130, 131, 132
Gray, Horace, 233
Great Britain: and captured slaves, 18; and slave trade, 19; slave law of, 28, 30; and Negro seamen acts, 38, 39; convention signed with, 55; and Texas, 59; and Oregon, 61; common-law tradition of, 102-103; colonial system of, 103-104
Greeley, Horace, 230, 239, 269
Grier, Robert C., 119, 149, 164; corresponds with Buchanan on DS case, 166, 167-68, 169; and substance of DS decision, 175, 178-79, 181; DS opinion, 216, 222
Groves v. Slaughter, 118-19
Gypsy (steamboat), 125-26

Hale, John P., 251
Hall, David N., 132, 139
Hamilton, Alexander (1757-1804), 105, 109, 139
Hamilton, Alexander (judge in *Scott v. Emerson*), 130-31, 131-32
Hammond, James H., 254
Harpers Ferry, 270, 289
Harper's Magazine: Douglas article in, 269-70
Harriet v. Emerson. See *Scott v. Emerson*
Hayne, Robert Y., 55

Hillhouse, James, 47, 49, 55
House of Representatives, U.S.: speakership contests, 79, 92. *See also* Three-fifths clause
Houston, Sam, 59
Hughes, Charles Evans, 303-304, 307

Illinois: sojourning in, 29; law of, concerning free Negroes, 33; indenture system, 44; nearly a slave state, 66; politics in, and Lecompton controversy, 248-49. *See also* Lincoln-Douglas debates; Scott, Dred, in Illinois
Illinois State Journal (Springfield), 255
Illinois Territory, 49
Independent, The (New York), 232
Indiana: law of, concerning free Negroes, 33; indenture system, 44; nearly a slave state, 66
Indiana Territory, 49, 87
Insular Cases, 302
Iowa Territory, 55, 127

Jackson, Andrew, 19, 59, 113, 241
Jackson *Mississippian*, 275
Jackson resolutions, 133, 134
Jay, John, 9, 18, 109
Jefferson, Thomas, 41, 46-47, 53-54, 94, 110, 241
Johnson, Reverdy, 148, 251, 269, 297-98; briefs and argument in *DS v. Sandford*, 153, 156, 159-61
Johnson, Richard M., 54
Johnson, William, 38
Jonesboro, Ill.: Lincoln-Douglas debate at, 262-63

Judicial review: sources of, 103, 104-105; in Constitutional Convention, 105, 107-108; categories of, 108-109; in Marshall Court, 110-12; in Taney Court, 115-16; and DS decision, 183, 205, 240-43
Judicial supremacy, 241-43, 307-308
Judiciary Act of 1789, 110, 111, 112-13, 210, 212

Kansas-Nebraska Act, 89-90, 98, 146, 151; passage of, 85-89; interpretation of, 93-97, 100
Kansas Territory: conflict in, 89, 91, 94, 97, 99, 151; statehood proposed, 93, 95, 98-99; as issue in 1856, 101; replaced by DS decision as central issue, 265, 268; legislates against slavery, 274, 275. *See also* English compromise; Kansas-Nebraska Act; Lecompton constitution and controversy
Kearny, Stephen W., 61
Kentucky: constitution of, 35; supreme court of, 135
Key, Francis Scott, 113
King, Rufus, 55
Know-Nothings, 90, 97, 155, 264, 287, 291

LaBeaume, Charles Edmund, 140
Land Ordinance of, 1785, 43, 201
Lawrence, Kans.: "sack" of, 91, 97
Law Reporter, The, 233
Learned, W. A., 233
Lecompton constitution and controversy, 258, 264, 266, 290, 292, 294; origins of, 247-48; in Congress, 248-57

Lemmon v. The People, 31
Lewis, Walker, 304
Liberator, The, 56
Liberty party, 68
Lincoln, Abraham, 255, 298; on DS decision, 154, 215, 238; and race as political issue, 238-39; and charge of conspiracy to nationalize slavery, 240; House-Divided speech, 240, 257-59; his administration nullifies DS decision, 240, 297; and judicial review, 242-43; debates with Douglas, 243, 259-63, 290; elected President, 244, 279, 290, 292; nominated for Senate, 257; and Freeport question, 260-63; defeated for Senate, 263; in Ohio campaign of 1859, 269; nominated for President, 277; opposes compromise, 282; first inaugural, 286
Livingston, Edward, 55
Louisiana: slave law of, 26; secession of, 285
Louisiana Purchase, 46, 220-21, 222; slavery in, 46-47, 48-49
Louisiana Territory, 47; slavery in, 48, 49, 87
Louisville *Democrat,* 230, 236
Luther v. Borden, 116, 117-18

McCulloch v. Maryland, 50, 111, 210
McLean, John, 118, 119, 149, 164, 173, 232; presidential aspirations, 154, 155; blamed for enlarged DS decision, 166-67; DS opinion, 169-70, 184, 210, 221-29; and substance of DS decision, 177-81; death of, 296
Madison, Henry, 295

Madison, James, 9, 11, 104, 106; on Northwest Ordinance, 42-43; and territory clause, 43-44, 160, 201-202; on Missouri Compromise, 53-54

Maine: and Missouri Compromise, 52; legislature denounces DS decision, 237

Mansfield, Lord, 28

Manumission, private, 25-26

Marbury v. Madison, 110, 111, 241, 307, 308

Marshall, John, 50, 103, 113, 114, 305, 308; and *American Insurance Company v. Canter,* 69, 173, 203-204; and judicial review, 109-12

Marshall Court, 110-12, 114, 115, 223

Maryland: manumission in, 8; fear of free Negroes in, 33; secession crisis in, 286

Massachusetts: supreme court of, 29-30; miscegenation law, 191; and Negro citizenship, 224

Memphis *Avalanche,* 268

Merryman, John, 286

Methodist Church: and DS decision, 232

Mexican Cession, 68, 72, 75, 76. *See also* California; New Mexico; Wilmot Proviso

Mexican War, 61

Mexico: abolition of slavery in, 59, 82; and Texas, 61

Michigan Territory, 49

Miller, Samuel F., 300

Minnesota Territory, 101

Miscegenation laws, 191-92

Mississippi: secession resolutions in, 31

Mississippi Territory: slavery in, 45, 49

Missouri: as border state, 133; politics in, 133-35, 136-37

Missouri Compromise: enacted, 52-54; success of, 55

Missouri Compromise restriction (36° 30′ line): ruled unconstitutional, 4, 174, 175, 208; enacted, 52-53; reaffirmed, 60; extension of, 63, 64, 70-71, 281-83; a policy of two policies, 65; endorsed by Calhoun, 66; and Compromise of 1850, 81, 82; repealed, 85-89; Pierce on, 92, 155; and *Scott v. Emerson,* 134, 140; in *DS* argument of counsel, 159-61, 162; in Court conference, 164, 166, 169; in *DS* concurring opinions, 165, 215, 216, 218-22; in DS decision, 174-80; in Taney's DS opinion, 199-209, 222; in *DS* dissenting opinions, 225-27

Missouri controversy (1819-21), 36-37, 49-54, 66, 220

Missouri Republican (St. Louis), 151-52

Missouri supreme court: *Scott v. Emerson* in, 30, 131, 132-33, 158, 159

Missouri Territory: slavery in, 48, 49

Monroe, James, 53, 54

Napton, William B., 134-35, 137

Nash, Frederick, 36

Naturalization: federal law on, 35; clause, 201

Natural law, 103, 104

Nebraska Territory, 84, 91, 274; organized, 85-89

Negro citizenship: in DS decision, 4, 5, 144-45, 167, 174-77, 179-82, 184, 185; as public issue, 34-40; not involved in *Scott v. Emerson,* 140; in *DS* argument of counsel, 152,

156-57, 162, 163, Taney on, 185-99; 245; Daniel on, 217; McLean on, 221, 223; Curtis on, 223-25; in critiques of DS decision, 235-36; Lincoln opposes, 239; in Lincoln-Douglas debates, 259-60; Bates opinion on, 297; established in 14th Amendment, 298, 300

Negroes, free: in DS decision, 6; population, 25; southern hostility to, 25, 186; in early Republic, 31-32; laws concerning, 32-34, 37-38; federal government and, 33-34; Taney on, 38-39, 235; and Missouri Compromise, 54; effect of DS decision on, 235-39, 244. *See also* Negro citizenship; and specific states

Negro seamen acts, 37-38, 39, 40

Negro suffrage: and DS decision, 237-38

Nelson, Samuel, 119, 149, 154, 163-64, 167, 168, 289; DS opinion, 165, 184, 199-200, 211, 214-16, 217; on substance of DS decision, 175-76, 178-79

New Englander, 233

New Hampshire: and Negro citizenship, 224

New Jersey: and Negro citizenship, 224

New Mexico, 63; in Clayton compromise, 73; Douglas bill for, 76; Taylor's policy concerning, 78

New Mexico Territory: organized, 79, 80, 82-83, 86, 87, 88; slavery in, 81, 84, 85, 91

New Orleans *Delta*, 280

New Orleans *Picayune*, 230

New York: sojourning law, 29, 30; politics in, 61; and Negro

citizenship, 224; legislative reaction against DS decision, 239-40

New York *Evening Post*, 241

New York *Herald*, 295

New York *Journal of Commerce*, 231

New York *Times*, 265, 298, 306

New York *Tribune*, 4, 230, 297

Nicholson letter, 64

Nonintervention: early practice of, 45, 65, 68; as doctrine, 58, 66, 68-71; in Calhoun's "Southern Address," 76; in Compromise of 1850, 81-82; in Kansas-Nebraska Act, 87, 88; in Utah and New Mexico, 91; Douglas reaffirms principle of, 263. *See also* Popular sovereignty

Norris, Lyman D., 132

North Carolina: laws of, concerning free Negroes, 38; land cession by, 44, 45, 220; and Negro citizenship, 224

Northwest Ordinance (1787), 18, 35, 48, 271; passage of, 9, 14, 41-43, 44; Taney on, 42, 135, 136, 201-203, 222; as model for other territories, 44, 47, 48-49; concurring justices on, 218, 220, 222

Northwest Territory: slavery in, 9

Nott, Samuel, 234-35

Obiter dictum: and DS decision, 180-81, 183, 240, 242, 303

Ohio: sojourning in, 29; effect of DS decision in, 237-38, 294

Ohio State Journal (Columbus), 255

Ordinance of 1784, 41, 46, 94, 271

Ordinance of 1787. *See* Northwest Ordinance

Oregon country: settlement of, 59
Oregon Territory: organized, 63,
    72-73, 75; as part of Com-
    promise of 1850, 83-84
Oregon Treaty, 61
Orleans Territory: slavery in, 47-
    49, 55, 87
Ottawa, Ill.: Lincoln-Douglas de-
    bate at, 259-60

Pennsylvania: abolition in, 8; so-
    journing law, 29, 30; Repub-
    lican gains in, 291-94. See
    also *Prigg v. Pennsylvania*
Personal liberty laws, 21
Philadelphia *Pennsylvanian*, 230
Pierce, Franklin, 19, 84, 97, 258;
    and passage of Kansas-
    Nebraska bill, 87, 89; Kansas
    policy of, 91, 93; on Missouri
    Compromise restriction, 92,
    155
Pinckney, Charles C. (1746-
    1825), 11
Pinckney, Charles (1757-1824),
    53
Plea in abatement: in trial court,
    144-45; in Court discussion,
    154-55; in DS decision, 162,
    163, 174, 184-85; Taney on,
    184-85, 199; concurring jus-
    tices on, 216-17, 220; dissent-
    ing justices on, 221, 223, 224-
    25
Polk, James K., 19, 60, 61, 73,
    75, 147
Polygamy, 97-98
Popular sovereignty: early prac-
    tice of, 45, 65; in election of
    1848, 64; as doctrine, 65, 68-
    71; and Oregon, 72-73; in
    Clayton compromise, 73; in
    Compromise of 1850, 81, 83;
    in Kansas-Nebraska Act, 85-
    88; Douglas version of, 93-94,

95; and polygamy, 97-98; in
    Kansas, 99-100; in election
    of 1856, 154; Buchanan in-
    terprets, 169; Taney on, 206,
    273; effect of DS decision on,
    245, 266; and Lecompton
    controversy, 252; in Lincoln-
    Douglas debates, 258-59, 261-
    62; Douglas article on, 269-72;
    in Davis resolutions, 274-75;
    in Douglas platform of 1860,
    276, 278. *See also* Freeport
    doctrine; Nonintervention
Potter, David M., 84, 240
Prigg v. Pennsylvania, 21-23,
    118-19, 252
Privileges-and-immunities clause,
    36, 145, 156; Taney on, 39,
    187-88, 193-94, 195-96
Privy Council, British, 104
Property-rights doctrine. *See*
    Common-property doctrine
Prosser, Gabriel, 26
Pugh, George E., 266

Race and racism: in *Prigg v.
    Pennsylvania*, 23; Taney and,
    38-39, 189-90, 235; as party
    issue, 236, 239, 240. *See also*
    Negro citizenship; Negroes,
    free
Rachel v. Walker, 130, 132, 218
Reattachment, principle of, 27,
    29, 30, 136, 158, 218, 228
Reconstruction, Radical, 299-300
Republican party, 94, 155; plat-
    forms, 45, 68, 97, 154; char-
    acter of, 90-91; founding of,
    151; reaction of, to DS deci-
    sion, 230-31; racial dilemma
    of, 236, 239-40; and slave-
    power conspiracy charge, 239-
    40; use of *obiter dictum*
    charge, 240; and Supreme
    Court, 242-43; and Crittenden

compromise, 282-84; Taney on, 285-87. *See also* Elections; and specific legislation

Republican party (Jeffersonian), 50; and slavery, 46-47

Reversion, principle of, 27, 136, 157, 210-11, 218, 228

Revolution, American: and slavery, 8-9; and theory of legislative power, 104

Richmond *Enquirer*, 231, 263, 272

Rodell, Fred, 306

Russell, Samuel, 128, 133

Russell, Mrs. Samuel (Adeline), 132

Ryland, John F., 134, 137

St. Clair, Arthur, 44

St. Louis: DS in, 3, 121-22, 128, 130, 295-96

Sanford, Alexander, 125, 127, 131, 132

Sanford, Eliza Irene. *See* Emerson, Mrs. John

Sanford, John F. A., 3, 4, 153; as executor of Emerson's will, 127-28; as his sister's agent, 132; as putative owner of DS, 140-42, 231; and origins of *DS v. Sandford*, 140-44; as defendant, 144-46

Santo Domingo: revolt in, 25, 46, 284

Schwartz, Bernard, 116

Scott, Dred, 3, 26, 155-56; travels of, 121-26, 128; description of, 122; marriage, 124, 227-28; initiates suit for freedom, 128-29; initiates federal suit for freedom, 140; question of ownership, 140-42, 231; manumitted, 142, 231, 295; pamphlet in behalf of, 147; death of, 295-96

Scott, Dred, in Illinois (comity question): in Missouri supreme court, 137-38; in argument of counsel, 152, 157-58, 162; in concurring opinions, 165, 215, 217-18; Taney on, 174, 210-11; in dissenting opinions, 227-28

Scott, Eliza (daughter of Dred), 125-26, 128, 296

Scott, Harriet (wife of Dred), 124, 125-26, 128-29, 130, 131, 133, 140, 296

Scott, Lizzie (daughter of Dred), 131, 296

Scott, William, 131, 137, 153, 158, 159, 162, 228

Scott v. Emerson, 30, 174, 217, 228; in trial court, 128-31, 132, 139; in Missouri supreme court, 131, 132-38; 218; and *Strader v. Graham*, 135-37; influence of, on *DS v. Sandford*, 140, 146, 153; in *DS* argument of counsel, 158-59; Taney on, 162, 211-12; Nelson on, 165

Secession, 279-81

Seward, William H., 78, 277; attacks DS decision, 251-52

Shaw, Lemuel, 29-30

Slaughterhouse Cases, 300

Slave code for territories, 208, 265-67, 274-75

Slave Grace, The, 30, 218, 252

Slavery: colonial origins of, 7-8; law of, 7-8, 15-17; abolition of, in North, 8; and Revolution, 8-9; and Articles of Confederation, 9; in Constitutional Convention, 10-15; as an interest, 15; federal government and, 18-25; in District of Columbia, 58. *See also* specific states

Slavery in territories: DS decision and, 4; from 1787 to
1803, 9, 43-46; federal acquiescence in, 18; under
Articles of Confederation, 41-
43; from 1803 to 1819, 46-49;
in Missouri crisis, 49-54; sub-
sides as issue, 54; and annexation of Texas, 60; from 1846
to 1849, 61-78; in Compromise of 1850, 79-84; and
Kansas-Nebraska Act, 85-89;
from 1854 to 1857, 91-101,
154; in *DS* argument of counsel, 159-61; in Taney's DS
opinion, 184, 200-209; in *DS*
concurring opinions, 215, 218-
21; table of judicial opinions
on, 222; in *DS* dissenting
opinions, 225-27; code for,
debated, 265-66; in Black-
Douglas debate, 270-72; issue
settled, says Buchanan, 273-
74; territorial legislation
against, 274, 275; 1860 congressional debate on, 275,
277-78; 1860 Democratic
platform on, 277-79; abolished by Congress, 297. *See
also* Freeport doctrine; Missouri Compromise restriction;
Popular sovereignty
Slaves, status of, in free territory,
26-31. *See also* Scott, Dred,
in Illinois
Slave trade, domestic, 76, 79, 80,
85
Slave trade, foreign, 8, 12-13, 19,
46
Slave-trade clause, 12-13, 14,
192, 207-208
Smith, Charles W., Jr., 304-305
Sojourning. *See* Slaves, status of,
in free territory; Scott, Dred,
in Illinois
Somerset v. Stewart, 28-29, 252

Soulé, Pierre, 82, 83
South Carolina: slave law of, 16;
law of, concerning free Ne-
groes, 37-38, 40
"Southern Address," 76
Southwest Territory, 44-45, 49
Spain: and slave trade, 19; ac-
quisition of Florida from, 55
Spector, Robert M., 304
Springfield (Mass.) *Argus,* 231
Springfield (Mass.) *Republican,*
231
State v. Manuel, 224
Statehood clause, 204
Stephens, Alexander H., 82-83,
164
Stone, Harlan F., 301
Story, Joseph, 21-23, 114, 159
Stowell, Lord, 30
Strader v. Graham, 135-37, 140,
141, 146, 218; and argument
in *DS v. Sandford,* 153, 154-
55, 159, 162, 163; in Nelson's
DS opinion, 165, 214; in
Taney's DS opinion, 210, 211,
212
Strong, George Templeton, 298
Sturges v. Crowninshield, 111
Sumner, Charles, 97, 251, 298
Supremacy clause, 107
Supreme Court: presents DS de-
cision, 3-4, 5; territorial issue
deposited with, 73-74, 82, 86,
101, 102; in Constitutional
Convention, 105, 107; early
years of, 109; reorganization
of, 298; and failure of Radical
Reconstruction, 300; and use
of DS decision as precedent,
300-302. *See also* Marshall
Court; Taney Court; Judicial
review; Judicial supremacy;
and titles of specific cases
Swisher, Carl B., 287, 304-305

Taliaferro, Lawrence, 124

Tallmadge, James, Jr., 49
Tallmadge amendment, 49-51
Taney, Roger B., 33, 40, 157, 159, 258, 300; opinion in *Prigg v. Pennsylvania,* 23; opinion on Negro seamen laws, 38-39; on corporations and citizenship, 39; becomes Chief Justice, 113; description of, 113-14; as nationalist, 115; and judicial self-restraint, 115-19; and *Strader v. Graham,* 135-37, 140, 214, 215; agrees to write DS opinion, 166, 167; and presidential influence on Grier, 167-68; and Buchanan's inauguration, 168-69, 251; quarrels with Curtis, 170-72; and substance of DS decision, 173-82; and order of opinions, 214, 220; and Cushing, 234; letter to Nott, 234-35; and *obiter dictum* charge, 240; and judicial review, 241-42; and election of 1860, 244, 284; manuscript on secession crisis, 284-86; and Lincoln's inaugural, 286; and *Merryman* case, 286; pro-Confederacy sympathies, 286-87, 296; motivation, 287-88; alleged antislavery convictions, 304; and Lincoln administration, 296-97; death of, 298; reputation of, 302-306
———Opinion in *DS v. Sandford:* read, 3-4, 169; on slavery in territories, 4, 184, 200-209, 222; on Negroes and citizenship, 4, 185-99, 216-17, 297; racial theory in, 5; content of, 6, 119-20, 172-73, 182-83; on slave-trade clause, 12; on three-fifths clause, 12; distinguishes between reversion and reattachment, 27; on

Northwest Ordinance, 42; anticipated by Calhoun, 58; on territory clause, 68, 93, 200-204, 209, 219, 225, 233, 234; on jurisdictional question, 146; alterations in, 171-73; on proceeding to merits, 184, 199; on plea in abatement, 184-85, 225; on citizenship, 186-89, 300-301; on privileges-and-immunities clause, 187-88; on Articles of Confederation, 195, 202-203; on federal government and slavery, 196-97; on DS in Illinois, 199-200, 209-11; on due-process clause, 205-206, 229, 233; on popular sovereignty, 206, 274; reaffirms principle of reversion, 210-11; on validity of Scott's suit, 211-13; compared with Curtis opinion, 229; revelatory value of, 288
Taney Court: and corporations as citizens, 39, 194; and judicial power, 112-13, 114-15; and judicial self-restraint, 115-19; data on, 149; and *DS v. Sandford,* 151-229
Taylor, Zachary, 63, 64, 76, 78, 79, 128
Tennessee: slave law of, 26; constitution of, 35; admission of, 45
Territories, congressional power in: DS decision as precedent, 301-302. *See also* Slavery in territories; Territory clause
Territory clause: framing of, 43-44; Taney on, 68, 93, 200-204, 209, 219, 225, 233, 234; Douglas on, 93; in *DS* argument of counsel, 160; in *DS* concurring and dissenting opinions, 218-19, 220, 222, 225-26; Benton on, 233-34

Texas, 66; annexation of, 59-60; and 36° 30′ line, 60; boundary of, 78, 79, 80; debt, 79, 80; secession of, 285
Thacher, George, 45-46
Thayer, James Bradley, 176
Thirty-six-thirty line. *See* Missouri Compromise restriction
Thomas, Jesse B., 52, 53
Thomas amendment. *See* Missouri Compromise restriction
Three-fifths clause, 10-12, 13, 14, 193, 282
Tocqueville, Alexis de, 109, 307
Toombs, Robert, 98
Toombs bill, 98-99, 100
Topeka government, 91
Trumbull, Lyman, 95, 99-100, 252-53
Turner, Nat, 17, 57
Tyler, John, 19, 53, 59-60

Utah Territory: organized, 79, 80, 81, 82, 83, 86, 87, 89; slavery as issue in, 84, 85, 91

Van Buren, Martin, 19, 58, 59, 60, 64
Van Evrie, John H., 235
Vesey, Denmark, 37
Virginia: manumission in, 8; slave law of, 16; law of, concerning free Negroes, 25-26; and Negro citizenship, 35; and Missouri Compromise, 53-54; anti-abolitionist laws of, 57
Virginia plan (1787), 106

Walker, Isaac P., 77-78
War of 1812, 49
Warren, Charles, 244, 289
Warren, Earl, and Warren Court, 306, 307-308
Washington, D. C. *See* District of Columbia
Washington *Union*, 246, 263
Wayne, James M., 119, 164; proposes that Taney write DS decision, 166, 167; DS opinion, 166-67, 214, 222; and substance of DS decision, 175, 178, 179, 181; loyal to Union, 296
Webster, Daniel, 19, 77, 81
Wells, Robert W., 144-46, 152, 157, 158, 186, 194-95, 221-22
Whig party: and suppressing of slavery issue, 56, 63-64; weakened in South, 78; effect of Kansas-Nebraska Act on, 89-90. *See also* Elections; and specific legislation
White, Edward D., 302
Wilmot, David, 61
Wilmot Proviso, 45, 64, 69; introduced, 61-62; reintroduced, 62-63; as doctrine, 68; rejected in Compromise of 1850, 80, 81, 94
Wilson, Henry, 98, 296
Wirt, William, 37, 38, 196-97
Wisdom, John Minor, 300
Women: and citizenship, 34
Woodward, C. Vann, 302

Yazoo land fraud, 111
Yazoo Strip, 45, 46